ALSO BY DANIEL SWIFT

Bomber County: The Poetry of a Lost Pilot's War

*Shakespeare's Common Prayers: The Book of
Common Prayer and the Elizabethan Age*

The Heart Is Strange: New Selected Poems of
John Berryman (editor)

THE
BUGHOUSE

THE
BUGHOUSE

THE POETRY, POLITICS,
AND MADNESS OF
EZRA POUND

DANIEL SWIFT

FARRAR, STRAUS AND GIROUX   NEW YORK

Farrar, Straus and Giroux
175 Varick Street, New York 10014

Originally published in 2017 by Harvill Secker, Great Britain
Published in the United States in 2017 by Farrar, Straus and Giroux
First American paperback edition, 2018

Owing to limitations of space, all acknowledgments for permission to reprint
previously published and unpublished material appear on pages 299–302.

The Library of Congress has cataloged the hardcover edition as follows:
Names: Swift, Daniel, 1977– author.
Title: The bughouse : the poetry, politics, and madness of Ezra Pound /
Daniel Swift.
Description: First American edition. | New York : Farrar, Straus and Giroux,
2017. | Includes index.
Identifiers: LCCN 2017007577 | ISBN 9780374284046 (hardcover) |
ISBN 9780374709587 (ebook)
Subjects: LCSH: Pound, Ezra, 1885–1972—Mental health. | Pound, Ezra,
1885–1972—Friends and associates. | Poets, American—20th century—
Biography. | Psychiatric hospital patients—United States—Biography. |
Saint Elizabeths Hospital (Washington, D.C.)—Biography.
Classification: LCC PS3531.O82 Z853 2017 | DDC 811/.52—dc23
LC record available at https://lccn.loc.gov/2017007577

Paperback ISBN: 978-0-374-53804-0

www.fsgbooks.com
www.twitter.com/fsgbooks • www.facebook.com/fsgbooks

For Jessie

Oh, do not ask, 'What is it?'
Let us go and make our visit.

T. S. Eliot,
'The Love Song of J. Alfred Prufrock'

Contents

Prologue: Liz Bish   1

Timeline of Pound's Years at St Elizabeths   22

PART ONE   1946
1   Hell-Hole   31
2   Kafferty   61

PART TWO   1947–53
3   Amurika   83
4   The Bughouse   122

PART THREE   1954–58
5   The Same Cellar   153
6   CasaPound   195
7   Ezuversity   221

Epilogue: Trying to Write Paradise   255

Essay on Sources   263

Acknowledgements   285

Index   287

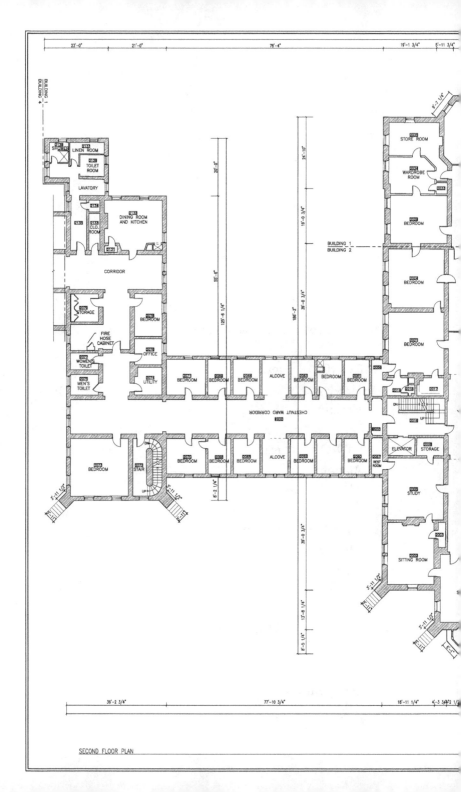

SECOND FLOOR PLAN

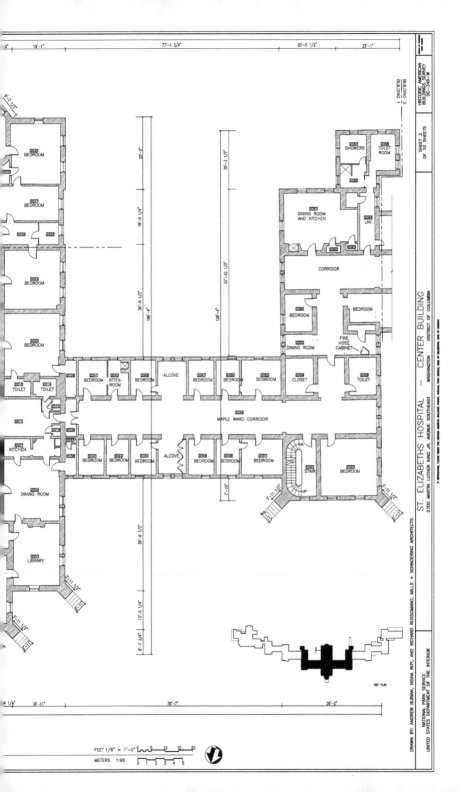

THE
BUGHOUSE

Prologue

Liz Bish

The Roman road runs north past Livorno, past fields of sunflowers dazed by the sun and mountains in the haze. This is the old Via Aurelia. Above it snakes a new motorway on stilts. Just after Pisa, the old road meets a sullen river and a forgotten train station. METATO, says the rusting sign, and here is the field that was the prison: bound to the north by river and to the west by road, while all around to the south and east are low hills.

Across the landscape there are lines: of cypresses, lines where the plough passed, lines from a tractor. There are lines of umbrella pines each one like a Y, while in the hills are marble mines, red squares boxed from brown hillside. The field that was the prison is now a nursery garden. At the north end is the Fiorista Gloria, and here are greenhouses filled with ferns for the stiff bouquets Italians give at funerals. At the south end is Ristorante La Rota, and behind the restaurant are nine more pale greenhouses. Some are empty and in some are tomatoes in rows, zucchini on the ground, white butterflies, blue beehives. The soil is rocks in the heat.

The woman at the fern garden tells me to go and see the old men at Circolo Acli, where they take their coffee each afternoon at two. The café is at the end of a road, with white gravel and brown plastic furniture, and they sit in the shade smoking slowly, not much talk. I ask, but they do not know about the field at Metato, for this is Vecchiano and Metato is a mile away. Then they remember Signor Bertelli. He lives in a green house by the old train station, over-looking the field and the river, and as I walk up he is sitting on his terrace. When I say I am writing a book about a story that began here seventy years ago, he tells me he is a writer too. He holds out a handful of pages. He has been writing a poem about his ninety-seventh birthday, last week.

Signor Bertelli remembers the camp on the other side of the river. It was all tents, he says, and first it was for Italian airmen, and when the Americans came they built a fence two metres high. Nobody local went inside. He laughs when I say there was a famous American poet in there. At the end of the war Signor Bertelli worked for the Americans. They sent him to Naples to direct the traffic, and he remembers the terrible traffic and how everybody thought he spoke English because he wore an American uniform, but he never understood a word.

Ezra Pound was the most difficult man of the twentieth century. He was an ardent fascist who wrote 'Never consider anything as dogma' and a rambling anti-Semite who believed that 'Fundamental accuracy of statement is the ONE sole morality of writing.' He was the densely allusive high modernist who wrote some of the tender-est poetry of his time and a boy from suburban Philadelphia who lived most of his life in Europe: London, Paris, Italy. His great work, which he wrote for fifty years, is the unfinished, 800-page *Cantos*. This is a poem of legendary complexity, as hard and rich as any art produced in that century, but Pound's difficulty lies not only in the challenge of how to read his poetry, but also how to reconcile it with his life's contradictions. He loved the American Constitution and spent the Second World War broadcasting anti-American pro-paganda from Mussolini's Italy; he was a racist who held that the summit of human truth was to be found in African myth, Chinese philosophy and Japanese plays. He is difficult because he is a man who may accurately be described by the most cartoonish names: fascist, madman, genius, traitor. He was the best and the worst, and just as his strengths seem to cancel his failings, so too do those failings falsify the strengths.

You cannot write the history of twentieth-century literature without giving Pound a starring role in the story, but you can call him the hero or the villain; both parts are his. Writing in *Poetry* magazine in 1916, the celebrated American poet Carl Sandburg claimed: 'All talk on modern poetry, by people who know, ends with dragging in Ezra Pound somewhere. He may be named only to be cursed as wanton and mocker, poseur, trifler and vagrant. Or he may be classed as filling a niche today like that of Keats in a preceding epoch. The point is, he will be mentioned.' In 1916 Pound was thirty years old and already the contradiction is set. For those who care about poetry, Pound is either the sign of all that is wrong or the best thing going, but he cannot be ignored.

Sandburg continues: 'One must know how to spell his name, and have heard rumors of where he hangs his hat when he eats, and one must have at least passing acquaintance with his solemn denunciados and his blurted quiddities, in order to debate on modern poetry, and in such debate zigzag a course of progress.' It is not enough to read his poems alone, for it is in his life that he becomes an emblem of what a poet is and should be. Sandburg mentions Keats, for Keats is the kind of poet who is easy to love: a boy of extravagant talent who lived a poet's life and usefully died young. He knew his niche and filled it beautifully. But Pound is not Keats; his place is not so certain; where he hangs his hat one day may not be the same tomorrow; and this is not all. Pound's contradictions remain with us. They are the uncertainties of our time, and if we wish, in Sandburg's phrase, to zigzag a course of progress, we must consider Pound and his place in our world.

A mile from where I work in central London is the National Portrait Gallery: an ornate Victorian temple which houses the faces of Britain's history. On the second floor is the Statesmen's Gallery. It is an avenue of important men – and a couple of women – of the nineteenth century, and the statesmen have monocles, watch fobs and splendid names such as Lord George Cavendish Bentinck. The portraits have black backgrounds and the only person in this gallery not wearing a black suit is the cricketer W. G. Grace and he is the most stately of the lot, a mountain of a man in cricket whites and wide, square beard. Here, decorum matters.

To the side of the gallery is Room 24, where the writers are, and they too wear black. Elizabeth Barrett Browning and Robert Browning are looking at one another, muted, ready for a funeral. Dickens is in very dark green trousers and frock coat; a tiepin holds a spray of black cravat. The Reverend Charles Kingsley, author of *The Water Babies*, looks like your headmaster's headmaster. Thomas Hardy wears a black suit and a white shirt. This was an age which considered writers lesser statesmen, and they dress the part.

Continue a little further now, to the end of the gallery, and left, and as you turn you leap into a new century. The portraits shrink and here at last is colour, and here at last the writers look alive. In the painting by Dora Carrington, Lytton Strachey is lying reading. He wears a fuzzy dressing gown with a red paisley blanket on top and he holds a book tenderly with long amazing hands. Dylan Thomas, painted by Augustus John, is wearing what looks like a woolly jumper made from a leopard's fur, and Laurie Lee is in a rich brown suit and blue shirt.

When you step from the Statesmen's Gallery you move from the Victorian age to the modern, and as much as Freud or Einstein, Ezra Pound invented the modern age. He edited T. S. Eliot's *The Waste Land* into what is routinely described as the most important poem of the twentieth century and he told Ernest Hemingway to use fewer adjectives. He encouraged E. E. Cummings to experiment with the layout of typewritten words on the page and he was responsible for the first publication of James Joyce's *Ulysses*. Wyndham Lewis called him the Trotsky of literature and the difference he made lies not only in anecdotes such as these. On the broadest possible scale, Pound's life was committed to the principle that writers are not lesser statesmen.

By May of 1945, when the soldiers came for him with guns, Ezra Pound had been living in Italy for twenty years. His was a generation of American writers who went abroad, but his entanglement in Europe was a little more extreme. In January 1941 – the year America entered the war – he began a series of radio broadcasts from Rome. He discussed monetary reform, his poetry and, most of all, the folly of this fight against the Axis powers; and he broadcast perhaps 200 times – rambling, passionate, in accents and impersonations – before 26 July 1943, when the US Department of Justice indicted him for treason. This charge carries the death penalty. Pound continued to broadcast. By the spring of 1945 the war was coming to an end and Italy was collapsing, and on the morning of Thursday 3 May he was at home in the village of Sant'Ambrogio, just above the northern seaside town of Rapallo, when two Italian Communists from a local anti-Fascist brigade rapped on his door. Pound had long believed in culture, that scholarship might save us, so he picked up a Chinese dictionary and a copy of Confucius and put them in his pocket. Then he went with the soldiers.

There are two ways to tell what happened next.

I.

The Communist partisans who captured Pound did not want to keep him, so at lunchtime they let him go. He went to the American military post in the next village and handed himself in. The American troops were uncertain what to do with this sixty-year-old poet with a pointy beard. The next day he was taken in handcuffs to Genoa, where he was questioned by the FBI. On 22 May the order came from Washington. 'Transfer without delay under guard to MTOUSA Disciplinary Training Center,' it ran: 'Exercise utmost security measures to prevent escape or suicide.'

The DTC at Pisa was a punishment and rehabilitation camp for military offenders: rapists, murderers, deserters, 3,500 men. Pound was put in a cage at the edge of the field, six feet by six, reinforced with strips of jagged steel of the sort used to construct emergency runways. He called it 'the gorilla cage'.

All other members of the camp, both prisoners and guards, were ordered to keep away from him.

Next to him were the cells where prisoners on their way to execution waited. Pound was permitted to keep his Confucius and the Chinese dictionary, and was given an army issue Bible.

The sun at Pisa is hot in May and June. Pound had no shelter. The dust and glare inflamed his eyes.

By the middle of June Pound has suffered a nervous breakdown. He is given a tent of his own in the military compound. He finds a poetry anthology in the communal latrine. He is allowed to use the typewriter in the dispensary at night. He starts to write.

He writes:

> No one who has passed a month in the death cells
>   believes in capital punishment
> No man who has passed a month in the death cells
>   believes in cages for beasts.

One of the guards makes a desk for him from a packing case. This is against the rules. In return, Pound includes the guard's name – 'Mr Edwards' – in his new poem.

He writes: 'the greatest is charity / to be found among those who have not observed regulations.'

Few stories in the history of poetic creation are more touching than this one: Ezra Pound in prison wrote himself into a state of grace.

He starts to notice the natural world around him: the insects and the birds, that which is growing, that which renews. He writes: 'Learn of the green world what can be thy place / In scaled invention or true artistry, / Pull down thy vanity.'

Sometimes, the other prisoners and guards took advantage of the poet in their midst. The guard Robert Allen later recalled: 'It was not unusual to see him typing a letter to some trainee's girl or mother with the trainee dictating at his shoulder and Pound interpreting for him.'

His nickname in the camp was 'Uncle Ezra'.

The commanding officer of the DTC was Lieutenant Colonel John L. Steele. He said: 'We weren't able to provide him with a library, but obviously he didn't need that; he carried that in his head.'

Pound's wife Dorothy was not told where he was until August, and once she heard she went to him. His son Omar – who was serving in the US army – also went to visit him at the DTC.

He writes: 'What thou lovest well remains, / the rest is dross.'

In Washington, the Department of Justice began to assemble the treason case. Despite the existence of recordings of Pound's broadcasts, the prosecution, in order to prove treason, were required to provide witnesses to the act. The government lawyers found five Italian radio technicians to testify that Pound had made treasonous speeches over the radio in Rome, and flew them to Washington. In the United States, awaiting the trial, these five radio men demanded their regular monthly salaries, but soon revealed that since none of them knew English they could not account for what Pound may or may not have said during the broadcasts. Later, the government paid for them to take a vacation at Hot Springs, Virginia.

Pound's defence lawyer, who willingly took on the case, was Julien Cornell. He was a Quaker and a pacifist and most experienced in defending conscientious objectors.

On 18 November 1945 Pound's plane landed at Bolling Air Force Base in Washington, DC. This journey – his rendition – was the first time he had flown. Upon disembarking, he was greeted at the runway by a crowd of reporters, and he asked them: 'Does anyone have the faintest idea of what I actually said in Rome?'

Pound was examined by army medical experts and civilian psychiatrists under the direction of Dr Winfred Overholser, who was a widely respected authority on the role of psychiatry in legal proceedings and the superintendent of St Elizabeths Hospital, the government hospital for the insane just outside Washington. On 21 December 1945 their joint report was presented to the court. 'He is now suffering from a paranoid state which renders him mentally unfit to advise properly with counsel or to participate intelligently and reasonably in his own defense,' the doctors conclude: 'He is, in other words, insane and mentally unfit for trial.'

He writes: 'Oh let an old man rest.'

Pound was taken directly from the courtroom to St Elizabeths Hospital. He was kept there for the following twelve and a half years.

2.

In early May 1945, when Pound was being held at Genoa, he gave an interview to an American journalist. In it he described Hitler as 'a martyr', Mussolini as 'a very human, imperfect character who lost his head,' and Stalin as 'the best brain in the business'.

On 15 June 1945 an army psychiatrist examined Pound and reported: 'There is no evidence of psychosis, neurosis or psychopathy. He is of superior intelligence, is friendly, affable and cooperative.'

The opening of Canto 74 – the first of *The Pisan Cantos*, written at the DTC – presents the fall of Mussolini as a tragedy.

He writes: 'poor old Benito'.

One of the most troubling of the *Cantos* is 73, which celebrates the death of a company of Canadian soldiers tricked on to an Italian minefield. Along with Canto 72, Canto 73 was written in Italian during the summer and autumn of 1944. Pound's publishers, New Directions and Faber, excluded these two cantos from the printed versions of the poems until 1987. Since then, editions include the two cantos in the original Italian along with an English translation of 72, but not of 73, meaning that the most extreme statement of Pound's political sympathy remains unknown to those who cannot read Italian.

It is hard to convey bad poetry in quotation. This is why Pound has tended to fare well in the hands of his critics. Anyone can find a good line or two, but the grand bad faith of the *Cantos* – its pomposity, its anger – is a constant, running line after line.

On 17 November 1945 Pound was flown from Rome to the United States via Prague, England and Newfoundland. He was escorted by Lieutenant Colonel P. V. Holder, and on the long journey they talked. Later, Holder wrote: 'Pound [. . .] is an extremely educated man with a wide divergence of knowledge and interests. His hobbies are the translating of ancient documents such as Pluto [*sic*] and Confucius. The bulk of our conversation was carried on concerning these matters. He explained in detail the source of his knowledge and the means by which his translations were accomplished.'

On 27 November 1945 Julien Cornell told the *New York Times*: 'Mr Pound is not sufficiently in possession of judgement and perhaps mentality to plead.' This was the first time anyone publicly declared that Pound was insane.

In a letter written after their first meeting, Cornell noted that Pound 'had no objection to the possibility of pleading insane as a defense [. . .] In fact he told me that the idea had already occurred to him.'

On 10 December 1945 Dr Marion King – the head of the prison medical service – reported his findings from three examinations of

Pound. He concluded that Pound was not 'a psychotic or insane person', and therefore 'should not be absolved from the necessity of standing trial'. His opinion was not included in the documents presented to the court.

At the end of December 1945 Dr Addison Duval – one of the psychiatrists who had told the court that Pound was unfit to stand trial – noted: 'I had assumed that he was psychotic because our boss had already made a diagnosis [. . .] But I couldn't elicit any symptoms of psychosis at all. There were no delusions, no thought disorder and no disturbance or disorientation. He definitely did not seem to be insane.'

At the hospital Pound was patient number 58,102. We can glimpse him in the description given in an article by Jack LaZebnik in the *New Republic* in April 1957. It is an almost comical scene. 'For eleven years he has held his own court where he has been able,' LaZebnik recounts, and goes on to itemize this fallen figure, part-clown and part-professor. 'There, in a loose sweatshirt, an old GI overcoat, baggy trousers, heavy white socks, bedroom slippers, long underwear showing at his ankles,' it lists: 'Pound sits on a chair warm afternoons on the wide, lush and sweeping lawns of the grounds and peers at his visitors from beneath a green eyeshade.' The spectacle was irresistible. The magazine goes on: 'He has the problem of too many visitors who seek advice, aid, answers, literary judgements, and just the thrill of looking at him.' The thrill lay in the contradictions: he was a traitor in an army overcoat, a poet in a sweatshirt. Ezra Pound – inventor of modern poetry, friend and editor of the most important artists of the twentieth century, the man who everybody said should win the Nobel Prize – was on show as a circus freak.

It was the world's least orthodox literary salon: convened by a fascist, held in a lunatic asylum, Tuesdays and Thursdays, Saturdays and Sundays, 2 until 4 p.m. Among the many who came to visit – tourists, young activists, ambassadors and academics – were foremost the poets. T. S. Eliot came to see Pound at St Elizabeths, as did Robert Lowell, Marianne Moore, W. S. Merwin, Charles Olson, Kathleen Raine, Allen Tate and William Carlos Williams. John Berryman visited twice; Louis Zukofsky brought his ten-year-old son, who played the violin on the lawn. A. Alvarez came, as did Paul Blackburn, Guy Davenport, James Dickey, Ronald Duncan, Randall Jarrell, Archibald MacLeish and Frederick Seidel. They were the most famous poets in the world and those who had not yet amounted to anything; they were the first generation of modernists and the still-young postmodernists, who in the years after their visits to Pound would reinvent American poetry. They brought him peach candy and jasmine tea, brownies and books, and they sat close by his feet and listened to him talk.

One suspicion has always circled Pound: that he was faking. This distrust takes several forms. It surfaces in the common claim that modern art is a clever fraud, and in this specific biographical episode it appears as the recurring hint that Pound was not insane but only pretending in order to escape the death penalty. This suspicion has as its opposite the idea, held with equal force by many, that despite it all – the broadcasts, Pound's allegiance to Fascism, his badness – here was a truly great poet, one apart from the rest, who cannot be judged by mere human standards. Beneath the case, and the allure of Pound, is this tension between genius and fakery.

Pound in the insane asylum encapsulates the central questions about art, politics and poetry of the twentieth century. These are questions about what madness is, and what makes genius; about the connection between experimental art and extreme, often illiberal political sentiment; about the consequences of the Second World War, and specifically America's post-war ascendance; and about the modern world's relation with its immediate past. Pound at St Elizabeths is the riddle at the heart of the twentieth century. This period of his life offers a rare luxury of records, for in his dozen years at the hospital Pound became an oddly public figure: one whose movements were observed and whose speeches were written down. One might see incarceration in a mental hospital as a style of silencing. But at St Elizabeths, Pound was on display.

The most famous account of a visit to Pound in the hospital is that given by Elizabeth Bishop in her wary poem 'Visits to St Elizabeths'. 'This is the house of Bedlam,' it begins, for Bedlam was the asylum for the insane in medieval London and has become a symbol for all mental hospitals. That she means a specific hospital is revealed only in the title; the name of the hospital in turn hints at which particular patient we are going to see.

> This is the man
> that lies in the house of Bedlam

runs the second stanza, and the half-rhyme of 'Bedlam' and 'man' whispers one more thing: that this is his proper place.

The poem mimics a visit. We start by looking upon the hospital and expect to meet the patient, but the peculiar motion of these crablike stanzas thwarts our approach. Each stanza swells, adding an extra line and changing the adjective qualifying the man. He is 'tragic' in the third stanza; he is 'talkative' in the fourth. It builds:

> This is a sailor
> wearing the watch
> that tells the time
> of the honored man
> that lies in the house of Bedlam.

We are approaching along the hallways now, passing others, coming close, but as the stanzas grow the man retreats, and those same words which promise to draw us near only serve to keep him at a deepening remove.

The poem is a version of the old nursery rhyme 'The House that Jack Built': 'This is the house that Jack built. / This is the cheese that lay in the house that Jack built. / This is the rat that ate the cheese . . .' and so on. Bishop's poem borrows the pattern of this sweet children's song but turns it sour. In the eighth stanza, which is eight lines long, we pass 'a Jew in a newspaper hat / that dances weeping down the ward' and now the man is 'cruel'. Something is broken and the poem is troubled. 'This is a world of books gone flat,' writes Bishop. There is one repetition too many:

> These are the years and the walls and the door
> that shut on a boy that pats the floor
> to feel if a world is there and flat.
> This is a Jew in a newspaper hat
> that dances joyfully down the ward
> into the parting seas of board
> past the staring sailor
> that shakes his watch
> that tells the time
> of the poet, the man
> that lies in the house of Bedlam.

It is here, as all the world tilts, that we first hear he is a poet.

'Visits to St Elizabeths' was written for a special issue of an Italian magazine dedicated to Pound in the early autumn of 1956. Its first context would therefore have made explicit the identity of the madman we are going to visit, but this identification works against the spirit of the poem, which has at its heart an endless putting-off, as if it were a clue in operation against itself. This poem, which promises to deliver us to him, never names Pound, and so much in this encounter is uncertain. Encounter, or encounters: the poem imagines only one but the title acknowledges several, for it is called 'Visits'.

Bishop visited Pound many times. In the first week of May 1948 she went to Washington to see her friend Robert Lowell, who was serving as the Consultant in Poetry to the Library of Congress, and he took her out to St Elizabeths to see Pound. In September 1949 Bishop moved to Washington to succeed Lowell in his post, and she returned to visit Pound. At Christmas 1949, she gave him a bottle of eau de cologne. On 21 February 1950 she took the poet Weldon Kees along with her, and Pound asked her to bring him books and magazines in foreign languages. On 27 June 1950 she wrote to Lowell: 'Pound is mad at me because I put off getting something microfilmed for him.' On 17 August: 'We had quite a pleasant visit, I thought, & Pound is very forgiving about my not coming oftener, although he sees right through me.'

Bishop always stood a little askew from her generation: she was, as she wrote in her poem 'Keaton', 'made at right angles to the world'. Her year as poetry consultant was an unhappy and uncertain time. She was drinking hard and often unwell, and her biographer Brett Millier suggests that Bishop hated having to visit Pound. 'These meetings with Pound were a confrontation between Elizabeth Bishop and a whole tradition of modernist poetry, a potential way of life,' Millier writes, and reads Bishop's poem as her final defeat of Pound: 'The poem put to rest Pound and what the example of his career had meant to her.'

This does not feel quite right: both too narrow and not particular enough. It does not account for why she waited six years and then wrote the poem, nor for its peculiar poise. The man in Bedlam is cruel and brave, tedious and tragic, honoured; this is no simple reckoning. The poem is a puzzle and there is no way to account for its force without participating in its madness: without, that is, conjuring in the spaces of all it withholds. Later, when Bishop told friends the stories of her encounters with the old mad poet, she made them laugh by listing the things he had asked her to bring: maps of the Paris sewer systems, journals in Bengali and Japanese, in languages she knew he didn't speak. She guessed he only wanted to see his name in them. In her poem, however, he would never see his own name, but he would see hers: Elizabeth, there at the head of the page. Pound liked nicknames, and he had one for Bishop: 'Liz Bish'. When Pound wrote letters from the hospital, he began by writing his location at the top right-hand corner of the page, and he called it 'S Liz'.

Elizabeth or Liz: the poet is the hospital. Just as the patient is never named, nor is the visitor mentioned, only implied by what she sees as she walks those crooked halls. She shares the view with madmen, and this is the poem's most troubling allegation: that visitor and patient are no different. The poem depends upon a series of unexpected doubles and alternatives, each switching back upon itself, buried in the language of this type of encounter. Take the words 'guest' and 'host': these are apparently opposite positions, yet in Latin – and Italian – the two are the same word. At the hospital, in the dynamic of the visit, the lines are blurred, and here is the poem's great twist. If the visitor is the patient then the mad are sane, too. This is the man that lies in the house of Bedlam, it repeats, but 'lies' means several things: to be recumbent, to remain and to deceive. Buried beneath the poem's childlike chorus is the doubt: that Pound belongs here for he is mad or does not belong here for he is only faking, and all of us are mad.

Later, after leaving Washington and moving to Brazil, Bishop liked to retell the story of her visits to Ezra Pound. She made it into a funny routine for her friends, and they laughed as she described Pound sitting beneath the hospital Christmas tree, or how he mistakenly used the eau de cologne as hair oil. Where once there were visits, now there are only versions. Just as her poem had shifted its adjectives, each stanza skewing the previous story, so too did Bishop's tellings shift over time. But always at the centre, as patient as a spider, waits Pound. The madman is locked for ever in his Bedlam, boxed up by jangly rhyme and crazed repetition. But even if the poem acts as a prosecution, putting Pound away, it equally works against itself, freeing Pound into multiple versions and into the eyes of others. Years later, long after all their visits, Bishop wrote to Lowell: 'I have received a rather strange note – my one repercussion, I suppose – asking me if I ever actually did meet Pound or if I made it all up.'

If you spend your life teaching literature, as I do, you cannot avoid bumping into Ezra Pound. I don't remember when I first heard his name, but what I knew of him was the same prose commandments that everybody knows. Literature is news that stays news, he said, and Make It New: his once-radical injunctions now reduced to the status of exam questions for reluctant teenagers. What I first knew of him was his certainty, and when in the summer of 2011 I found myself in an uncertain time, living in a small college town in a cold, northern American state, far from home and far from my young son, then Pound's commandments came to feel a little like salvation. You can read and write your way out of trouble: if there is a lesson inside the mountain of Pound's life and works, it is this. The consolations I have sought throughout my life have always been bookish, but the best of Pound is his insistence that thinking must begin with an intimate response. 'The critic who doesn't make a personal statement, *in re* measurements he himself has made, is merely an unreliable critic,' Pound wrote in his *ABC of Reading*: 'He is not a measurer but a repeater of other men's results.' I liked that, and noted it down, so as not to forget.

I have not written many books, but enough to know that our subjects find us, and once they present themselves then they chime in unexpected ways, rhyming against the happenstance of life at that particular moment. I thought this was my idea, but inevitably, as I read my way after Pound, I met it again in his own words. In his *Guide to Kulchur* – another of his schoolmasterish handbooks – Pound set out a test of true poetry. 'No man can read Hardy's poems collected but that his own life, and forgotten moments of it, will come back to him, a flash here and an hour there,' he wrote, for we bring our own unexpected familiarities to each new reading. He continues: 'The domain of culture begins when one HAS "forgotten-what-book".' Art starts when sensation glimmers at the edge of recall, almost known, already.

Forget the books, for a moment: step outside. The great Pound scholar Donald Davie calls for a 'pedestrian reading' of Pound's poetry. He writes, 'the first requirement for a study of Pound is a set of maps (preferably ½" to the mile),' for Pound's poetry is geographical, concerned with the writing of places. A map is the first requirement but better still is to make the journey. 'To do that poetry justice,' Davie continues, 'the critic must turn himself into a tourist,' but literary critics often look down upon such leisurely work, as if this were the province of Jane Austen book clubs and Civil War re-enactors, equivalent to collecting typewriters or admiring a long-dead writer's desk.

I took Davie's prompt literally. In the year before I left the United States and moved back to London, where I was from, I went to St Elizabeths Hospital and spent a day walking its halls. The hospital is abandoned now, so to people it with memories I tracked down as many of Pound's surviving visitors as I could. I visited a beautifully dressed poet on the Upper West Side of New York City and took a slow train to Princeton to see an ex-soldier and literature professor. I drove four hours across two states to listen to an ageing poet laureate do an impersonation of Pound's voice, and I found a woman who had played tennis with Pound at the hospital. Back in Europe, as I tried to settle the pieces of my disjointed life, I went to the castle in northern Italy where Pound retreated after he left the hospital and where his daughter still lives, and I found the field at Pisa. 'His thought was not dry on a shelf,' wrote Pound in Canto 99, while he was at St Elizabeths, and I went too to speak with those for whom Pound is still alive and whose ongoing devotion has given the poet an unexpected afterlife. They were in unlikely places: a painted squat in Rome, a gathering of Poundian obsessives in Dublin, a grey seminar room at dusk in a tower in central London, where a group of amateur Poundians spend their Friday evenings unpicking each allusion in the *Cantos*. Wherever people speak of Pound, there I tried to go.

Their stories differed, of course; or rather, their Pounds differed; and this is just as Pound would have wanted it. In a cryptic phrase in Canto 59 he describes one way of witnessing the world:

> periplum, not as land looks on a map
> but as sea bord seen by men sailing.

The odd term 'periplum' comes from the name given to the records of the wanderings of Hanno, an explorer from Carthage in the fifth century BC, whose unsystematic compilation of useful information – on local commerce in the territories he visited, on the times of tides and winds, on all the things a wanderer might learn and like to know in a strange land – was titled *Periplus of Hanno*, 'periplus' being the Latin form of a Greek word for a circumnavigation or, literally, 'a sailing-around'. Pound got the Latin slightly wrong, but what he meant was a story told from the sides: as if the storyteller were not a god looking down from above but instead a sailor on a ship imagining the landscape behind the shore he can see far off. Any story told like this will necessarily be imperfect, for our vision has limits and faults; it might at times be contradictory. But this is, perhaps, precisely the style of telling – occasional, fragmented, in glimpses – that the complex figure of Pound invites.

Pound's biographers have sought to harmonize differing accounts of Pound into a single portrait of the truth of the man; this book attempts something close to the opposite, which is to permit rival tellings to sing their discord. Each of the following chapters opens with an encounter between Pound and another – six poets, and a doctor – at St Elizabeths, and follows this as a way into the enigma.

This involves trying to see him through the eyes of others, which means that at times I have let misunderstandings tell their own story instead of trying to settle them into mine.

I have been led by archives and by what they are willing to tell. My account of Pound is therefore necessarily partial. Dorothy, Pound's wife, was his most regular visitor, yet precisely because she moved to an apartment near the hospital and went to see him so often, she did not need to write to him; and has therefore left fewer traces. By contrast, those most vocal in their responses were the poets who visited Pound, and these are therefore the heartbeat of my study.

All archives are incomplete; this was one of Pound's great themes. I have made visible the records upon which my account relies, and when those records are unavailable, I have acknowledged this too. When Pound arrived at St Elizabeths on 21 December 1945, he was taken to Howard Hall, which was the high-security block for the criminally insane, and the restrictions of this locked ward echo its unknowability. There is little archival evidence left from Howard Hall and the building was torn down fifty years ago. But at the start of February 1947 Pound was transplanted to Cedar Ward in Center Building, and then the following year he moved downstairs to the ward directly beneath: Chestnut Ward, which was his home for a decade and which still stands today. I could walk within these buildings and touch the walls and floor, and then pursue what took place there through the huge Pound file kept at the National Archives in Washington, DC. The hospital files were one central resource; less scientific, more impressionistic but equally powerful for my purpose were the diaries kept and letters sent by each of the visitors, as well as, best of all, the poems they went on to write about meeting Pound. As far as possible, then, this is the periplum of an entrapped man. He was kept in a narrow space, but he was various enough to appear different to each who looked upon him.

Much in the story of Pound now reads like a dispatch from a foreign land. It is the saga of a figure from a distant time and perhaps what makes Pound appear most antique is his insistence upon the urgency of poetry. In an age in which we are often told that few people care for or read poems – except at a funeral or a wedding – it is worth asking a simple question, here at the beginning. What do we lose, if we lose poetry? I don't think anyone but the strictest formalist would mourn the passing of particular poetic forms – the English sonnet, the sestina, pentameter, rhyme – for themselves, but I hope that all would mourn the loss of these many rich ways of recording and in turn reinventing human experience. Poetry has the capacity to be a radical art form: one which transforms society. This idea used to be more familiar than it is now. There is a long tradition, in the West, which holds that poets can and must better the world. In the sixteenth century Sir Philip Sidney insisted that the poet 'lifted up with the vigour of his own invention, doth grow in effect another nature, in making things either better than nature bringeth forth, or, quite anew, forms such as never were in nature.' This new poetic world is, he wrote, 'golden', and when in the early nineteenth century Percy Bysshe Shelley defended poets as 'the unacknowledged legislators of the world' he shared this same hope that in poetry man might improve the world. Poetry: the name comes from the Greek word for 'making', and each poem is a possible utopia.

Pound was perhaps the last believer in this traditional claim for poetry's public role. He wrote: 'When words cease to cling close to things, kingdoms fall, empires wane and diminish,' and he believed that the poet's responsibility was to keep the language pure and to teach his fellow men to see the world right. This idea lay behind his elaborate ambitions for his poetry, which he believed would restore justice and fairness to human society. But his life is also a parable of the dangers of precisely this style of thinking and this faith in grand social schemes. This same principle led him to the darkest reaches of the twentieth century. It led him to fall half in love with authoritarian politics, with cruelty and violence; to hatred and confusion. Whether or not we believe that Pound was a traitor to the United

States of America depends upon our political opinions. But it is hard to deny that he did betray the other kingdom of poetry. 'Every artist's strictly illimitable country is himself,' wrote E. E. Cummings in a comment upon the imprisonment of his old friend, and perhaps Pound's final betrayal was of all the things he stood for, and believed himself to be.

I cannot go to visit Pound now, for he is long dead; cannot ask him my questions. But his visitors, and their records, are waiting.

Timeline of Pound's Years at St Elizabeths

1945
21 December: Pound is admitted to Howard Hall at about 5.30 p.m. The following morning he undergoes his admissions interview with Dr Edgar Griffin.

26 December: Pound sits for his mugshot.

1946
3 January: William Joyce – known as Lord Haw-Haw, and convicted of treason against the United Kingdom for his broadcasts during the Second World War – is executed in London.

4 January: Charles Olson visits St Elizabeths for the first time. He is a regular visitor for the following two months.

5 January: Dr Jerome Kavka interviews Pound for the first time.

18 January: A brief pre-trial hearing is held at the District Court, before Judge Bolitha J. Laws. Pound is present.

30 January: The sanity hearing, scheduled for today, is postponed. During these weeks, psychiatrists at Howard Hall intensively examine Pound.

13 February: The sanity hearing finally takes place at the District Courthouse. The jury finds Pound to be 'of unsound mind'.

4 March: Pound is permitted to go into the enclosed area around Howard Hall, known as 'the Moat'. The following day, in Fulton, Missouri, Winston Churchill gives his famous speech warning of the 'Iron Curtain' between the Soviet Union and Europe. This is subsequently seen by historians as the start of the Cold War.

7 July: T. S. Eliot visits for the first time.

10 July: Dorothy Pound visits for the first time. From now on, she is his most regular visitor, coming out to the hospital perhaps three or four times each week.

September: Dorothy is granted power of attorney over her husband.

1 October: Sentences are read out at the first Nuremberg war trial of twenty-three Nazi leaders.

1947
3 February: Pound moves from Howard Hall to Cedar Ward in Center Building. This is the coldest day on record in North America: −63°C in Alaska.

April: Pound's daughter Mary gives birth to a boy, Walter de Rachewiltz. He is Pound's first grandchild.

May–June: Pound transliterates the 305 Confucian Odes into a 'singing key' in his notebook.

18 October: William Carlos Williams visits after lunch.

1948

January: Pound moves from Cedar Ward to Chestnut Ward.

9 February: Pound's mother Isobel dies in Italy. This month Julien Cornell files – and then withdraws – an appeal with the District Court.

February, March and April: Robert Lowell, John Berryman and Randall Jarrell visit Pound, along with many others. Superintendent of the hospital Winfred Overholser attempts to limit the number of Pound's visitors.

20 July: New Directions publish *The Pisan Cantos*.

1949

February: Pound wins the Bollingen Prize for *The Pisan Cantos*. In the early months of this year he is translating Sophocles' *Elektra*.

June: The radio police drama *Dragnet*, about the laconic sergeant Joe Friday, airs for the first time. Pound later becomes a regular listener, on a radio on the ward.

July: Pound is permitted to go out on to the lawn, under Dorothy's custody.

October: New Directions publish *The Selected Poems of Ezra Pound*.

1950

14 June: A young neo-Nazi called John Kasper writes to Overholser to ask permission to visit Pound. This is granted and Kasper travels to the hospital shortly after.

Elizabeth Bishop visits Pound throughout this spring and summer.

27 June: America enters the Korean War. It lasts three years.

1951
9 May: America tests a thermonuclear fission bomb for the first time.

16 July: The publication of *The Catcher in the Rye* by J. D. Salinger.

26 December: Sheri Martinelli, an out-of-work painter and muse to the Beats, writes to introduce herself.

1952
January: Sheri Martinelli starts visiting. This year, Pound translates Sophocles' *Women of Trachis*.

28 April: The war between America and Japan officially comes to an end, meaning the conclusion of the Second World War.

21 June: T. S. Eliot meets Pound on the tennis court at St Elizabeths.

1953
20 January: Dwight D. Eisenhower becomes thirty-fourth President of the United States.

5 March: Joseph Stalin dies. This month, Pound's daughter Mary arrives in Washington, and stays for ten weeks.

15 May: Charlie Parker plays the *Jazz at Massey Hall* concert in Toronto, along with Dizzy Gillespie, Bud Powell, Charles Mingus and Max Roach.

July: Faber publish *The Translations of Ezra Pound* and Pound tells Guy Davenport that he wishes to return to writing cantos. This month a doctor diagnoses Pound as belonging to the 'narcissistic personality type'.

23 November: The Harvard undergraduate Frederick Seidel visits Pound and stays for Thanksgiving weekend.

1954

January–February: Publication of *Women of Trachis* in the *Hudson Review*, as well as *Literary Essays of Ezra Pound*, edited by T. S. Eliot.

17 May: The Supreme Court rule in *Brown v. Board of Education of Topeka* that the segregation of public schools by race is unconstitutional.

June–November: Pound is writing Cantos 91 to 95.

7 August: Eustace Mullins, a conspiracy theorist, comes to visit. This month Pound writes to his daughter: 'I don't even feel licked / merely caged.'

September: Harvard University Press publish Pound's *The Classic Anthology Defined by Confucius*.

29 October: Ernest Hemingway, who once gave boxing lessons to Pound, wins the Nobel Prize in Literature. In an interview, the new Nobel laureate comments, 'This would be a good year to release poets.'

1955

May: Overholser diagnoses Pound with 'Psychotic disorder, undifferentiated'. This month centenary celebrations take place at the hospital, which received its first patient in 1855.

June: Pound writes Canto 90.

September: *Section: Rock-Drill de los cantares* (Cantos 85–95) is published, for the first time, in Milan. This month *Lolita* by Vladimir Nabokov is also published, in Paris.

1 November: The Vietnam War begins.

1 December: In Montgomery, Alabama, Rosa Parks refuses to give up her seat on a bus to a white passenger and is arrested.

1956
This year Pound contributes eighty or more pseudonymous or unsigned articles to the *New Times* of Melbourne, as well as *Edge*, *Strike* and *Voice*.

5 June: Elvis Presley appears on the Milton Berle show and grinds his pelvis while singing 'Hound Dog'. The newspapers are outraged. 'Mr Presley has no discernible singing ability,' notes the *New York Times*. 'His one specialty is an accented movement of the body.'

August: John Kasper is arrested in Tennessee for trying to prevent the desegregation of a high school.

1 November: Allen Ginsberg's *Howl and Other Poems* is published in San Francisco.

1957
March: Pound is writing Canto 99. By the end of this year he has completed a first draft of *Thrones de los cantares* (Cantos 96–109).

4 September: In Arkansas, Governor Orval Faubus calls out the National Guard to prevent nine African-American children from entering the high school.

4 October: Sputnik is launched. The following month a dog called Laika is the first living being to be sent into space.

October to December: Pound is writing Cantos 107 to 109.

1958
January: Pound finishes Canto 100. He had promised that this would be the final canto, but it is not.

14 April: Pound's lawyer Thurman Arnold files a Motion to Dismiss Indictment with the District Court in Washington, DC.

18 April: Following a short hearing at the District Courthouse, the indictment is dismissed.

7 May: Pound is officially discharged from St Elizabeths.

PART ONE

1946

you do meet someone

as I met you

on a printed page

Charles Olson,
'Letter 5', *The Maximus Poems*

Charles Olson reading the *Cantos,* 1949

I

Hell-Hole

On the night before he first sees Pound he takes his words and cuts them up. They fall like ash, a storm.

It is Monday 26 November 1945 and an exceptionally tall and ruffled man somewhere between youth and middle age is at home in his small apartment in the outskirts of Washington, DC. He is so tall that he breaks beds and has to have his shirts made specially; so tall that he was exempt from military service during the war. His name is Charles Olson. Later, he will be celebrated as the father of postmodern American poetry, but this evening he is not quite yet a poet. Before him is the new issue of *PM* magazine, which includes an outspoken, perhaps foolish, interview with Ezra Pound. 'If a man isn't willing to take some risk for his opinion, either his opinions are no good or he's no good,' Pound declares in the interview and Olson notes this down. He copies out two phrases from his volume of Pound's *Cantos*, too, and he takes lines from the strange and rambling essay called *Jefferson and/or Mussolini*, which Pound wrote in early 1933 and which now, after the war, looks like his most incendiary book. 'Stand with the lovers of ORDER,' Pound instructs, and Olson notes it down, and then: 'a one-party system is bound to appear'. These are troubling phrases. It is a careful jumble, and at the top of the page, as if this were a legal proceeding, Olson adds a title: 'Your Witness'. The next day he goes into the centre of the city and in the pillared courthouse just after lunch he hears Pound described as a traitor, then as insane, and last of all as one of the greatest literary geniuses of the time. Olson watches as Pound stands silent, and he catches the look in Pound's eyes: dark, full of pain and tired. He thinks for a moment about reaching out to touch him.

At the end of 1945 St Elizabeths Hospital housed 7,031 patients. There were 4,109 men and 2,922 women; 4,835 were white and 2,196 were, in the language of the time, colored. In December 102 arrived, almost all of them servicemen who had come back from the war but stayed touched by it, and these numbers tell us two things. They suggest the overcrowding that had cursed the hospital since its first construction, and they reveal the huge scale of life here, how this is a place where one man might get lost. On 21 December the patients in occupational therapy finished wrapping 1,425 Christmas gifts in bright tissue paper. These were for the women but almost everybody got something for that afternoon the more mobile patients distributed through the wards 3,096 green and red rough muslin bags, each filled with an apple, salted nuts in cellophane and a pack of chewing gum. That evening, as the wards of Center Building were echoing with the laughter of humble gifts being handed out, Ezra Pound arrived at St Elizabeths.

Pound did not receive a gift because he was not on the wards. He was brought direct from the District Courthouse to Howard Hall, a separate and enclosed building to the west of the hospital grounds. This was the maximum security section, for the most dangerous patients, and it was designed to keep the criminally insane and the violent apart from the war-shocked soldiers who filled the rest of the hospital. It was three storeys, square and brick, with a tower at two corners; a low garden around it, and then a high wall. 'Howard Hall is totally inadequate,' notes the hospital's 1945 annual report: 'it lacks hydrotherapeutic, recreational, occupational and various other facilities.' Pound stopped his ears with paper and spent the night trying to escape the cries of the other patients.

In the morning he reported to his admission interview. 'This patient this morning strolled into the examining room, seated himself wearily in the chair offered him, sighed deeply, held his head, and immediately began to complain about his Howard Hall surroundings,' begins the lightly sardonic account kept by the doctor who conducted the interview. Dr Edgar Griffin was clinical director of Howard Hall and saw many patients in many states of various distress, but this patient insisted he was different. His shirt was untucked and his buttons were undone, and he talked about Confucius and the founding of the Bank of England. At one point he took out a small notebook and from it made a short speech about Italian politics and how he was not a traitor but a saviour. 'Delusions of persecution and grandeur,' noted the doctor and wrote it all down.

To the doctor that morning Pound told a colourful story. He recounted how he had moved to Italy because he and his wife Dorothy could afford to live there on their small income, and how when the war began he knew his ideas could help, so he sought out the microphone and started to broadcast. He told the doctor that he had been misunderstood, and how they had held him in a cage at Pisa. He slept on the floor there, he said, and then he suffered from 'great confusion and loss of memory'. At the start they treated him like a criminal, but later they were kind. When they brought him to America he was first held at the city jail, and then the old symptoms started to return, but he recovered once he was transferred to a public hospital in early December. Now he feared he would fall ill again, because of the noise and bright lights. 'What is wrong with you?' the doctor asked, and Pound replied: 'All of Europe upon my shoulders.' He was, he repeated, just so tired, and soon he became angry. 'I want quiet,' he said, raising his voice, and 'If this is a hospital, you have got to cure me.' Cure you of what? asked Dr Griffin, and Pound replied, 'Whatever the hell is the matter with me – you must decide whether I am to be cured or punished.'

Howard Hall was a place of both punishment and cure. The original plan of St Elizabeths, dating from the 1850s, had no separate, enclosed ward for the criminally insane. Howard Hall was added in 1891: 120 single rooms set in two L-shaped buildings, interlocking to frame a quadrangle. That year, the superintendent described this as 'a perfectly secure ground where the inmates can be at will in the open air and sunshine. Here they can grow plants, keep their pet birds and animals, and make it their home.' On the original plans the structure looks fine and elegant. There are walkways marked 'veranda', which suggests lemonade and civil afternoons in the Old South. It did not turn out this way. The verandas were iron-barred external walkways, while the courtyard was shadowed by the high buildings ringing it. All was tall and narrow. The doors were seven feet high and two feet ten inches wide, each a single plate of metal with three hinges, two locks and an anchor bolt at the top and bottom. On each window was a diamond-pattern iron lattice, as if the whole building were made from lopsided squares, each one locking into the next.

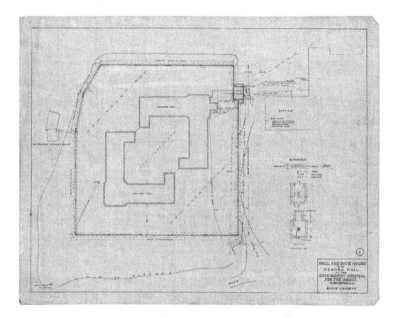

It was imagined as one thing, but soon became another. Howard Hall was built to house those patients whose insanity had turned to crime, but a second subset of the hospital population were soon moved here too: the violent patients. These required greater restriction. The original building had no perimeter wall but in 1915 one was added: twenty-two feet of reinforced concrete, sitting fifty feet from the building. Paradoxically, this permitted greater freedom to the patients, for now they could go out into what they called 'the Moat', the contained area running around the hall. There were cement benches and drinking fountains, concrete walkways and gardens. A photograph taken during the First World War shows the patients surrounded by growing crops, beneath the high wall. Cucumbers, cabbages and corn were grown here, as well as sorghum, whose stems were then turned into brooms in a workshop in the basement. In June 1946 the garden at Howard Hall produced 400 bunches of radishes and 12 bushels of green beans, and these were served to the patients at Thanksgiving in what the annual report called 'a tasteful and bountiful repast'.

The annual reports from Howard Hall record this curious double history: there are crops and there are spasms of violence; there is cruelty and care. In the first months of 1946 the doctors arrange weekly screenings of movies for the inmates, and in March the building is sprayed with DDT and a patient stabs an attendant between the eyes with a spike of wood torn from the floor. 'There are a great many patients in Howard Hall with extremely assaultive tendencies,' notes the annual report, which goes on to recommend replacing the old wooden floors with concrete or tile. In May the floors were tiled, and this was Pound's time here. He was held at Howard Hall for thirteen months, from the end of 1945 until the start of 1947.

Ezra Pound arrived at St Elizabeths with the following possessions: twenty-one stamps, a broken watch, a fifty-dollar cheque from *PM* magazine, a bone-handled cane, seven books and a hairbrush. The hospital inventory is dated 26 December 1945 and also mentions a 'briefcase with papers of unknown value', which were his manuscripts of translations from Confucius and new cantos. Inside the briefcase were his sunglasses, chequebook and a comb. $18.70 of his money was taken to the hospital's finance office, and he was issued with a receipt.

In addition, the following items were carried in an old mailbag:

> 1 bottle of instant coffee
> 1 box of cookies
> 8 pairs of underwear
> 4 towels
> 11 undershirts
> 2 facecloths
> 2 shirts
> 1 blue cardigan
> 2 pairs of slippers
> 2 pairs of pyjamas, one checked and the other blue
> 6 pairs of socks
> 1 pair of shoes
> 1 canvas knapsack
> Unlisted toiletries.

The books – including a poetry anthology, two copies of the New Testament and an army-issue volume of *Jewish Holy Scriptures* – were locked in the hospital vault for the next eight months.

Although Pound was formally admitted to the hospital on Saturday 22 December, his possessions were not inventoried until the 26th, for he had arrived in the middle of the holiday season and the hospital was running with limited staff on duty. So they waited until the next full working day after Christmas, and this slight delay meant also a curious stutter in his check-in. On the 26th Pound sat for his arrival photograph. He had spent the last four days in the hospital in an untucked loose shirt but now he dressed up in the wide, double-breasted suit he had worn on his journey to America, a blue-checked white shirt with a soft collar and a dark wool tie. He brushed his hair. Four days after his arrival at the hospital, Ezra Pound put on a costume and began again.

There are two halves to his arrival mugshot. When they turned him to take his photograph in profile he closed his eyes and held his head straight, but when the camera was directly before him he opened his eyes and tilted his head, just a fraction to the right. The suit sits a little large on his shoulders. His hair is starting to stand up, again. In the eyes, something is missing. He looks as though he has been left behind.

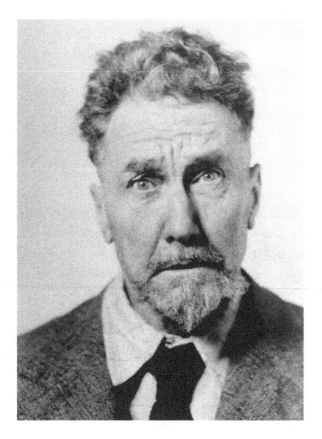

Charles Olson is the first to visit Pound at St Elizabeths. He had been waiting for this. During the war he had worked at the Foreign Languages Division of the Office of War Information, and when that got dull he took up a post at the Democratic National Committee, encouraging Spanish-speaking Americans to vote for Roosevelt. His political opinions are pious and all-American. When he speaks, he sometimes uses teenage slang. He is bored by his years of work for the government and now he wants to be a poet, but he does not know, quite yet, what this might mean. He is thirty-five years old and has published two articles and four slight poems. It is Friday 4 January 1946 and on his way in to Howard Hall he notices the door: heavy black iron, with nine peepholes drilled into it, three by three.

In the visiting room on the first floor Pound is kind, uncertain, open. He talks about his children, the war and how he came to be at the hospital. He tells Olson about the day the soldiers came with guns and about the cage at Pisa. He is confused, too; he does not know the name of the current president. 'Who is this Truman?' he asks, and when he stumbles over his words Olson does not correct him. Instead, he takes notes: he notes how Pound worries at the frayed cuffs of his shirt, and how his jacket has no buttons. 'I wish only to offer him some personal comforts, do some chores for him,' writes Olson in his notebook, and he records how Pound had asked, 'Is it possible I have seen your name somewhere in print?' This pleases Olson and as he stands to leave he promises he will come again, and he suggests that next time he might bring his wife. Pound likes the idea and Olson writes it all down.

Modernist poems often pose an apparently simple question: how, and where, do we begin? Pound's *Cantos* open in a tangle of origins. Pound published three cantos in *Poetry* magazine during the summer of 1917, so this might be one starting point, but he soon abandoned the first of these and heavily rewrote the second and third; he published the first volume of cantos in 1927, under the almost apologetic title *A Draft of XVI Cantos*. Now, this first canto begins:

> And then went down to the ship,
> Set keel to breakers, forth on that godly sea, and
> We set up mast and sail on that swart ship,
> Bore sheep aboard her, and our bodies also
> Heavy with weeping

The opening denies us any once-upon-a-time certainties of context or character. Instead, the poem begins mid-scene, upon a journey already underway, just as it apparently begins mid-sentence, with an 'And'. This present moment is merely continuous with whatever came before. Something is missing – the pronouns, the people – and as readers we must deduce; try to see the relations between those few things we are given.

The scene continues. These are sailors, on a ship, and they sail on to the 'bounds of deepest water' and dark cities covered by mist, and beyond these to a place where the seas flow backwards. Here they perform a sacrificial rite and as the blood runs, the dead come to them with curses and pleas. Among the dead is Elpenor – 'our friend Elpenor' – and once we hear this name we know a little more of who they are: the crew of Odysseus, on their interrupted journey home from the Trojan War to Ithaca. Behind this new poem is an older one, perhaps the oldest of them all: Homer's *Odyssey*.

Now Elpenor recounts how he came to be here. He died a shameful death, drunk on Circe's island, and the sailors left him there, but he asks them to make a monument for him and to inscribe upon it: '*A man of no fortune, and with a name to come.*' This is how the *Cantos* begin: with this doubling, recalled scene, with a journey and an encounter with someone strange yet familiar, a man changed by time and fate, but one whom we once knew. As an opening, it is about the demands of a past which comes to overwhelm our present, which asks almost too much of us now, and which feels like a threat.

Yet it is also – oddly, starkly – about the opposite of this, as the present telling comes to undermine any story of the past. For having conjured this rich scene, thick with poetry, Pound breaks the spell. From nowhere, the poem turns to Latin:

> Lie quiet Divus. I mean, that is Andreas Divus,
> In officina Wecheli, 1538, out of Homer.

He gives the publisher and translator's names of a sixteenth-century Latin translation of the original Greek of the *Odyssey*, and in doing so Pound reminds us that he has only been retelling an old story. It's just a book, held on pages, shifted through languages, from Greek to Latin and here into English. This is nothing but a bundle of documents, each as frail as paper, and the poem is a magician's trick, cruelly pulled off: where you thought you were beginning something new, you are only reading a dead language.

On 10 January, the week after Olson's first visit, Pound sat for a Rorschach test at Howard Hall. The methodology is simple: he was shown ten inkblots and told the doctor what each recalled to him. 'A brilliant but pedantic individual,' concluded Dr Kendig in his report, in possession of 'abstract and theoretical intelligence of a high order and unusual creative gifts', and so far, this sounds as though he is saying nothing more than that Pound is a poet. He goes on:

> His whole responses, however, are cheap and popular and he gives no original interpretations at all, suggesting in part indifference and contempt for the test procedure (very apparent throughout) but probably also certain retrogressive changes accompanying his advancing years.

Perhaps once, when he was a young man, Pound's responses would have been richer and stranger, but now, the doctor finds, 'he gives no original interpretations at all'. This is a cruel judgement to pass upon a modernist whose most famous poem offers a ruthless assault upon the idea of originality, but this is the drama of Pound at St Elizabeths. You put the old man in a new context and now he looks different. He is lit up by their systems, and everything he says and does is noted down.

The report continues with its description of the patient's habits: 'withdrawal from reality into a more satisfying world of fantasy is a fundamental personality trait'. The opening scene of Canto 1 is a retreat from this daily world into another, as Odysseus and his crew go down into the classical underworld. This moment is drawn from the opening of Book XI of the *Odyssey*, and scholars refer to this as the *nekuia*, which means necromancy or the art of summoning ghosts so as to speak with them. At the start, then, the poem invites us down to a place we can never reach, and it gives us a clue as to how we might get there: with a specific translation of the *Odyssey*, published in 1538. This is rare, but not impossible to find, so one day in the British Library I call this book up from the vault. It is a handsome little volume, bound in soft brown leather, and although it is close to 500 years old it is still good to the touch.

Not knowing what else to do, I turn to the *nekuia*. Here, the beginning of Book XI is still a descent to the underworld, for this is simply a Latin translation of the original Greek, but in this specific edition a series of additional notes propose that we must understand this equally as a journey to hell. In hell – 'in inferno' – the souls meet Ulysses, runs the note at the top of the page, and on the following page, a side note: 'Inferorum locus.' Ulysses is the Latin name for Odysseus. The two landscapes – the pagan, classical world of Homer, and the Christian cosmology of heaven and hell – are not the same; and the *Odyssey* long pre-dates Christianity. This is why we need this specific volume of 1538, for only this edition lays one place over another. The underworld is hell; one place might be both. At Howard Hall Pound devised a new name for his surroundings. In letters to his lawyer and friends, he began to call it 'hell-hole'. He is hearing the rhyme between place and place, between sound and sound. The canto leads us down to hell, and on to Howard Hall.

We begin with a journey to hell. In March 1946, while appealing for Pound's discharge from the hospital, his lawyer Julien Cornell initiated the process of transfer of the power of attorney. It was not granted to Cornell, but to Dorothy in September 1946, and this gave her the authority to make decisions about Pound's treatment and his movements. She took control of his financial affairs, publishing contracts and income, and in this legal arrangement Pound relinquished his right to personhood. He seems to have interpreted this development in a particular way. Pound's first letters from St Elizabeths are signed with his name – EP or Ez, the swirl of his signature – but sometime in the middle of 1946 or towards the end of that year he stopped signing his name to his letters. He became anonymous. As Elpenor describes himself in Canto 1: 'a man of no fortune, and with a name to come'.

This all might be coincidence, this mix of naming and losing names, these fears of hell and flimsy places, each fading into each. Or it might be something closer to literary prophecy. We might see Pound's early weeks at St Elizabeths as a history oddly fulfilled, one written out in poems long before and waiting for its characters to assemble and perform their scheduled roles.

A man loses his name and another man makes his. The day after his first visit to St Elizabeths, Charles Olson wrote to Dr Winfred Overholser, the superintendent of the hospital, to ask if he might see Pound again. The letter reads as though he were applying for a job. Olson drops a name – 'at the suggestion of Mr Pound's publisher, James Laughlin, of NEW DIRECTIONS' – and states his wish – 'to visit Ezra Pound occasionally while he is in your care' – and adds with best humility: 'My motive is the simplest: I wish to proffer a helping hand to him, and a sympathetic ear.' But he cannot help himself; perhaps he recalls Pound's flattery of the previous day, that politeness about having heard his name before. 'I think that both you and Mr Pound will want assurance,' he adds, 'because I am a writer, that there is no hidden motivation of publication.' There is none, he immediately insists, but the little boast stands: I am a writer.

On 7 February Olson arrived at the hospital at three, and this time he brought with him his wife Connie and a bottle of wine. This was his fifth visit, for Olson had travelled out to the hospital once or twice each week during January, but today Pound was low: his eyes like mud and full of agitation. The jury hearing to settle the question of Pound's sanity and future incarceration had been scheduled for 30 January, and on that morning Pound had got back into his suit. He sat and waited, until late in the day an attendant came to tell him that the hearing had been postponed, and then for the following week Pound had waited for any news. By 7 February he was desperate, uncertain. Perhaps to raise his spirits, or as a compliment, Olson this afternoon opened himself up to Pound. He records, in his notes: 'Mentioned I had stolen a poem from him.'

In Canto 53 Pound includes the Chinese figures for axe and tree, combined to mean something like renovate or, in Pound's version, 'make it new'. Between them is the sun: each day make it new, the ideograms command, and this was a phrase much loved by Pound. It came from an anecdote he had found in Confucius, about a Chinese nobleman who had these three figures engraved upon his bathtub, and Pound used it several times: as a title for a collection of essays; as an expression of what he found most attractive in Fascism. It is now famous as the great modernist slogan, but 'make it new' was never new. It was always quotation and repetition, and, as if to complete the cycle, Olson took the three characters and from them wrote a version of his own, which he called 'A Translation'. Olson's poem simply lifts Pound's own phrases and – as he had done once before – rearranges them on the page. As Olson was explaining all this, Pound raised his right hand like a salute. This meant, Olson thought, 'take it away'.

Each previous visit, the two men had spoken – or rather, Olson listened and Pound spoke – about American history and economics, about the questions the doctors put to him each day, about how the diamond market is rigged, and what Pound called the cultural lag in America, but this was their first discussion of poetry. Once they began speaking about the *Cantos*, Pound mentioned that two he had written could not be published in America, and started to explain. They tell, he said, the story of an Italian girl who has been raped by Allied troops and takes revenge by leading a company of Canadian soldiers on to a minefield. She was, Pound said, 'one of the resistance'. Olson paused for a moment while he deciphered what Pound meant by this, and in his notebook, later that evening, registered his shock. He moves into capital letters. He writes, 'we were listening not only to a fascist, but the ENEMY!' He repeats, 'Pound was talking like no American but an out and out enemy,' and notes again in caps, 'TREASON'. The visit lasted fifteen minutes and Olson and his wife took the bottle of wine home with them, unopened.

Olson drew upon the details of these exchanges for the rest of his writing life. It is tempting to read all this as psychodrama: to see in Olson's gift and his borrowing, in his confession followed hard upon by condemnation, a cycle of trying to please and then falling to hate. We might think, that is, in Freudian terms about fathers and sons and the violence which can pass between them. Olson's notebooks certainly invite this reading. His own father had died suddenly in the summer of 1935, not long after the two had quarrelled, and in late 1939 Olson read Freud's study *Moses and Monotheism*. In his notebook Olson copied out Freud's definition of a hero: 'a man who stands up manfully against his father and in the end victoriously overcomes him'. In early 1945 Olson had been down in Key West, staying with Ernest Hemingway's ex-wife Pauline, and while there he sat at Hemingway's old desk and read Hemingway's copy of an early volume of Pound's poems. 'Maybe Pound discloses you a method,' he wrote in his notebook, and then: 'Let yourself be derivative for a bit. This is a good and natural act. Write as the father to be the father.' Back in Washington, in the early winter of 1945, Olson heard that Pound was to be tried. To get into the trial he needed a press pass, so he convinced the editor of a local magazine to give him a day's work as a reporter. On the day he first saw Pound, Olson was playing a role.

This is, again, the modernist point: that our origins trail a little trouble behind them. In each of his encounters with Pound, both before and after he met him in person, Olson is carefully establishing his authority as a poet. His first glimpse of Pound was in court, and his visits in the early weeks of January were in the shadow of the imminent jury hearing, scheduled, then postponed. Although he has no part in the legal process, the language of trial and judgement soon seeps into Olson's own accounts of his visits. Among his notes is a fragment from the period between Pound's rendition to the United States and his first hearing. Olson observes that the Department of Justice may try 'the citizen Ezra Pound', but neither 'I nor any other writer can allow Ezra Pound the writer to go untried'. Both parts of Pound must stand judgement: the citizen charged with treason and the poet charged with bad faith. 'Because he is a writer, this case of Ezra Pound deserves to be examined by the men who share his responsibility,' Olson explains, and the poets share in Pound's crime because they have all taken from him. 'He is as gifted and skilful a poet as any man who has written the English language in these years of our century,' Olson notes, and asks: 'Shall we learn from his line and not answer his life?' To read only his poetry and ignore his crimes would be the grand betrayal, for it would be to admit that poets are fools and bohemians, not men of the world. He adds: 'a poet must be tried to prove that poets are responsible citizens.'

Olson's meetings with Pound therefore became a kind of theatre, as Olson dressed as a friend but played the role of prosecuting poet. This is what he is doing with his careful notes: he is a poet trying a poet, fixing him in words. As Pound's trial was deferred then postponed during January, Olson's focus sharpened. If the Department of Justice would not try Pound, then Olson would do it himself. On 15 January he compared Pound to the Nazi prisoners tried for war crimes at Nuremberg, and wondered how he might preserve Pound's poetry from the destruction of the man. Even as he feels himself drawing close, he writes, 'I must confront him again soon.'

Each time Olson went to visit Pound at Howard Hall he arrived and waited downstairs in the entryway. An attendant then led him upstairs, passing through the black iron door with nine peepholes and into the first-floor waiting room, with its high ceiling and windows barred by a lozenge-shaped iron lattice. Here, in this straitened setting, Pound was brought to him, and here Olson began thinking about the relation between poetry and place. Among his notes on Pound assembled after these meetings there is a mention of something Olson refers to as 'my SPACE idea'. He had tried to explain this to Pound, he records, but Pound was not interested. With this idea, and its rejection by Pound, Olson is starting to dream up the poems which later made his name: the sprawling *Maximus Poems*, which he began writing in the summer of 1949, and which he wrote for the rest of his short life. *The Maximus Poems* are the epic of a fishing town called Gloucester, Massachusetts, on the east coast of the United States, written as a series of letters and fragments, and they are crucially a record of a specific place and an experiment in how we may capture a place – its limitations and its richness – in poetry. 'Limits,' Olson wrote, 'are what any of us / are inside of' and 'it is elements men stand in the midst of'. In the early weeks of 1946, at Howard Hall, Olson was thinking about place, and how where we put things matters. *The Maximus Poems*, that is, were begun at Howard Hall in the meetings with Ezra Pound in January and February of 1946.

From Pound at Howard Hall Olson learned a simple lesson: where we are might come to define us. It is one thing for a visitor to acknowledge this, and another for a patient trapped inside. In early January 1946 a young doctor called Jerome Kavka noted that Pound 'continually makes extraordinary requests, even so far as to roam beyond the "wall" surrounding Howard Hall'. Pound was at this time confined to Howard Hall and to its inner courtyard, but he was dreaming of the world outside. 'The patient,' Kavka adds, 'does not appreciate his status as a patient.' By February Pound had learned to limit his ambition. He told Olson, 'I want to get out into the yard,' meaning the area beneath the wall, known as the Moat. He is not asking to leave Howard Hall, but only to walk in the area inside its high external wall, which was a privilege granted to those patients who worked on the crops growing there. On 4 March Pound was permitted to do so, and this looks like a mercy, but it is only half so. Both confinement and then its slight relaxation are elements of the essential control over his person, and both say: your movements here are not your own.

It is a teaching that must occasionally be rehearsed. Not long before midnight on 22 April 1946 two military prisoners escaped from Howard Hall. One was captured in the Moat, while the other scaled the wall and vanished. Four days later another prisoner, who had escaped months before, was returned to Howard Hall. He had killed a man in Maryland before they brought him back, and these wilder prisoners share with Pound a single dream of elsewhere. 'I want to get out,' Pound implored Olson. But Olson wished to keep Pound in place.

A poem can be a space of its own. Six years after that afternoon in early February 1946 Olson wrote a composite scene of visiting Pound. He does not give a date, and the scene is so strange that it cannot describe any single visit, but it was only this day, 7 February, that he took his wife with him and she appears in his retelling. In 'Letter 6' of *The Maximus Poems* Olson is remembering the men of Gloucester he sailed with in his youth, and he opens a parenthesis to describe the day of the visit:

> when Con suggested we have fried chicken,
> and get him out of S'Liz for the afternoon,
> eat alongside the tennis courts
> out over the Anacostia.

It is a charming fantasy, to take the patient out on a picnic, but it cannot be. For Pound roars 'pick-nicks' in mockery – and 'pick-nicks' is the only word he speaks in Olson's poem – and Olson adds:

> I was against it
> for another reason, because of the Navy planes
> roar in just there, and the chatter of the patients
> was more to my liking as background
> for the great man, in his black coat and wide hat

On the hill beneath the hospital is the Anacostia River, and next to the river is Bolling airfield, where the Navy planes land, and this was where Pound arrived when he was brought back to America. Olson wished, however, to fix Pound within the rumble and chatter of patients in Howard Hall, inside the hospital sounds. The context is a judgement. There is a little cruelty to the phrase 'more to my liking', for it is not to Pound's own tastes. I want quiet, he pleaded to the doctors, as he was admitted, but they did not grant him this. Pound wished to leave, and was denied, but Olson is the fantasist, for the poem suggests that it is Olson's wish and not hospital orders which keeps Pound indoors that day. He is dreaming of what it would be to have mastery over Pound.

*

In the hospital, context was control, and Pound's most immediate and literal context was what he wore. Clothes were the signs of his status, clear for all to see. In his notes, Olson returns often to Pound's attire. He records that at their first meeting Pound worried at his shirt cuff with his fingertips and that his jacket had lost its buttons; Pound told him that his hospital clothes were so distressed because he had been wearing them since he had been captured in Italy. There is some pathos in his outfit and Olson noticed Pound's discomfort at this. He speculated that 'his worry springs from his normal fastidiousness about laundry.'

In *Maximus*, Pound is no longer this anxious scarecrow but now done up in an unlikely, otherworldly costume. Here is 'the great man, in his black coat and wide hat', and this is the dress of a figure out of time, a preacher or a romantic. It is what you might expect a poet to wear if you had never met one. In the following letter, the poem returns to the scene, and now Olson's wife interrupts with a question. 'Why did you give him a black hat, / and a brim?' he quotes her as asking:

> when he wore tennis shoes,
> and held his pants up
> with a rope?

Of course a patient in a mental hospital does not wear a black coat and wide hat, and Olson has dressed Pound up only to diminish him. For his wife's question has the effect of stripping Pound once more, and the quotation returns him to his hospital uniform. Olson has dressed him up and then dressed him down, and each move in this slow game is one more placing of Pound.

Olson was watching Pound's clothes and making his careful notes, and approaching Pound from this question of dress might give us his whole history: a biography in rags. In the spring of 1895 he leaned for a portrait against the wooden banisters of the porch of Wyncote Public School just outside Philadelphia. His classmates scowl in double-breasted jackets and high-necked gowns and Pound is like them in old-time garb, narrow boots with many lace holes, a black jacket with lots of buttons. He was nine years old and the only one wearing glasses. His hands were delicate. In the fall of 1897 Pound was sent to Cheltenham Military Academy, where he learned to walk in lines and how to drill. The uniform was square and grey with a high collar. He was still wearing glasses. At the start of the academic year 1901 Pound arrived at the University of Pennsylvania. He was fifteen years old, the youngest in his year, and in the freshman class photograph he is the only one wearing a hat – a beret, and a white scarf – but from now on he no longer wears his glasses when he is photographed. Around him are thoroughly modern young men, their faces open with wealth and open to the century, and all except Pound are dressed in dark suits, white shirts and narrow ties.

His clothes – recorded in letters, photographs, memoirs – tell us when he starts to be himself. The poet H.D. met Pound at a Halloween party in 1901 and he was wearing a green Moroccan robe. In April 1905 Pound wrote to his mother from Hamilton College in upstate New York. He told her that he had been eating properly and, in terrible spelling, 'Ive enough collors here to ware for some time,' and then, 'I earnestly desire my diamond tiara gold shoe buckles & my jewelled gallouses.' It is a joke about the money he is spending and also the wishfulness of one who believes he is destined to be a great poet but was stuck in a small northern college town. He arrived in London in August 1908 and soon equipped himself. He bought a suit, a hat and new socks, and wrote home: 'I've got to get a vest some new neck ties hand kerchiefs etc.'

He was dressing to become the thing he wished to be. In March 1909 he wrote to his father to explain that he now had two suits, 'which is precisely one suit of clothes more than I have any real need of,' and added: 'I shall never allow my self to be so encumbered with excessive possions in the future.' Here is the pose of an unworldly poet, at odds with all possessions, but immediately he goes on: 'The only thing I object to is the cut of the english neck tie. but as my waistcoat happens to be cut ungodly high this dont matter.' In July 1909 the literary magazine *Bookman* ran a photograph of him: high starched collar, rich soft coat. Ford Madox Ford met Pound that year and described his outfit: 'a purple hat, a green shirt, a black velvet jacket, in addition to an immense flowing tie that had been hand-painted by a Japanese Futurist poet'. In their letters and diaries his contemporaries notice a grey overcoat with lapis lazuli buttons, spats, a large turquoise earring, floppy berets, a sombrero, a cane, a cape, and always deep colours of shirt, dark blue, pink. He is the bohemian poet, dazzling, ready to stand upon a table and recite his verses.

A photograph: Paris, 1923. Nine men are gathered to celebrate the opening of a nightclub in Montparnasse and eight of them wear white shirts, dark ties and suits. Tristan Tzara has a monocle and neatly parted hair, and Man Ray is wearing a trim bow tie. This is how the serious modernists dressed, like businessmen or the bureaucrats of revolution, and this is only one of the ways in which Pound was never a pure modernist. He liked soft collars, things unbuttoned, and all the old garb of a bygone poet, and in the photograph the collar of his dark shirt flows over his lapels and his big tie is loose.

His clothes speak of his dissent. In the spring of 1939 Pound travelled back to the United States. He had hoped to speak with the president about his economic views and the upcoming war, but this was not possible. On this trip, Pound collected an honorary degree from Hamilton College, dressed in a long black academic robe which soon slipped from his shoulders, and was refused entry to the Stork Club in New York, because he was wearing a loud, striped, purple shirt and no tie. In the city, in late April, he met a young poet called Mary Barnard. In her memoirs she mentions his shabby dark-blue pinstripe suit and his shirt with its wide collar, and as if anticipating Olson's later fantasy she recalls also 'a large, broad-brimmed hat'.

Pound returned to Italy, where he stayed for the war, and in the *New Yorker* on 13 April 1940 he is described as strolling across Rapallo in a white suit, 'tall and broad, with a pointy beard'. In early 1941 he walked through Rome to the Ministry of Popular Culture for his first broadcasts, and he was wearing a huge, double-breasted tweed overcoat with wide lapels, six buttons and deep patch pockets on the front. The pockets are big enough to hold a book and they are often stuffed with papers. In the late summer of 1945, in the military prison at Pisa, he wore a dark shirt with large, pale buttons. It is so soft and loose that it might be the jacket from a pair of old pyjamas.

On his first morning at St Elizabeths the psychiatrist observed 'a rather dishevelled appearance. His shirt tail protruded from his trousers, shirt was completely open at the front, and also unbuttoned at the sleeves.' This year an attendant at Howard Hall glimpsed Pound standing in his cell, looking out of the window with his back to the door. He was wearing trousers, a hospital gown and a bathrobe. He was pale, his beard unkempt, his hair uncombed, and at Howard Hall this was how all the patients looked. 'I saw this everywhere and so it made little impression on me,' the attendant noted in a later memoir. After the years of dressing up – of turquoise and lapis lazuli, of spats and hats and a cane – now Pound is the same as everybody else.

Look again at the list of possessions he arrived with. It is a record of things held on to through the storm. But it is also the mirror of this: an invisible inventory of all that he has lost, all that he has thrown away or has been stripped from him.

On 14 February 1946 Olson arrived to find Pound a little lighter. He had typeset page proofs of new cantos in his hand, and he had been proofreading. 'The whole sense of this meeting was Pound in power, anew,' Olson wrote: 'Flushed with his return to work.' Today, Pound pressed Olson, asking about his own prospects and how his income looked. Olson answered that he was finding it hard to interest publishers in the book he was writing on Melville, and that he had made $60 last year, so little that he had needed to ask his wife to work. On hearing this, Pound laughed. He told Olson that when he was in London there was a year he made only £40, and once a publisher came and offered him £5,000 for his autobiography, but he had turned it down. They were close that day, and perhaps their laughter was a little loud, and at 2.45 the guard came over to stop them. Before Olson left, Pound asked a favour. He handed him an envelope with the corrected page proofs of the new cantos and told Olson to deliver them to James Laughlin at New Directions. These were the cantos he wrote at Pisa, and they were being readied for publication. Olson felt honoured by this, and as he stood to go, Pound said: you are a container for me. He repeated the word: a container. On the envelope he drew a pattern a little like an upside-down staircase, five boxes resting upon one another. My container.

The day before – 13 February – had been the long-postponed sanity hearing. Pound was taken back to the District Courthouse and he listened while the doctors pinned him like a butterfly. A trial is an exercise in applying words to things and this one began with his name. The Clerk of the Court announced 'The Case of Ezra Pound' and then four doctors under the direction of Winfred Overholser spent the morning and early afternoon laying out a train of terms: remarkable grandiosity, considerable distractibility, paranoid, confabulation, delusional, a mentally sick person, psychotic. Pound was not invited to testify and through all this he spoke only once when he cried out, 'I never did believe in Fascism, God damn it!' He was trying to take back one word. After listening for four hours the jury deliberated for four minutes, and when they returned they had a new name for the man in the dock. He was officially 'of unsound mind' and this had the immediate consequence of preserving him from the treason charge and the possibility of the death penalty. He was returned to Howard Hall in the late afternoon.

The jury found him of unsound mind and Olson called him the enemy, and beneath these early weeks at Howard Hall we might see a squabble over ownership: over who has the right to contain Pound and to interpret him. During January 1946, as Olson was weekly visiting Pound, the poet was also the subject of a series of intensive medical interviews: the Rorschach test on 10 January and then regular meetings with Dr Kavka. Pound liked to complain to Olson about the medical men and their questions, how they would come in groups and pester him: they were 'hammering' at him, he said, and grumbled, '4 medicos at me this morning'. Olson's attitude towards Pound was contradictory and shifting, but his record of their encounters is marked by constant, anxious identification with the older poet. Often he mimics Pound's attitudes and adopts Pound's mannerisms as his own. In passing, Olson refers to Kavka as 'this Jew' and speculates that perhaps he changed his name. Pound told Olson that Kavka had laughed at him; 'I tried to get him to take Kavka less seriously,' Olson notes, 'And that he's no more than a graduate student, trying to act professional.' But this graduate student controlled access to Pound, and Olson went to speak with him before several of his visits. He lent him a book of poems, and invited him to dinner, but Kavka refused, explaining that he did not wish to breach confidentiality. The two men are playing the game of ownership, and Pound is playing with them too. In March Pound told Olson that he had asked his publishers to send Kavka copies of all his books. 'God damn Laughlin he'd send them to a doctor but not to me,' Olson furiously wrote: 'I'm damn well going to take them away from K.'

At the end of Olson's first visit, on Friday 4 January 1946, and just as he was leaving the room with high, barred windows, an attendant told him to wait for a moment, down by the entrance to Howard Hall. The doctor wished to speak with him. After so long looking through Olson's eyes, it is strange to see this moment from the perspective of the doctors, but they were taking notes too, and in the case file kept by the medical staff, Kavka recorded 'a very tall and burley individual with ingratiating manners who described himself as a writer'. Olson is not a writer, yet, and now, in the hallway of the madhouse, a few feet from the famous poet, the doctor measured up to the tall writer-to-be. Kavka recounted: 'Throughout the discussion, Mr Olson apparently attempted to gauge the attitude of the writer toward the patient,' and when he uses the word 'writer' he is referring to himself. The doctor is the writer. But Olson pressed on, telling Kavka that 'the patient has always been a strong and mentally egocentric individual', and now he is using the language of psychiatry. Now the future poet is speaking as a doctor.

In a scene this fraught with wishfulness nothing is stable. In his notes Kavka records that Olson described Pound as 'a misunderstanding genius', and this may have been Olson's error – perhaps he meant 'misunderstood' – or Kavka's truth. Perhaps Pound's misunderstandings had led him here to Howard Hall. Perhaps only Olson could understand Pound now, and the doctors with all their questions could only misunderstand. This might be a slip of the doctor's pen or the poet's tongue; it might be error or accusation.

The two men shook hands, parted. Kavka kept the patient Pound but Olson took the envelope of new cantos home with him. Before he delivered it to Laughlin, as he promised he would, he opened it and took the pages out. These were the corrected page proofs of Cantos 74 and 75, and, as Olson read, he copied out phrases into his notebook. Here is Pound at his most defiant, mourning the death of Mussolini: 'The enormous tragedy of the dream in the peasant's bent shoulders.' Here is Pound at his most lyrical: 'The suave eyes, quiet, not scornful, / rain also is of the process.' Here is Pound dreaming: 'To build the city of Dioce whose terraces are the colour of stars.' And Olson thought: I should like to keep this for my own.

The encounters with Olson are one way into the enigma of Pound at St Elizabeths. On his third visit, Olson signed in as usual and, next to his signature – in the space in the entry log in which a visitor declared their relation to the patient – he wrote 'friend'. The guard could not read his handwriting. 'Are you his brother?' he asked. Olson was as yet nobody, but he was planning, and it was by puzzling out his relation to Pound that he became himself.

During the early winter of 1945 Olson was thinking of a long poem. It was to be called *West*. According to George Butterick – Olson's friend and editor – Olson planned to 'cover the history of Western man for the past 2,500 years', beginning with Odysseus and ending on a mysterious figure, 'yet unnamed'. This is the first plan for what became *The Maximus Poems*. They are a remarkable cycle: huge, avid, hungry for change, and most of all marked by vast ambition. They take their title from Maximus of Tyre, a second-century philosopher, but the name suggests their scope. The philosopher with a big name is a stand-in for the tall poet. As he looks upon the American coast Olson declares 'I compell Gloucester / to yield, to / change,' and these poems celebrate the wilful imagination, a kind of seeing elsewhere. In them, one world slips to another. 'The Continental Shelf // was Europe's / first West,' he writes, for the east coast of the United States was once the western edge of Europe. Place is upset by the passage of time. In Gloucester, the merchants who built the city 'hid, or tried to hide, the fact the cargo their ships brought back / was black', for the money that went into making the town library was money made from the traffic in slaves. 'One's forced, / considering America, / to a single truth,' he writes:

> the newness
> the first men knew was almost
> from the start dirtied
> by second comers.

Our origins are never clean and 'knew' rhymes troublingly with new. That which we know is always old.

'It isn't so decisive,' Olson writes, 'how one thing does end / and another begin.' The price of his rich and generous vision of the world sliding through forms is that he cannot be wholly himself, for his own invention is always indebted to others. Olson's poetry is distinguished by two typographical eccentricities. First is the virgule, which is the technical name for the slash in the middle of a line: '/'. Traditionally, this symbol marks when one is quoting verse and wishes to indicate a line break in the original poem, but Olson includes the virgule within a line of poetry. This gives the illusion that all he writes is a quotation. Second: he opens parentheses which he never closes, which has the effect of up-ending the apparent priorities of a sentence. Both are means to preserve the many-ness of things, and to estrange our relation with the words before us on the page. Both appear in *The Pisan Cantos*, which Olson carried out of Howard Hall.

The crucial term for Olson is place. *The Maximus Poems* gather up lists, fragments, inventories, paragraphs from local newspapers, and his own memories, and weave these into a portrait of the fishing port of Gloucester and, by extension, America. But place is not only the subject of these poems; it is also their most abiding metaphor for what a poem is or must be. On one page is a prose account with a note: 'In this place a poem I have not been able to write,' and it gestures to a poem, made from these materials, to be assembled or imagined by the later reader. That is: the poem is larger than the page it sits upon. Olson's most famous contribution to literary criticism is an essay of 1950 called 'Projective Verse'. This is now a classic anthology piece and has been, writes the literary critic Marjorie Perloff, 'safely enshrined as a cornerstone of avant-garde poetics, perhaps the key theological statement in defence of the "new poetry"'. At its heart is a claim for the space of a poem. Too much poetry has been closed, Olson argues, and by this he means poetry in which a set pattern of metre determines the length of the line and by extension the shape of the poem. In a Shakespearean sonnet, for example, each line has five regularly repeating metrical feet, and the sonnet is fourteen lines long. Olson, by contrast, proposes open composition. Now the poem can take not formal measure but the human breath as its building block.

He calls this process 'COMPOSITION BY FIELD' – we are back with his excitable Poundian capitals – and it has two simple consequences. First, form must now emerge from content ('FORM IS NEVER MORE THAN AN EXTENSION OF CONTENT'), and second, the poem adopts a new 'stance towards reality'. In Olson's new poetics, the shape of the poem is defined by that which is inside it, by that which it contains, not by some outside rule. These ideas have long been celebrated and are at the heart of American poetry written in the second half of the twentieth century; they are also far from new. Perloff traces how each of these claims, as well as the terms in which they are expressed, were drawn by Olson from Pound's own critical writings, and goes on to describe Olson's 'Projective Verse' as 'essentially a scissors-and-paste job, a clever but confused collage made up of bits and pieces of Pound' and others. Olson was the father of postmodernism, and his essay its founding document; all are equally second-hand.

This is perhaps as good a definition of postmodernism as any: a confusion of the categories of old and new, of theft and inspiration, and each new work is equally a place of repetition. The poem is not a report upon an external reality but instead an attempt to transfer energy from its subject to its reader. As Olson put it in his essay 'Human Universe': 'Art does not seek to describe but to enact.' My favourite of the *Maximus Poems* is six words long. It is a list of categories from 'The Account Book of B Ellery,' an eighteenth-century merchant who lived near Gloucester, and it runs:

> vessels
> goods
> voyages
> persons
> salaries
> conveyances.

This is a poem, complete. These are the categories by which one merchant believed he could sort his immediate world, but they are also – almost by accident – the skeleton of a great classical poem. The *Odyssey* tells of vessels, voyages, persons and goods, and the old poem is glimpsed behind the new. The archive is a poem and an inventory becomes an epic.

It is too simple to say that *The Maximus Poems* are about Pound. But they are marked by his tricky presence. In one, written in late 1960, Olson lists the characters of his epic, and first on the list is: 'Pound, a person of the poem.' *The Maximus Poems* play with strategies of naming and containing, of a determined space and its slippage, and in all they are the product of Howard Hall. After his run of visits in January and February 1946, Olson went less often in March. This was not quite his final break with Pound, which happened a couple of years later, but their relations began to sour, and Olson's notebooks are increasingly bitter about Pound. It was time to move on. In April 1946 he wrote a new poem. 'We are the new born,' he announced. The poem is called 'La Préface' – promising, again, a start – and when Olson came to assemble his poems into his first collection, called *X&Y*, he put this one first.

The poem continues with an instruction:

Draw it thus: ( ) 1910 (

This looks like a hieroglyph, some strange equation, but as so often with Olson, it appears far less legible than in fact it is. 'The closed parenthesis reads: the dead bury the dead, / and it is not very interesting,' he explains in the following lines, for there are histories which find an end; some stories do simply finish. But this is not one of them. He continues:

> Open, the figure stands at the door, horror his
> and gone, possessed, o new Osiris, Odysseus ship.
> He put the body there as well as they did whom he killed.

The open parenthesis is the unfinished past: the unburied body, the task still left. It is Elpenor, the sailor Odysseus must return to, whose debt begins the *Cantos*. The open parenthesis says that something remains to be settled. We are all new born, once, but we are also built from the past, and the title of the collection refers to those chromosomes which compose us. Olson was born in 1910 but in 1946 he is beginning, and the only way to do so is to go back to the old men who still make claims upon the living, to Pound and to Elpenor. Once you have gone back to honour them, you may move forwards. Once you have gone down to Howard Hall, you may start to make it new.

2

Kafferty

It is Saturday 5 January 1946 and Dr Kavka and Pound are speaking of grandparents when a great noise strikes up in the hallway outside. The patient choir – in which all the singers are criminally insane – are rehearsing, and as well as loud they are a little out of tune. The doctor and the poet get up; the doctor collects his papers, and the two men walk down the hall to a new examining room, farther from the squawk. Pound sits on the long low couch once more, and begins again.

This was their first interview. Kavka has been asked to prepare a complete family history and diagnostic background: education, religious interests, occupation, and sexual and venereal history, although he decides he will leave that last and intimate topic for another day. He does not know what to expect but he finds the patient expansive, pedagogical, willing. Tell me about your family, the doctor asks, and Pound tells without hesitation a grand story of American wile and poetry, of independence and the frontier. There was his father's father, who made and lost three fortunes and served as a congressman for Wisconsin in the 1870s. This was a man who 'wielded considerable National influence', Pound boasts, and he married – and abandoned – a woman from an old, honourable family called the Loomises, who held 'one of the oldest homesteads in America'. If his father's side was politics and pragmatism, then his mother's line was something more poetical. Her father was a northern cavalry captain in the Civil War and a man who had ideas, and he married a woman Pound described as 'a romantic', who loved to read novels to her grandson and was related to the famous American poet Henry Wadsworth Longfellow.

Pound was proud of this history, and in these stories he found sense, and he offered Dr Kavka a helpful symbolic scheme by which to understand all this. 'You have the Colonial family on one side,' he said, 'and the pioneer on the other,' as if all of the nation's history were tributaries flowing into the American river of Ezra Pound. The doctor put this, without further comment, into his report, and in those pages, seventy years later, we can still glimpse something like pleasure: the pleasure Pound felt at talking, at being listened to. He is laying it all out, speaking with his hands, and his voice is warming. It is almost too rich. 'Damn it all,' he told the doctor: 'if I was a novelist or could write history, I would write the entire American history from this family cycle!'

Pound loved to talk. After 5 January Kavka met with Pound almost every day, in order to prepare a complete evaluation to be presented at the sanity hearing, and in their interviews Pound sprawled out low upon a couch and spoke fast, occasionally rising to a fury. Their meetings took place in the mornings, in an examining room at Howard Hall. They were a break in the drudgery of Pound's cell, and in response to the questions posed by the young doctor Pound recounted a brightened vision of his past. The family history is a part of any psychiatric evaluation, and it seeks the origins of today by tracing upstream through the previous generations. It seeks, that is, the traits which repeat in a family, and beneath the apparently formulaic questions – tell me about your grandparents, tell me about your childhood – the doctor was asking Pound to consider his own life as a pattern of symbols, and Pound played along.

He was born happy, he said, and his hair was curly. His first memory was of giant sheepdogs on a farm, and when he was four the family moved to a suburb of Philadelphia. He went to school, where he published his first poems, and on to the University of Pennsylvania, where he studied 'Latin and chess', he said, and where he took his first degree, and then on to Hamilton College in upstate New York for further study. He was boosting his actual academic achievements here, for he never completed either of his degrees, but the doctor wrote it all down. After this American childhood, Pound recounted how he moved to Europe, where he mingled with artists and writers, and settled in Italy after, in a little euphemism, 'becoming interested in the developments of the Italian form of government'. When asked about religious interests, he mentions tennis. He was not a drinker, he said. He married a respectable Englishwoman called Dorothy Shakespear, the daughter of a solicitor, and she gave birth to a boy called Omar. He also told the doctor about his daughter by another woman, and he called this little girl 'the light of my life'.

He did not tell the doctor that he was not Omar's father, but he did imply that Dorothy was descended from William Shakespeare, and while even the doctor was suspicious of this untruth – Kavka's note in the case file is tactful, but unconvinced – it reveals the essential quality of Pound's version of himself. In their interviews Pound was fashioning a persona with a specific genealogy: he was, he was telling the doctor, a true individual born from a line of proud men, free thinkers and, most of all, poets. He mentioned his distant cousin Longfellow and his grandmother who used to write verse; when asked about his own writing, Pound said, 'I took off from Browning,' the English Victorian poet.

The doctor was asking about his background and Pound preferred to see it as a question not of psychiatry but of lineage, what he called his 'stock and hereditary drive'. We might also call it destiny:

Pound recounted his background, that is, as a story of the gifts of blood and acts of will, and this is perhaps what is most striking about the genealogy Pound laid out for Kavka in Howard Hall in January 1946. Even here he still has faith that he is the true interpreter of his past. Kavka noted that Pound 'initiated an elaborate discussion of American Colonial History, pointing out the significance of viewing his personality against such a backdrop, in order to get at the brass tacks of his upbringing'. He is refusing to be judged by the standards of his immediate context; he is reaching instead for the past, and it is purely in this act of selecting and explaining that he presents his own identity. The self, Pound insisted, is an act of will, not psychiatric habit. 'A lot of the psychological bullshit doesn't apply to my case,' Pound told Kavka: 'I don't mean to my breakdown, but to my entire life.' He will teach the doctor what that essential personality is. He will select its symbols and speak it into being.

In the examining room at Howard Hall Pound spoke and Kavka took notes. 'At times,' the doctor observed, 'he would soliloquize in a manner typically found in his poetry,' and explained: 'apparently disconnected thoughts and ideas strung together in a pattern'. Pound was talking about poets and, as the doctor saw, his speech soon turned into something like a poem of a specific type. For in listing his predecessors, Pound mentioned Robert Browning, who is most celebrated for his dramatic monologues: these are poems which are also speeches, or speeches which are also poems. In Browning's monologues a single character speaks, uninterrupted, in the presence of a silent interlocutor, and as he speaks he gradually betrays his secrets and desires. These are poems whose drama turns upon the revelation of character, and this too is the central technique of Pound's early poetry.

In 1925 Pound had selected his early poems into a single volume and he called it *Personae*. For this new edition he chose to put a poem called 'The Tree' first. 'I stood still and was a tree amid the wood,' it begins, and this is an eccentric opening both for a poem and for a collection, but it demands that we imagine being something else, from the inside. From the start, the volume insists that a very foreign thing can speak of its own being, and throughout the poems take the voices of characters from distant times and places. The speakers are troubadours and wanderers, from ancient China and medieval Provence. Here is a caustic old Italian bard ('Bah! I have sung women in three cities, / But it is all the same'), and here a bashful Chinese bride addressing her absent husband ('While my hair was still cut straight across my forehead / I played about the front gate, pulling flowers. / You came by on bamboo stilts, playing horse'); here is an old warrior, restless in a time of peace ('I have no life save when the swords clash'), and what draws them together is that they are reckless exhibitioners of their inner lives. The great assertion behind Pound's early poetry is that the self is formed by speech: our personality does not predate what we say, but instead comes into being only as we speak, and as we speak, we are always giving ourselves away.

The classic objection to modernist poetry is that it is cold and only intellectual, but in reading early Pound we see that this need not be so. For here are love poems, tender with care:

> I would that the cool waves might flow over my mind,
> And that the world should dry as a dead leaf,
> Or as a dandelion seed-pod and be swept away,
> So that I might find you again,
> Alone
>
> ('Francesca')

Here are great shouts of joy and company:

> And yet my soul sings 'Up!' and we are one.
> Yea thou, and Thou, and THOU, and all my kin
> To whom my breast and arms are ever warm,

For that I love ye as the wind the trees
That holds their blossoms and their leaves in cure
('In Durance')

These are songs of longing, and exile, and those cast astray by history, richly imagined, precise. Each poem is a piece of a person, but in the fragment – in this one moment from a life – they stand before us whole.

The poem of Pound's which I knew first is one which is often published without his name. It is his version of the Anglo-Saxon lament 'The Seafarer', and it appears in undergraduate anthologies of medieval verse as a standard translation. This is fitting and suggests that Pound has so completely abdicated his own personality that the poem becomes anonymous, but it is characteristically part of the Poundian game of shifting self-narration. His version begins with a demand:

May I, for my own self, song's truth reckon,
Journey's jargon, how I in harsh days
Hardship endured oft.

The speaker is a wanderer, far from home and with a lifetime of struggle behind him, and he wishes to teach a lesson:

Lest man know not
That he on dry land loveliest liveth,
List how I, care-wretched, on ice-cold sea,
Weathered the winter, wretched outcast
Deprived of my kinsmen.

The seafarer's reward for all his struggle is the right to explain his own life. What he has to say now is perhaps the oldest spiritual lesson of them all. 'Days little durable,' he says, and once a man comes to the end then he will, in a curious, lovely phrase, 'Nor eat the sweet nor feel the sorry,' but instead find that 'His born brothers, their buried bodies / Be an unlikely treasure hoard.'

The poem was written in perhaps the mid ninth century, and Pound's version, done in 1911, sounds at once medieval and modern: it achieves this effect of dissolving history through careful poetic artifice. As is clear from the lines already quoted, it is filled with clipped repetition, of sounds and of struggle, and that the sound works with the sense is what makes it a poem. There is tension, too: between what is particular to him and what repeats for all. Much has been changed in Pound's new version, but equally much has been preserved, for Pound renders the Anglo-Saxon original in modern English vocabulary and yet retains the original poetic form of alliterative verse, which is built upon a skeleton of four strongly stressed, repeated sounds, two in each half of the line. This is a very showy style and one which draws attention to itself; it is hard to reconcile such careful poetic formalism with the speaker's insistence upon his own distinctive individuality, but we may. The poem says: let me tell my own version of events and in the telling let me invent my self. It will be unreliable, of course; it always is. But it will also – at least for this moment, in this place – be me. 'May I, for my own self, song's truth reckon,' the first line demands, both firm and polite. In the old language of song, he is inventing his own self and his own past.

At Howard Hall the doctors were reckoning up their patient and telling his story in their jargon too. But in the examining room with Kavka on those January mornings Pound replied with a performance of his own. 'The patient spoke rapidly, with a faint suggestion of an "English" accent, and modulated his voice frequently,' Kavka noted, and he observed how Pound was apparently 'uninhibited in the choice of words, often using the most profane language and vilification'. This is another persona, and now Pound is playing the defiant poet, a little larger than the restraints of this narrow place, a little outside the conventions of submission and despair. He is a man versed in all the ways of speaking – in profanities, in accents – and all of his speaking is also a work of art.

On 20 January Pound and Kavka met for what the doctor later remembered as 'an emotionally charged session'. On that day Pound turned upon the doctor and asked him about his own parents and his background. Kavka replied that his family was Polish, but the question – where are you from? – is always more trouble than this. It is an allegation: you are not from here. It is also a judgement: you do not belong here. Kavka later suggested that this was simply defiance, as if Pound were questioning the doctor's right to analyze him, but beneath it all we might also hear some racial code. What Pound is really saying is: are you Jewish?

Kavka was Jewish. His parents were first-generation immigrants from Poland; they had eight children, and Kavka was the first to be born in America; St Elizabeths was his first posting as a psychiatric resident. He was twenty-four and just beginning his career. Perhaps Kavka said none of this, but at some point in their weeks of interviews Pound gave the doctor a nickname. Throughout his life, Pound bestowed new names upon the people and places around him. Sometimes they were kind and sometimes mocking, but they were his way of redefining the world, and he called the doctor 'Kafferty'. This is a generic outsider name, a composite of Irishman, Jew and old fashioned racist slang – Rafferty, Kaffir – and a free-floating anti-immigrant slur.

In his report, Kavka noted Pound's unruly gestures and lack of inhibitions. 'Gesticulation was frequently used to press home points,' Kavka observed, 'and his facial expressions were animated, expressive and emotionally appropriate.' Appropriate, that is, to his own emotions, but not polite, and perhaps what the doctor is alluding to here is an extraordinary moment in their meetings. This week – the exact date is uncertain, but it was before 29 January – Pound stood for Kavka and, with his elbows at right angles from his body, and his knees bent almost double, he launched into a song.

Pound sang what he called the 'Yiddisher Charleston Band', which was a bawdy and bad-taste chant he had written twenty years before and named after a satirical old klezmer song about Jews prospering in American society.

> Gentle Jheezus, sleek and wild,
> Found disciples tall an' hairy
> Flirting with his red hot Mary

it begins, and in passing takes in 'ole king Bolo's big black qween / Whose bum was big as a soup tureen' and 'Calvin Coolidge dh' pvwezident'. The song – composed as a game with T. S. Eliot, thirty years before – is a generation out of date, and a cartoon of bigotry. Its prejudices must have felt antique even in 1946, and it is hard at this remove to grasp quite what Pound could have meant by this: to shock the doctor, to make him laugh, to test him? The next day Kavka told Olson that he regretted not having recorded this astonishing performance.

It is tempting to read the case file prepared by Kavka as a record of scientific observation, doctorly and precise. Kavka does not mention the Yiddish Charleston – we only know that Pound did the dance for he boasted about it to Olson – and nor does he ever admit to the patient's antagonisms and challenges. Many years later, after Pound was dead, Kavka wrote a series of short memoirs of his encounters for the journal *Paideuma*, and these present a less guarded account. Kavka recalled how Pound asked for a quart of milk to be delivered to his cell each day, along with a copy of the *Washington Times*, and Kavka arranged all this. These are kindnesses, and Kavka adds, almost as an explanation: 'my father was about the same age and had a somewhat similar sense of humor'. The two men were joined in something more than a strict relation of doctor to subject; it is hard, reading Kavka's later accounts alongside the original report, to escape the sense that he is protecting the older man. Just as he had to Olson, Pound mentioned to Kavka that he was once asked to write a memoir, but that he had refused. Kavka concluded, many years after: 'In a way, we were continuing his unfinished autobiography.'

Reading all this we might think again about Pound's nickname for Howard Hall. It does not seem so hellish now, with fresh milk and the daily papers, and the sense that arises most of all is of vast sympathy: of the kindness of this young doctor, fresh out of school, and his willing engagement with a difficult man. Kavka's description of Pound's speech habits – 'he would soliloquize in a manner typically found in his poetry: apparently disconnected thoughts and ideas strung together in a pattern' – is both respectful and surprisingly specific, and reveals something important, but simple: Kavka read Pound's poems.

At the start of March, after receiving the package of Pound's books sent by James Laughlin, Kavka asked Pound to sign them for him. In his memoirs, Kavka notes that he bought an additional volume, *Make It New*, a selection of Pound's literary essays, but he does not mention other specific titles. Which books did Laughlin send? He would certainly have avoided the prose on economics, for he refused to publish these volumes, as well as Pound's recent book about Mussolini. He would almost certainly have included *Personae* and – from what is left – perhaps one or two volumes of Pound's early *Cantos*. Kavka mentions soliloquies, and this is the distinctive style of the early poems; he also alludes to what sounds like the collage technique of the *Cantos*. Although this is not everything that Pound had ever written, it is a sufficient anthology of the best of Pound, and Kavka read carefully.

This is one way of reading Pound's poetry, and this is the spirit in which I have so far approached it. As a style of reading it depends upon the assumption that something valuable is present in this man and in his works; we grant the poem power which we trust it will repay. We might call this goodwill. Not everybody reads this way. In preparation for the sanity hearing, which at last took place on 13 February, Pound's lawyer Julien Cornell sent extracts from Pound's poetry to the four doctors who would provide the expert testimony. Cornell selected passages from the cantos that Pound had written in his prison cell at Pisa. These 'show a reaction to his imprisonment', he explained to Dr Wendell Muncie, a respected psychiatrist who taught at Johns Hopkins University, 'and which might afford some evidence of his mental condition at that time.' He does not quite say this, but he is presenting the poetry as proof of insanity.

At the sanity hearing Dr Muncie noted Pound's grandiosity and vagueness, and Cornell pressed him to explain his evidence: 'Did you examine sufficient of his writings, and so on, to be able to determine whether or not this condition may have arisen in his earlier life?' The question appeals to Muncie's professional pride, for it suggests that some doctors do not do all of their homework, and on cue Muncie replies: 'I have read a great deal of his writings in connection with preparing this case, and it is my idea that there has been for a number of years a deterioration of the mental processes.' Dr Marion King was examined next. King was Medical Director at the Bureau of Prisons, and had grave doubts over the diagnosis of Pound; when questioned, he was wary. Cornell asked about the poetry, but then Donald Anderson from the Department of Justice pushed him in cross-examination.

Q. Have you read his poetry?
A. Some of it.
Q. And have you read poetry by other poets?
A. Some.

Anderson returned to his point. 'Did what poetry you read make good sense?' he asked, and King replied, 'I think what I read was all right.' The doctor is working as a literary critic; the question asked of the poetry is whether it makes sense, and this is precisely the suggestion that Pound's own legal defence wished to avoid. Cornell returned with more questions. 'Doctor, you mentioned having read some of his poetry which seemed to you rational and poetic,' he led, treating the psychiatrist as if he were quizzing a teenager about his homework, and King recalled what he was supposed to say. 'Well, I saw one of his poems,' he answered, 'which, of course, was incoherent and impossible for me to understand.' So much depends upon the way in which we might be willing to read Pound's poetry.

On 1 April 1946 Kavka left Howard Hall. He had been drafted into military service as an army physician, and he handed his responsibilities over to his colleague Dr Harold Stevens. Pound's sanity hearing had been completed and his file prepared, so there were no further regular interviews between Pound and the doctors, but he continues to feature from time to time in the general file for the ward, and the doctors continue to puzzle at this unusual patient. On 31 March – Kavka's last day at the hospital – Dr Stevens added a summary note. 'His present style of speech and writing resembles his poems and other artistic productions,' it begins, and so far this only concurs with Kavka's own opinions, but Stevens goes on to propose vaguely that Pound is 'apparently a true Symbolist' and confesses that he finds Pound's manner of speaking obscure. 'It seems that a distinct remark is meaningful to him,' he writes, 'but the complete meaning is lost to others,' as if the patient is talking to himself. The poems do not help. Stevens records that he tried to read one, and then asked Pound to explain it, but Pound's explanation was more confusing still, and 'conveys very little of the original meaning'.

After the departure of Kavka, Pound's doctors worked from a different set of assumptions about the patient and his poems, and the relation between the two. In August another doctor notes that Pound's room is dirty and that he is always complaining, and adds: 'I confess again my great difficulty in following Mr Pound's reasoning.' Like the others, he imagines that this apparent obscurity in speech is connected to Pound's poetry, and when he asks Pound about his poems, Pound offers to lend him a pamphlet recently issued by New Directions, 'which he assures me will give me a little better insight into the workings of his mind'. The pamphlet does not help; in the next entry the doctor reports their subsequent discussion. 'I asked him today why he did not at some time write material for purely popular consumption as a sort of "Potboiler" to bring in some money,' the doctor notes. Pound is understandably dismissive. 'He states that it would be impossible to write that sort of thing,' the doctor adds. This is how Pound's poetry looks from the perspective of an unsympathetic reader: like noise and confusion; a clever game of wilful obscurity, too clever for you, and you are locked out.

Some readers are hostile; some documents betray you. One minor irony of the trials of Ezra Pound is that it was precisely his restless self-narration, both in poetry and in the broadcasts, which led him into trouble. His own belief, held as a poetic principle, that the hidden self is shown in speech, was turned by the doctors and lawyers into a political and psychiatric test. He was caught precisely because he was so endlessly willing to reveal his mind in words. This is surely a hard way to catch a poet, but Pound's case is also a parable of the dangers of speech and its contaminations.

On 5 May 1945, at the US army's Counter-Intelligence Center in Genoa, Italy, Pound sat upon a leather couch and spoke to Major Frank Lawrence Amprim of the FBI. This interview provided the central materials for the Department of Justice's case against Pound. I worked for the Republican Fascist Ministry of Culture, Pound said, and he told Amprim everything: how they paid his expenses and gave him a pass for discounted train tickets; how he cashed the cheques at the Banco di Guavari in Rapallo. I am willing to return to the United States to stand trial on the charge of treason, he said, and Amprim wrote it all down. From Amprim's account, as well as everything we know about Pound, it appears likely that he told his story willingly, and that he trusted Amprim, even as he gave himself away. This moment is therefore both Pound's confession and betrayal.

When Amprim appears in the biographies of Ezra Pound he remains a murky and enigmatic figure, one whose role is a walk-on part in the grander tragedy of someone else. So in the summer of 2012 I filed a Freedom of Information Act request with the FBI. Eight months later an envelope arrived, of about one hundred pages, not in any order I could understand, with a note on top: 'Deletions have been made.' I admired the turn of phrase and began to read.

Amprim was born in Pennsylvania, but grew up in Detroit, Michigan. He went to high school and university there, and then to law school not far away. He once received a parking ticket for leaving his car too long while he was sitting an exam. He wore reading glasses and he had been working as an attorney in Wyandotte, Michigan, for seven years when America entered the Second World War. Four weeks later, in January 1942, he applied to the FBI. He was single, thirty-one years old, and his country was at war.

Amprim believed in America, but his family was Italian. He was a member of the Italian-American Fraternal Association of Detroit, which the FBI looked into; in the file are letters to his business associates, asking what this is. He lists his parents' names as Jack and Anna Amprim, but these are not Italian names, and they must have changed them at some point after they left Turin or arrived in America before 1910, when Amprim was born. Perhaps Jack was Giacomo, and Amprim Amparo. They had eight children, a big immigrant family like Kavka's, and they did well in the New World. The file lists a straight-A average at high school and 'nothing subversive'. 'He wears a mustache that doesn't enhance his appearance any,' runs a note in the file, 'and he would probably look better without it,' but Frank Amprim is nonetheless hired on 13 April 1942 as Special Agent, at $3,200 per year. He completes a personal history, including qualifications – 'Knowledge of Italian language. Fluent knowledge of Piedmontese dialect (northern Italian)' – and swears to defend the Constitution of the United States against all enemies, foreign and domestic.

Now the redactions begin; now Pound enters. Three days after Amprim is hired by the FBI, Pound addressed Americans in one of his broadcasts from Rome. 'For the United States to be making war on Italy and Europe is just plain nonsense,' he declared, 'and every native born American of American stock knows that it is plain downright nonsense.' The next day – 17 April 1942 – the Department of Justice began enquiries into Pound's nationality and place of birth, for treason depends upon where you are from. On 25 July 1943 Mussolini fell from power in Rome and a Federal Grand Jury in Washington indicted Pound for treason. Two months later Amprim was given a medical check-up and declared fit for active duty, and the following day he went on leave from the Department of Justice. He was sent to Italy on what is described only as 'a liaison assignment', presumably attached – although the file does not quite make this explicit – to the intelligence service of the US army. On 1 March 1944 he received a pay raise and a promotion in rank. American troops entered Rome and Amprim was with them. He was hunting through the ruined bureaucracy of the Fascist state, waiting for the war criminals to emerge, and he was good at his work. In August he found a set of Mussolini's personal calling cards and sent them to Washington.

The file reveals many things, but two stay with me. The first is that the Department of Justice sent the child of Italian immigrants to catch Ezra Pound, who had betrayed his own country for Italy. This little historical irony is elegant, and equivalent to the anti-Semitic Pound finding in a Jewish doctor his most sympathetic reader. The second revelation is a little sharper. In the closing months of 1944, as Amprim was nearing Pound, the file records that he fell sick. By December he was so ill that he was sent back to America, and at the Naval Hospital in Bethesda the doctors found that he was carrying the parasite *Entamoeba histolytica*. These live in the intestines and burrow into its walls, but Amprim returned to Rome. By the first week of May, when Pound is brought to him, Amprim had the rank of Major, but he had not recovered. At the end of the year, after the war is over, he returned to the Naval Hospital. They found that his parasites had blossomed into full amoebic dysentery, and they noted that he had probably had it for two years, undiscovered, and that it was due to 'unsanitary conditions in Italy'. On 12 March 1946 Frank Amprim retired from the FBI and left no forwarding address.

The pieces of Pound's history are now held in many files. We have Amprim's FBI folder and the medical records kept by the doctors, as well as the treason case, which was prepared by the Department of Justice and which is largely made up of incriminating extracts from the broadcasts and Pound's own earlier writings on politics and economics. In addition, his poetry is another unlikely archive. The confession of an invented self is the distinctive mode of the early poetry, but behind these early poems is a fear. Pound's poetry is marked – from early until late, this is his most powerful concern – by an anxious, repetitive worry at the distinction between history and its tellings. In the place of the past, his poems say, we have only documents, and our voices in the end are only versions. We may not, these poems whisper, ever know the past.

In 1915 Pound wrote a poem called 'Near Perigord', which attempts to describe the life of the troubadour Bertran de Born. As the title suggests – 'near' not 'at' – the poem is concerned with the approach to that life, and Pound begins by addressing the historical facts: what he knows of this one man and his times. 'Take the whole man, and ravel out the story,' he commands, but this proves hard, for the record is incomplete, and he moves on to a new approach. 'End fact. Try fiction' begins the second section, and now he conjures up a scene of the poet at work:

> a tower-room at Hautefort,
> Sunset, the ribbon-like road lies, in red cross-light,
> Southward toward Montagnac, and he bends at a table
> Scribbling, swearing between his teeth

But this too is outside, and cannot quite penetrate the man. In the third section, the poem invents a voice for Bertran, now addressing his lover. 'And all the rest of her a shifting change, / A broken bundle of mirrors . . . !' it ends, and we are left with the shiny, enigmatic pieces.

'Near Perigord' was written in early 1915, and that summer Pound began work on his cantos. He wrote these for the rest of his life, but they build crucially upon the sense of documentary frailty suggested in this earlier poem: upon the awareness that, as he puts it in 'Near Perigord', our historical records are nothing more than 600-year-old gossip. In the *Cantos* this becomes a more focused concern with the relation between specific documents and the history they purport to tell. 'And even I can remember,' writes Pound in Canto 13, 'A day when the historians left blanks in their writings, / I mean for things they didn't know.' He is following Confucius, and he adds, 'But that time seems to be passing.' The *Cantos* are acutely aware that the history told in documents is always prey to falsehood, is always tentative.

The early cantos are called 'drafts' – *A Draft of XXX Cantos* in 1930 followed by *A Draft of Cantos XXXI–XLI* in 1935 – to remind us of their preliminary status. No document is whole and faithful; it is always bound by time and decay, and this is the insight out of which all Pound's late poetry grows. This is a hard scepticism, and it results in a constant strategy of interference and distraction. The cantos, that is, refuse to let you forget that this is only one preliminary version of history; they refuse transparency and will not let the reader look through them as a window to the truth beneath. From Canto 8 onwards, Pound not only fills his poem with documents borrowed from elsewhere, but he also makes increasingly clear that these are only documents. Canto 8 begins with a letter from Sigismundo Malatesta, the fifteenth-century Lord of Rimini and patron of the arts. He is one of the strong and cruel heroes Pound's imagination was drawn to, but his presence in the poem is hardly noble. On the page are pieces of the letter – '*tergo* / . . . *hanni de* / . . . *dicis*' – followed by the announcement 'Equivalent to:', which in turn begins an awkward translation of the original medieval Latin into a mash of formal, business English and out-of-date slang. 'The lines, in short, do not convey information,' writes Marjorie Perloff, 'rather, they take certain facts and present them from different linguistic perspectives (formal, florid Italian; broken Italian words; English translation) as if to undercut their historicity. Fact, in other words, is repeatedly transformed into fiction.'

What we see on the page is the mishandling of records, their failure, treason, collapse. The documents which carry history may in turn – in an image drawn from Canto 24 – be crumpled up and used to wrap the nails bought in a hardware store. Our laws and histories are held on paper; these cantos are a warning, and it is a cruel irony that this man who was so acutely aware of the limitations of documentary evidence came to be charged on the basis of uncertain documents.

We may tell a history in lists and pieces; we may have the poem or the archive. The great theme of the early cantos is the failure of any smooth transition between single document and whole story, between inventory and epic. In Canto 25 two pages are drawn from the records of the Palazzo Ducale in Venice. We hear of the lions who once lived there and the laws restricting gambling, and these give way to receipts, for the cost of the lion statues made in stone and further building works. All this in turn breaks to Pound's own invention of the scene. He is looking upon dry laws and the kinds of dusty, historical trivia which fill the archives of the city, but all these pieces will not on their own cohere. They need him, and his later imagining. 'Which is to say,' he translates – list to fantasy, archive to idea –

> they built out over the arches
> and the palace hangs there in the dawn, the mist,
> in that dimness

In the mist of the morning, through the mist of the centuries, we move from archives to stories, but something obstructs our view. We may imagine the grand building at a little distance, but as yet we see it only through a haze and incomplete.

Dr Kavka once asked Pound how he felt, and his report records the reply: 'I am so shot to pieces that it would take me years to write a sensible piece of prose.' Howard Hall was the end of one version of Ezra Pound: the celebrated poet of insistent multiple selves, the brash prose-man who believed he might by speaking change the world. It was also, curiously, a place of occasional ease, and Kavka's report goes on to describe how Pound passed the many hours when he was not being interviewed. 'He spends most of his time lying on his bed in his room,' explains the report, 'reading a Chinese text and a few slim volumes of poetry, making a few notes on random slips of paper.' They were watching him even when he did not know it, and he sounds almost idle.

Howard Hall was an ending, but it was equally the setting for another beginning. In July 1946 Pound's wife Dorothy arrived in Washington. She had been delayed in Italy, waiting for her passport to be renewed, but now she rented a room in a house near the hospital and took over control of Pound's legal affairs. In the autumn Julien Cornell entered an appeal for Pound to be released on bail, and while the Department of Justice denied him freedom, they did permit some lesser movement. On 31 January 1947 the hospital superintendent Winfred Overholser informed the District Court that Pound would be transferred to another ward at St Elizabeths. Here, Overholser explained, 'he would have somewhat more latitude and somewhat more free privileges of receiving visitors', and on 3 February Pound was escorted two hundred paces from Howard Hall to the hospital's imposing Center Building. In Cedar Ward, on the third floor of the east wing, Pound was given his own room among other troubled but non-violent patients. He would stay in Center Building for the next decade.

Howard Hall was the first draft of Pound's years at St Elizabeths. As he walked up the slight hill from hell-hole towards the grand red castle of Center Building, he began to write the second. Howard Hall was torn down in 1960, so it must remain for us only a half-known place: glimpsed in archives, through the tussle of records and the haze of a half-century's misunderstandings. But Center Building still stands, and here we may follow him down real halls and out into the surrounding green. We may find him in another way, too, for at Center Building he returned to writing once more. He promised Dr Kavka that he wouldn't produce any sensible prose for years and this is half-true, but he said nothing about the poetry to which he would now turn.

PART TWO

1947–53

Pound is now static with a vengeance – in an insane asylum.

> William Carlos Williams, 'A Study of
> Ezra Pound's Present Position'

3

Amurika

It is Saturday 18 October 1947. In the street outside the recording studio he turns and looks for a taxi. He had not meant to go that day but he had finished earlier than expected; the weather was fine, and he had a free afternoon; he had no excuse not to. For a moment the thin buzz of microphones returns to him, and the irritation that there had been background noise while he was trying to read his poems. This is a side-effect of success. He lifts his arm. 'No creative action is complete but a period from a great action going in rhythmic course,' he had written, thirty-five years before: 'Each piece of work, rhythmic in whole, is then in essence an assembly of tides, waves, ripples.' A friendship, too, is creative action. The taxi stops and he reaches for the door. Something is drawing him, some force beneath the day. From the Capitol the road runs east to Benning Bridge and then a turn south to the neighbourhood of Anacostia. It takes twenty minutes. There is no traffic this afternoon. When he reaches the hospital he is surprised to find no guards at the gate. He asks the taxi driver to wait while he goes in. At the desk in Center Building a nurse tells William Carlos Williams that Ezra Pound is sitting out on the lawn.

*

To get out to St Elizabeths I first go into Washington among the rush-hour traffic. There are men in suits in the soft spring heat and women on their way to work in trainers. At the fronts of buildings are guards with gold patches, and when I arrive at the square office of the General Service Administration, I sign the register and wait for Carter Wormeley, the asset manager for the redevelopment of St Elizabeths through the GSA, as they call it. DC is a city of acronyms and Masonic temples, and the neoclassical office blocks and great cross of monuments at the centre all reach up into a vision of governmental power. It was the perfect place to bring Pound.

Carter is wearing a dark suit and a white shirt, and by his car he takes off his jacket to show a pair of blue-and-yellow braces. As we drive he tells me the history of the site. In 1987 the hospital stopped being a federal institution, he explains, and this was the culmination of a longer movement away from the institutionalization of the insane and towards community-based care. There was no demand for grand asylums any more, and the number of patients dwindled. There are two sides to the St Elizabeths site, east and west, divided by Martin Luther King Avenue. In 2001 the Department of Health and Human Services declared that it no longer needed the west campus. By 2003 the last patients had left, and the following year the GSA took over the 176 acres to redevelop it as government offices. We are driving south in the hot morning glare, and because there is construction work we don't take the direct road to Anacostia, but instead curve west as the river opens out; now we are going against the traffic. I thank him for taking me out there today, and he says it is a pleasure to talk about books, and poets, and Pound, anything other than the development. He tells me that he loves James Joyce so much that when he was nineteen he went to Dublin to see the house where Leopold and Molly Bloom live in *Ulysses*, and soon we pull to a stop. At the gate the guard greets him by name, and he laughs. I know the staff of a mental hospital, he says. That's like being on first-name terms with your bug exterminator.

We are on our way to Center Building on west campus, but our first stop is at east campus, where the new hospital stands and where we collect a doctor who wants to come along on our visit. Carter calls her 'Dr K' because her name is hard to pronounce, and she was the last director of the pathology lab, before they closed it down. Now she considers herself the historian of the hospital, but today she is a tourist with the rest of us: the doctor, the government man and me. We drive a little around east campus, past red-brick buildings with Italian tile roofs. They couldn't build fast enough during the war, says Dr K, but now they are empty, and from a distance they are pleasant: screen porches, white wood pillars, green-framed windows. Later in the day a doctor will tell me that before the tranquillizers arrived in the 1950s they would take patients out on to those screen porches and hose them down. There were farms on the grounds of the hospital, Dr K tells me: flowers, vegetables, orchards. There is a huge white tree growing through the steps of the disused women's receiving building and on the walls are stubs where people have stolen the copper from the gutters.

St Elizabeths has fallen into a doubled neglect. These old formal buildings are used no longer and neither are the methods for which the hospital was designed: what has been abandoned is the idea that a mental hospital needs breezeways for the summer days, a farm and screen porches. We drive by the Blackburn Laboratory, square and low. This was the pathology lab, where doctors cut into flesh to find the origins of distress. It was opened in the 1920s and named after a pioneer in the field of pathology who performed two thousand post-mortems at the hospital and died from the septicaemia he caught while dissecting a diseased brain. In the 1930s the lab was run by one Dr Walter J. Freeman, whose nickname was 'the lobotomist' and whose collection of brain samples I see later in the day: slices of putty, bruised and blurred, framed with a board of calligraphy. Dr K says that the amphitheatre inside is beautiful. I ask what they will do with these buildings now. They're talking about retail, says Dr K, and Carter adds that the Coast Guard are moving into offices on the west campus, as part of the new headquarters for the Department of Homeland Security.

'Two days, the wide bayou or inlet / Lay flatland above it busy by night with fires,' writes Pound in Canto 40. The heroes of the *Cantos* are those who build new cities – those whose imagination outstrips the landscape before it – and here he is with Hanno, the fifth-century BC adventurer who founded seven towns on the Atlantic coast of Morocco. Hanno and his men are onboard ship, in a bay, watching the unknown shore and its hills above them, and Pound goes on, in a garbled, rewritten version of Hanno's own account:

And by day we saw only forest,
          by night their fires
With sound of pipe against pipe
The sound ply over ply; cymbal beat against cymbal,
The drum, wood, leather, beat, beat noise to make terror.

Ply over ply: Pound repeats this phrase in the *Cantos*. New buildings rise upon the old, rise and shimmer like waves, one upon the next, and each place may be two, may be forest by day and terror by night. As we leave the east campus we turn on to Martin Luther King Avenue. It used to be called Nichols Avenue, Carter says, after the founder of the hospital, and before that it was Asylum Road. We drive past beaten shops and Carter says, this place was a hotbed of bluegrass music after the war.

To get into the west campus of St Elizabeths we turn left on to a brief driveway guarded by two stone eagles on posts. The sign is a metal plate and the guardhouse on the right has a decorative border on the roof and boards over the windows. A policeman looks at our IDs and checks that I have signed the indemnity waiver, then opens the chain-link fence. Now we turn right, on to Golden Raintree Drive, and slowly past greenhouses where glass is tumbling in, past fallen trees on patchy lawns, past bricks and rubble stacked by the road. There is the peep of trucks reversing and there are yellow tractors with the words 'American Infrastructure' stencilled on their sides. Now we pass a small car park, where black cylinders sit in piles. The Ezra Pound Memorial Tennis Court, Carter says, and there is a sign: OUTSIDERS NOT ALLOWED. The old court markings are just visible beneath the dust.

We drive up a light hill to a bluff, park beneath a tree and get out. As if we were standing upon the raised lip of a great plate, Washington is stretched out beneath us and ringed by low hills. You can see the most important sights, says Dr K, and she points to the Capitol, the Washington Monument, the Pentagon. There are helicopters flying beneath us. Much is water. The bluff is ringed by rivers, as the Potomac and Anacostia meet. Carter says he grew up in DC, but he did not come to this spot until ten years ago, and when he saw the view he thought, where have you been all my life?

To our left is the new Coast Guard building: a cluster of glass boxes, cascading down the hill. This was the site of Howard Hall. Dr K says: we had Holstein cows, two hundred of them, and lots of pigs, and fruit orchards. It was like a village, she says, it had a postal service. Today there is noise of traffic and trucks, from the construction and from the new highway beneath us down the hill, built in the 1960s. We see a deer just past a yellow tractor. Dr K says, this was his view, he had luxury quarters, and he did his best writing here. Carter says: I always thought he was crazy like a fox.

In the summer of 1941 William Carlos Williams heard a rumour. At the local bank his wife was trying to deposit a cheque when the teller told her that Ezra Pound was on the radio, talking about old Doctor Williams of Rutherford, New Jersey. In 1941 Williams had for thirty years been a suburban doctor, delivering babies, keeping people well with his steady hands. He was far from the war. But then a young man from the FBI showed up one morning at his surgery. First he asked Williams if he had heard Pound speaking on the radio, and Williams said no, he had not. Then the young man proposed that Williams should listen to a recording of Pound speaking one of his broadcasts, to identify the voice. Williams paused, for there was something sinister about this circular proposal. 'How can I be absolutely sure?' he asked. The FBI man pressed him: 'All we ask is that you identify the voice as that of Ezra Pound.' Williams was cautious. 'I can say that the recording I hear sounds like the voice of Ezra Pound,' he offered, but this was not enough. The FBI man asked: 'Are you a loyal American citizen?'

Some friendships are a quiet world: conducted in hints, affection-ate in misdirection. Their friendship was not like that. When Pound and Williams fell out, they did so loudly, and when they wished to express affection, they did it in print. For forty years their friendship had been a robust, out-loud conversation about how a poet should sound, and where he should draw that sound from. They met in 1902 in the freshman dorms overlooking the college triangle at the University of Pennsylvania. Later, Williams recalled that at their first meeting Pound read a poem so badly that 'it was impossible to hear the lines'. Pound remembered it differently. 'My early rekolektn,' he wrote to Williams from St Elizabeths, 'is you in a room on the south side of the triangle, and me sayin come on nowt, and you deciding on gawd and righteousness.' At Penn, Pound wrote and then tore up a sonnet every day. Williams planned an epic in the style of Keats. When Williams sent Pound his first collection of poems, in 1909, Pound sent back a reading list.

What they shared was a rage for America. On their honeymoon in December 1912 Williams took his new wife Flossie to visit the places where the War of Independence had begun. That year, in London, Ezra Pound wrote a series of essays called 'Patria Mia', my homeland. Both were dreaming of what America might be and both were drawing from studiedly American sources. Beginning with the second volume – *A Draft of Cantos XXXI–XLI* (1935) – the scene of Pound's *Cantos* turns to America. He includes clippings and sometimes swathes from the writings of Thomas Jefferson and his correspondence with John Adams. 'His methodology is largely a collage of quotations from the Founding Fathers,' notes one admiring critic. Williams wrote poems whose line breaks mimic the slink and pounce of a cat; poems from a note of apology left stuck to the fridge; poems including neon signs he saw in the street. Their works look so different, but are answers to the same question: what are the borders of a poem and what fits into its territory? Pound moved to Italy and when he started a journal he called it 'Exile'. Williams stayed in New Jersey and when he started a journal he called it 'Contact'.

There is no America without Italy: no home without the imagination of abroad. Beneath the squabbles and conversation of forty years was an ideal America, imagined just for two. In 1912, in London, Pound read Williams's recent poems and relief washed over him. 'I was more glad than I can rationally explain to a critical audience,' he wrote in *Poetry Review*: 'I had found at least one compatriot to whom I could talk without a lexicon.' In 1932 Williams wrote to Ford Madox Ford and mentioned he had just read and adored the first volume of Pound's *Cantos*. They are, he said, 'a bulwark against this destructive America I detest', for they resist the disfigured modern world. Pound and Williams shared one idea of home, and Pound called it Amurika.

And when they failed one another, the blame was always this: you are insufficiently American. Williams's father was English, and his mother from Puerto Rico, and Pound returned to this with increasing bite. November 1917, Pound to Williams: 'America! What the hell do you a bloomin' foreigner know about the place?' September 1920: 'you haven't a drop of the cursed blood in you.' They needed their antagonism: each fed upon it. In his prologue to *Kora in Hell*:

Improvisations (1920) Williams described Pound as 'the best enemy United States verse has'.

Once the war began these terms all looked a little sharper; what had been metaphor now felt like politics. The FBI questions – do you know the voice of Ezra Pound? and are you a loyal citizen? – demanded slightly too complex an answer. The two men did not correspond during the war. In the fall of 1945, as Pound was brought back to the United States for trial, Williams contributed a cautious essay to a Washington magazine. It would be a miscarriage of justice to shoot Pound, Williams suggests, but he does not go much further than this. A brief exchange of letters in the spring of 1946 soon turned to name-calling. That summer, while on vacation in western Massachusetts, Williams wrote a piece for an Australian journal called the *Briarcliff Quarterly*. They were preparing a special issue, all about him, and had asked for his remarks on something general, perhaps the present state of poetry in the United States. He chose, instead, to describe what he was not. 'Ezra is one of my oldest friends,' he wrote, but they have drawn apart: by now, 'how diametrically I am opposed (in my work) to such a writer as Ezra Pound'. Poetry now, instructs Williams, must be 'a direct expression of the turmoils of today', and it must do so in radical new forms: 'in forms generated, invented, today direct from the turmoil itself'. Pound is only, by way of contrast, a 'translator', one who composes in the forms of the past. Williams concludes: 'His mind is troubled.'

It was altogether more reasonable in 1946 to place Pound back in the old kingdom, the safe house of the past. So Williams made no plans to visit Pound, and when he was invited in the autumn of 1947 to come to Washington to record his poems at the Library of Congress he was pleased to accept this honour for an American poet.

'This is the Italian broadcasting system,' begins the announcer in clipped English, and introduces the next speaker: 'Dr Ezra Pound.' All is polite and proper and the English voice goes on to explain that he is welcomed on to the air 'in the tradition of Italian hospitality' and that 'he will not be asked to say anything whatsoever that goes against his conscience, or anything incompatible with his duties as a citizen of the United States of America.'

The orderliness of this is thrown when Pound comes to the microphone. He wishes to read a poem aloud. 'Contains things or at least hints at things that you will have to know sooner or later,' he warns, and because this is important, 'I'm feeding you the footnotes first in case there is any possible word that might not be easily comprehended.' He mentions the 'Decennio' – 'the exhibition in Rome at the end of the first ten years of the Fascist regime' – and 'Antonius Pius, a Roman emperor'. He mentions the law of Rhodes and a phrase in Greek, 'more or less twisted from a line of Aeschylus'. This is a scramble of languages, a whole classical education, and all the index of his mind, and as he lists any chance of comprehension is slipping away. He mentions a Latin tag and an image from Dante, Geryon, Propertius. 'It don't matter who it's quoted from,' he says.

When he starts to read his voice changes: thickens. Now he halts, and chants, in an accent which sounds as if he learned it from a nineteenth-century Irish poet. He reads:

> That day there was cloud over Zoagli
> And for three days snow cloud over the sea
> Banked like a line of mountains.
> Snow fell. Or rain fell stolid, a wall of lines.

He picks out each word and rolls each 'r'. When the poem turns – as the *Cantos* often do – from clear lyric to a parade of characters, Pound follows it, moving in and out of voices. When he comes to the Fascist exhibition, he is flattened American – 'Didja see the Decennio?' – and next he is Egyptian camel-driver, then British imperial administrator. Each character has an accent, but it does not correspond to nationality. The camel-driver, as a working man, speaks American, and one 'Mr Rothschild' has a haughty, mock-English villainy. Pound reads as if the poem were only temporarily in any language, were only passing through.

Pound read these lines over the air on 12 February 1942 in Rome, and those details matter, for treason is a function of both place and time. On the page the canto is poetry; aloud to the Italian microphone, the same lines become a crime. He was speaking in Rome but could be heard at the Federal Communications Commission monitoring station at Silver Hill, Maryland, where agents recorded 105 broadcasts between October 1941 and July 1943. It is unclear exactly how many programmes Pound did. He refers, in February 1942, to the 70 or 100 done already, while he also spoke of planning to publish 300; he wrote scripts for others to read and his own were aired repeatedly. Although he often repeats ideas and phrases from the *Cantos*, the broadcast on 12 February 1942 was the only one given wholly to a poem. The broadcasts are prose: erratic, circular, occasionally funny, often rhetorically complex, and almost always a little sad. Their subjects are stockbrokers, political syphilis and the 'cloistered apes of Oxford'; he mentions 'the kikes' and Tennyson, and promises, 'you are learning Hitler's basic text'. These are his key motifs, repeated sickeningly, but most of all he keeps coming back to one idea. 'There ought to be more Americans with me,' he announces on 9 May 1942, and the broadcasts lay out an old fantasia of conservative America: a never-never land of homesteads and the Constitution, of 'Yankee curiosity' and common sense. 'You have chucked away our national, cultural heritage,' he declares, and in Maryland the federal agents wrote it all down.

Williams and Pound shared this dream of a poetic America and an American poetry. Williams had been thinking of writing a long poem about the town of Paterson, New Jersey, since at least 1926. It was to be, he knew from the first, an epic of America, told through the history and myths of one particular place, and he had written many plans and projections, but it was not until the

Second World War broke out that he found the form it needed. As he assembled the pieces during 1942, New Jersey was far from the fighting, but Williams had long thought about how poetics and the war might not be so distant. He was a student of American history and admired how, during the War of Independence, the American soldiers used flexible open formations to defeat the British troops, who were closed in ranks and order; his new poem was doing its own war work in flexible, American formations. 'Almost from the beginning of America's entry into the war, Williams had matched his own progress on his American epic with the progress of Allied troop movements, especially in Europe,' writes Paul Mariani in his biography of Williams: 'When he spoke of *Paterson* it was in terms of pushes, assaults, retreats.' As the US army neared Paris in 1944, Williams wrote to his publisher that he, too, was ready for the 'final push'.

When the first volume of *Paterson* was published in the spring of 1946 Williams added a brief note to the start. The poem was, he explained, 'a local pride' and – more warlike – 'a column', but it was also 'a reply to Greek and Latin with the bare hands'. *Paterson* was his challenge to the American writers who had gone abroad, a local poem to affront the modernism of Europe, and most of all an answer to Ezra Pound, whose *Cantos* were an alphabet of foreign voices, and who, while Williams wrote, was speaking dead languages into a microphone in Rome. *Paterson* is war poetry, but its terrain is not only the Second World War. It is one more skirmish in Williams's forty-year conversation with Ezra Pound.

When Pound was at the microphone in Rome, we might see him as the opposite of stay-at-home Williams. It is an easy scheme: Williams writing an American epic, Pound with his broadcasts; patriot and traitor, poet and fallen politician; and such binaries are pleasing. We might, however, equally find here a deeper proof of their conjunction, and might then see radio as a sign not of distance but of destiny.

Pound made his first recording in the spring of 1913, when he read his poem 'The Return' into a phonoscope machine devised by the Abbé Pierre-Jean Rousselot, the pioneer of experimental phonetics, in Paris. The phonoscope converted spoken sounds into a seismo-graph of vowels, consonants, tempo and pitch, and could show the patterns hidden behind free verse. In 1924, notes Richard Sieburth, 'a mere two years after the BBC had started regular programming, Pound was (in an unpublished letter to his father Homer) already comparing the montage technique of his *Cantos* to the medley of voices produced by turning a radio dial'. Pound was fascinated by its power. In 1934 he heard Mussolini speaking about economic reform over the radio from Milan: in one moment, Pound noted in awe, the leader reached '40 million Italians together with auditors in the U.S.A. and the Argentine'. Pound did not own a radio in Rapallo. He listened in the local bars to the news as the war approached, then began; he felt as if radio was a crowd, was people all together. In March 1940 Hitler and Mussolini agreed to ally their armies against the United Kingdom, and a friend gave Pound a gift. It was, he wrote to another poet back in the States, 'a goddam radio', and he concluded, with regret: 'God damn destructive and dispersive devil of an invention. But got to be faced.'

He had long been waiting for this. He went on, in the letter – a letter about a radio, as if for a moment all technologies of com-munication were contemporaneous – to describe it as familiar. 'I anticipated the damn thing in first third of Cantos,' he wrote, as his own poetic technique had once dreamed of competing voices and static cutting across. History is catching up with him. He went on, in the letter, a little ruefully, that he had been able to finish his most recent volume only 'because I was the last survivin' monolith who did not have a bloody radio in the 'ome', but now it was here and he might as well take it up. In November 1940 Pound submitted his first script for a radio broadcast to the Ministry of Popular Culture in Rome.

Pound was waiting for radio, and it awaited him. At Howard Hall he told Kavka of cavalry captains and pioneer poets, of congressmen and colonials, but there is one family story he did not tell: that of Mahlon Loomis, born in 1828, died in 1886. Loomis was a distant cousin of Pound and they shared a common ancestor in the puritan and pioneer Joseph Loomis, who settled in Windsor, Connecticut, in the late seventeenth century. Mahlon Loomis was an inventor, of small success. He held a patent for false teeth and another for a 'convertible valise', but he has one larger claim to history: by many accounts he was the first man to send a message by wireless radio. In 1866, in Virginia – just outside Washington, DC – he demonstrated his invention by communicating between two towers fourteen miles apart. In 1872 he was issued a patent for a new mode of telegraphy, which, he claimed, would draw energy from the atmosphere and with it send not only words but also waves of heat and electricity through the air.

Did Pound know of Mahlon Loomis? One day in the New York Public Library I call up *Descendants of Joseph Loomis in America, and his Antecedents in the Old World*, and when it arrives at my desk it turns out to be eight hundred pages of lists detailing the trials and triumphs of eleven generations of the Loomis family: those who had been killed in wars, held patents, graduated from Harvard and Yale. This was a family busy with genealogy and proud. The big volume was compiled in 1875 by Elias Loomis, professor of natural philosophy at Yale and author of numerous popular textbooks on meteorology and astronomy, and then revised by his son Elisha S. Loomis, who also wrote a book about Pythagoras and another on cousin Mahlon and wireless telegraphy. Every biographer of Pound makes the same point about his family. He was, they say, obsessed with the paternal line, his father and grandfathers, and they often note the neat little quirk that the poet so concerned with the wrongs of money should have the surname he did, but they perhaps forget that his middle name was Loomis and that here in his grandmother's family his own story finds its echo and origin. The Loomises were men who invented things to improve the world around them, and their family history reads like a gospel of the nineteenth-century religion of improvement. Elias, Elisha, Ezra: a line of prophets. Early technology always feels a little like something from a dream of possibility, and Mahlon Loomis was the dreamer of them all: he wanted to send messages through the Virginia air, to light up people's homes. In 1928, at the furthest reaches of his exile from America, Ezra Pound signed an article with the pseudonym 'Payson Loomis': Loomis is my countryman.

Mahlon Loomis is a glorious story and a parable of failure. In 1872 he presented the 'Loomis Aerial Telegraph Bill' to Congress, along with a request for $50,000 to complete his invention. The congressmen discussed his ideas and found them as fickle as moonshine: there were no witnesses that his experiment had ever worked, so they called him absurd and denied him the funds. One of his supporters addressed Congress. 'The visions of the seer are wont to be mistaken for the raving of insanity,' he told the government of the United States: 'The announcement of important truths have oftentimes been deemed the vagaries of those whom much learning hath made mad.' Loomis died forgotten in 1886. Less than a decade later, the Italian Marconi sent a wireless message a distance of nine miles in England and was greeted as a genius. In April 1899 the evening newspaper in Mahlon Loomis's hometown of Washington, DC, ran a feature which tried to restore him to his place in the history books, but in the headline printed his name wrong: Mahlon Lewis.

This is the risk with repetition: it makes the second time look foolish. Pound in his broadcasts is Mahlon Loomis, the genius bringing light to a darkened world, spinning truth from the air and conjuring the waves. Pound in his broadcasts is Mahlon Loomis, the crackpot inventor and laughable madman, thwarted and then mocked by the US Congress.

*

Center Building stands above the view of Washington, the yellow trucks and the car park that was a tennis court. As we approach on foot it rises like a castle. It is four storeys, with crenellations at the roof; red brick and stately, the windows boarded up; backed by wings, receding, and at its heart a tower with bay windows at three balconies. Center Building is as geometric as a bird.

In the shadow, Carter points up and to the left. Pound's room was on the second floor, close to the centre tower, but what was its window is now a dark red board. We move towards the base of the tower. For a moment I am surprised that the front door is open, but then I see the panel of the green door has been ripped out, leaving the hinges, handle and frame, so that the door, while closed, is always open. We step inside, into the dark and smell of mould. Carter says: welcome to your new home.

There are boards on the floor and upon them, grit, and on the walls the paint is peeling. The long hallway is low and wide, with arches repeating in the distance, and it vanishes at the far end into the light of another door. To the left and right are dispensaries and offices, some shut off with yellow tape, and we walk into others. Each room contains a sink. Here in the old hospital all is peeling back. The squares of fitted carpet curl up to reveal floorboards, and roof beams emerge from the broken ceiling. The world is turning upside down: leaves of paint upon the floor and roof tiles beneath our feet.

The old hospital is a chart of its own construction and it is also a map: the walls are stained with rough coastlines and clues. Outside patient reception are two small black boards with white plastic, stick-on letters. Once these gave the rules and order for the place, but half the letters have been lost. 'ENTR FIR TOR,' says one, and you can come close to reading what this once said. Others are opaque, impossible: 'TIN C F F E D MIO.' The temptation is obvious. To the right, someone has taken the old hospital letters and from them written new phrases. 'MTG WAS HERE,' it says, and just above: 'OBAMA THE GREATEST IDIOT.'

As we three stand in the half-dark at the base of the tower, Carter says he thinks we are at the oldest spot in the building, for it would be sensible to build from the middle out – to grow the spine before the wings – but he is not sure. He proposes that we go upstairs to see the superintendent's quarters, and in single file we climb a narrow staircase, each footstep testing the crunch upon the floor, left hand upon a metal rail. At the top of the stairs we turn right through an open door and into a hall too long and dark to see to the end, lit by lines of light through narrow shutters at the sides. This is Chestnut Ward, where Pound lived for almost a decade. The walls and floor shake a little, for the trucks outside are working the earth, and a fine dust falls through the air. Dr K says, the good patients were nearer the superintendent, and the rowdier ones farther away, down the ward, and she points out Pound's room. It is numbered 2E-3, and it is the second on the left side of the hall.

It has no door. There is one window, slightly to the left. The room is perhaps ten feet by twenty. Next to the window two thin iron pipes run up to the high ceiling. The blue, heavy wallpaper is peeling, and on the wall is an X of masking tape. The window is boarded and the gaps cast a strange pattern: the lines of light are so bright that they darken the shadow, as if the day were sucking its advantage from the room or the sunshine were losing a war against itself.

Halfway down the hall are two alcoves, one on each side, and I step into the one on the left. The paint is like earth upon the floor and against the wall old windows lean broken. The carpet is blue squares and the window shutters are firmly closed. I step back out into the hall and start to draw a map. On the left wall, starting from where we entered: cell, Pound's cell, cell, alcove, cell, cell, cell, staircase, cell. At the end: another room, an office. And then back along the opposite wall: cell, cell, cell, alcove, cell, kitchen, cell. As I sketch this simple plan into my notebook I reach the far end of the ward, and here I see that around a corner the ward snakes on, so I follow, with crunch underfoot and echo about me. At the next corner I turn left and into a wall of wire. An iron grid covers the width and height of the hallway, and the shock is to see, for an instant, that where I had thought I was a visitor I was already in a cage. The door in the wire wall is open and I test the handle. It locks from both sides. I can see the next ward stretching out before me, but I do not step into it, because once I pass this gate it can be locked behind me.

By now Dr K and Carter have grown restless and gone on, for they want to see the superintendent's quarters. I walk back along the ward and through the stairwell and immediately right into a wider and genteel set of rooms. There is smoked glass with a pattern of stars in the internal doors and carved decoration beneath the ceiling. These walls have been painted over: pink, green, white. The windows are unboarded and open on to a terrace with a low rail. We step outside for a moment to see the view once more. I make a joke about ghosts. Carter says, I've never had that kind of sensitivity, but . . . He trails off. Outside, the trucks peep as they reverse, and inside, the dust rains from the walls on to the carpets, the carvings and the ward. The building is dissolving.

On New Year's Eve 1946 William Carlos Williams wrote to President Truman. He did not deny Pound's crime – which he refers to as 'Mr Pound's actual sins' – nor did he deny that Pound was 'a political propagandist', but he went on to plead that nonetheless his imprisonment was not right. 'Pound is a distinguished poet,' he wrote, 'and though in many ways a fool he does not rightly belong in an insane asylum as a criminal.' But where did he belong? In 1947 this became an increasingly complicated question.

The history of psychiatry is a parade of theories about man's relation to his environment, and even more than other hospitals St Elizabeths begins with an idea of the resonance of place. The story of its founding is a well-worn myth and during my visit to the hospital I was told it several times. In the middle of the nineteenth century a reformer called Dorothea Dix was horrified to learn that insane prisoners were kept in unheated cells. This was an old idea of insanity: that it is the same as insensibility, and that sufferers are in effect inhuman as they cannot feel the place in which they are. Dix believed the opposite: that the mentally ill were acutely sensitive to their environment, and that environment – poor treatment, brutal urban childhoods, deprivation, malnutrition – had been the original cause of their distress. The answer to this was what became known as 'moral treatment', which held that if the environment could draw the soul down low, then the environment might too light a path away from trouble. Dix convinced Congress to fund the construction of a hospital to care for the insane of the District of Columbia, as well as of the army and the navy, and the first patients arrived in 1855.

Its design casts in bricks and wood a theory of care. 'The moral treatment of the insane, with reference to their cure, consists mainly in eliciting an exercise of the attention with things rational, agreeable, and foreign to the subject of delusion,' wrote Charles Nichols, the first superintendent:

> Now, nothing so gratifies the taste, and spontaneously enlists the attention, of so large a class of persons, as combinations of beautiful natural scenery, varied and enriched by the hand of man.

Position is important, for position is cure. The hospital must be apart from the city, to keep the patients from the original stresses of urban life, and to provide them with wide spaces and views. The grounds were therapy: laid out to please and in turn landscaped by the patients, who spread gravel on the paths and painted the benches. There were lily ponds and cast-iron fountains; a small zoo, where, in the 1880s, lived a bear; a preserves room for making jams from the fruit grown in the orchards: peaches, pears, apples and figs. In 1927 the vineyard produced 18,000 lb of grapes and that year a baseball field and three tennis courts were built on the grounds. In the spring of 1946 17,000 plants were added to the gardens and 60,000 cut flowers were brought to the wards from the greenhouses. There were lilies at Easter, poinsettias at Christmas, the seasons passing in what Nichols called 'the grand panorama of nature and art', all orchestrated to be 'effectual in recalling reason to its throne'.

The grandest elaboration of this ideal was Center Building. It followed the design established by the architect Thomas Kirkbride, a Quaker and proponent of the moral theory. He had written in his 1854 manifesto *On the Construction, Organization, and General Arrangements of Hospitals for the Insane* that 'a hospital for the insane should have a cheerful and comfortable appearance, every thing repulsive and prison-like should be carefully avoided', and he drew a generic plan: for a central building with wings on each side; the wards divided by sex and race, and the superintendent living in their midst; ceilings of at least twelve feet and no more than 250 patients.

Kirkbride believed in ventilation, in fresh air and lots of water, and he insisted that 'The floors of all patient's rooms, without any exception, should be made of well-seasoned wood.' There were rocking chairs and the furniture was heavy. In early photographs the wards look like a grand Victorian house: framed prints on the walls, little rugs upon which to rest your feet. At St Elizabeths, Center Building was oriented east to west, and the wards looked north over the river or south on to the orchards, so that the view which patients gazed upon might harmonize the discord in their heads. In the grounds beneath Center Building were Japanese maples and magnolias: in total, ninety-four different species of plant.

Literary critics have a term for this enchanted vision of place. They call it a green world: the rural space to which courtly young lovers in trouble retreat and which resolves their contradictions, returning them to themselves. It is the Forest of Arden in Shakespeare's *As You Like It* and the magical woods in *A Midsummer Night's Dream*, and it is an essentially comic idea. It holds that the natural world may buttress our best self and bring us to sweet concord, and in this light we may read the dream of St Elizabeths as a comedy. The Kirkbride plan instructs us on how to build a place and also how to imagine it. When he insisted that all 'prison-like' aspects should be kept from view he did so precisely because a prison is one obvious metaphor for a lunatic asylum. In the early years the crops and orchards of St Elizabeths, writes the official historian Thomas Otto, 'must certainly have made the campus look more like a farm than a hospital', and he, too, is a sharer in the dreamwork, the magical thinking. A hospital, a prison, a farm: close your eyes and open them upon these different worlds. They are all the same place viewed anew.

The ideal was elegant, spacious, pastoral, and always out of reach. In 1878 the hospital had capacity for 563 patients and housed more than 800. In the 1880s work began on a new series of buildings on the west campus, and these departed from the Kirkbride plan. They were cottages, each small and separate, and in turn permitted the further segregation of the patients, now not by race and gender, but by type and condition. Now the epileptics had a separate ward, as did the violent. Where the moral theory had believed in a universal cause and cure for mental distress, and therefore one environment for all, now the science of psychiatry was developing into specialization. 'Long-held notions that environment was the main cause of mental illness slowly gave way to a greater reliance on neurology, anatomy, physiology, organic chemistry, bacteriology and general medicine,' writes Thomas Otto. The hospital opens a pathology laboratory in 1884 and hires a dentist in 1886; at the start of the 1890s a nursing school opens in the grounds and in 1891 Howard Hall takes its first patients. These are all signs of the new theories of a patient's place.

At St Elizabeths two histories lie side by side: a history of the dream of space and gardens lined with magnolias; or a history of overcrowding and the construction of walls. Kirkbride's plan included a ten-foot wall around the grounds, but this was, he makes clear, 'to protect the patients from the gaze and impertinent curiosity of visitors'. At St Elizabeths the walls were begun after the arrival of the first patients, and the brick wall around the hospital was completed only during the Civil War to keep starving citizens from coming in and stealing the crops. The first walls, that is, were meant to keep people out. Later, the walls were designed to keep the patients in, and they built them high: at Howard Hall, twenty-two feet of reinforced concrete. The hospital was to protect its patients from the world outside, and then one day the hospital was to protect the world from the patients it held within.

Since they met, Pound and Williams had been trading ideas of how poetry might tell of their ideal America, how place might be made to sing. In November 1928, from Italy, Pound wrote an essay for the *Dial* magazine about his old friend. Called 'Dr Williams' Position', the piece begins with a lightly mocking anecdote about Williams as an uptight schoolboy and goes on to never quite praise him. The word 'position' means both location and attitude, and Pound takes as his theme the relation between these two. America, he writes, is 'a land teeming, swarming, pullulating with clever people all capable of competent and almost instantaneous extroversion', but it is precisely the absence of this quality that distinguishes William Carlos Williams. Williams looks soberly upon the scene before him. He seeks the longer cause. 'Where I see scoundrels and vandals,' Pound continues, 'he sees a spectacle or an ineluctable process of nature,' but explains this distinction in a dig at Williams's heritage. 'He has not in his ancestral endocrines the arid curse of our nation,' Pound observes, and in case we missed the point, he goes on to describe Williams as 'the observant foreigner'.

In January 1947, with Pound once more on his mind, Williams recalled his piece in the *Dial* from twenty years before, and he replied to it in an essay he called 'A Study of Ezra Pound's Present Position'. Here, 'position' is a delicate way of saying incarceration, but it also means beliefs, and the problem is precisely Pound's beliefs and the place to which they have brought him. Williams praises Pound's technique and particularly 'his abilities as a creator of the sensitive line', but he has strayed from the exercise of this sensitivity. Now 'he has lost faith in the efficacy of the poem and gone over to ideas, using poetry as his stick'. In the essay Williams is delicate, but his teeth are never far from sight. 'He is a very dear old friend,' he writes, but 'He has wanted to make me "like" him and therefore always inferior.' He answers Pound's racial speculation with his own musing on origin. 'He came from the frontier and has never got it out of his liver,' he suggests, and he alludes to St Elizabeths, the pun inside his title, only once and in a grinning parenthesis: '(Pound is now static with a vengeance – in an insane asylum).'

Williams did not publish this piece in his lifetime – it was first printed in 1973, in the *Massachusetts Review* – but he dated it: 21–23 January 1947. This was three weeks after his letter to the president in which he questioned whether Pound rightly belonged on the criminal ward; the following week, on 31 January, there was a hearing at the District Courthouse, and Overholser informed the court that Pound would be moved from Howard Hall to Center Building. In January 1947 many different people – poets, doctors, lawyers – were all reflecting once more upon the tricky question of where to place Pound.

As Pound walked between two wards on the morning of 3 February 1947 he was walking between two theories of psychiatric care, and backwards in time: from the specializations and confinements of the scientific, punitive 1890s at Howard Hall to the moral theory of the 1850s in Center Building. Since opening, St Elizabeths had housed a substantial military population. During the Second World War, however, the responsibility for the military insane was transferred to the new psychiatric ward at Walter Reed Army Hospital, and from 1946 no more military patients were admitted to St Elizabeths; all servicemen who had been patients were transferred out. The hospital is changing. Since the 1890s a herd of Holstein cows and another of pigs had been kept on a stretch of farmland a couple of miles to the south of the hospital, overlooking the Potomac. In 1947, however, a change in local law made it illegal to feed rubbish to pigs near a public road, and by the end of the year 500 pigs were butchered and fed to the patients and the piggery was closed. In 1947, too, a report by the US Department of Agriculture recommended that it would be cheaper for the hospital to source their dairy from elsewhere than to maintain a herd of cows, and by June 1948 all the cattle had been sold. The closure of the piggery is no major fact in the history of American psychiatry, but in it we might see in miniature the metamorphosis of St Elizabeths from one state to another, from the dreams of farmland to stronger medicine. While Pound walked uphill that morning in early 1947, the hospital was shifting around him.

We have no immediate knowledge of the visit. What we have are repetitions, tellings after the day, and these are always justifications: of something said or left unsaid; of a failure of sympathy or an excess of care. William Carlos Williams's visit to Pound at St Elizabeths is well-documented. It is the subject of a whole chapter of Williams's autobiography, and he described it in letters. The pressures of their friendship surface in the poems Williams wrote in the years just before and after his trip to St Elizabeths in October 1947. But all these paper traces do not necessarily draw us closer to the events of the day. Rather, they have the opposite effect, of turning the visit into something as slippery as a story.

Back at home in Rutherford, New Jersey, six days after his trip out to the hospital, Williams wrote to Dr Overholser. He was, he said, moved by all that he had seen and heard that day, and he was writing now, doctor to doctor, to report his impressions. 'To me Ezra Pound seems about as he has always been, not any worse or any better,' he wrote. While he found it 'quite inexcusable' that Pound was isolated at Howard Hall during his first year, the new open ward was very fine, and 'Certainly at the moment he is being very humanely handled.' He gives his thanks and then he adds, almost as an afterthought:

> Mrs Pound has asked me to suggest to you that Pound be released from the hospital under my custody as a physician. I explained to her that the nature of the charges against her husband precluded such a move but that I would mention the matter to you as I am now doing.

One poet might take into custody another, as if literature were a world apart from law; the idea is tender, but as soon as Williams proposes it, he disowns it. It is only Mrs Pound's suggestion, he emphasizes, and the retreating syntax of his sentence – that cowardly, redundant 'as I am now doing' – flags his doubts.

We might see in this gesture another striving for position: as Williams's final triumph over Pound, the moment at which the doctor owns the traitor. We might in it also see the mirror of a familiar poetic strategy: to take Pound in, incorporate him, shape him for oneself. To take possession, to rewrite. The first book of *Paterson* had been published in the spring of 1946. The early reviews were positive; through the summer and autumn of that year, and during the first months of 1947, Williams had begun to assemble the pieces for a second volume. While he never names Pound in Book II of *Paterson*, a poet's name is not his only signature, and in this second volume Williams writes a short parody of one of Pound's most famous cantos. 'With usura,' Pound begins Canto 45, and lists the wrongs fed into the world by the complex of trickery and capitalism which he called, in the Old Testament way, usury or usura. 'With usura hath no man a house of good stone,' he writes, and, rising: 'WITH USURA / wool comes not to market / sheep bringeth no gain with usura.' In the second book of *Paterson*, Williams replies. 'Without invention nothing is well spaced,' he writes:

> unless the mind change, unless
> the stars are new measured, according
> to their relative positions, the
> line will not change.

Williams had long objected to one particular habit of thought. In the first book of *Paterson* he mocks those who have 'Minds like beds always made up, / (more stony than a shore).' His poem will be flexible, will welcome in the world. In Book II of *Paterson*, and increasingly so in the subsequent volumes, the poem draws into its field voices, fragments and pieces of life from the world outside.

One way to measure the impact of Williams's visit to St Elizabeths is to trace the differences between those poems he wrote before and those he wrote afterwards. Williams sent Book II of *Paterson* to his publisher James Laughlin in May 1947, and the pages were set in proofs in the autumn of that year; he began work on the third volume of the long poem in January 1949. So Williams's first visit to Pound in October 1947 falls between the second and third books, and what changes between *Paterson* Books II and III is simple. Whereas before Williams's handling of Pound had been anonymous and conducted in Williams's own words, after the visit Pound's own voice enters the poem. In the third part of Book III there is a page of wonky lines, running at askew angles as if the poem were beginning to fall apart, and immediately following this, set on a separate page – according to Williams's specific instructions – is the transcript of a letter from Pound. 'S. Liz 13 October,' it is headed, and the familiar heckling voice picks up mid-conversation. 'Fer got sake don't so exaggerate / I never told you to *read* it,' it exclaims, 'let erlone REread it.' Then follows one of Pound's customary reading lists. He had been handing these out to willing and unwilling recipients since he was a teenager, and the contents rarely vary: the Greek tragedies – in the Loeb edition – then Brooks Adams and Arthur Golding's translation of Ovid.

In drawing this alien letter into the country of his poem, Williams has made two changes. He shifts the lineation of the original, so it lies on the page like verse, and he alters Pound's wayward spelling: not to correct the frequent errors but to make them differently wrong, so Pound's 'gor Zake' becomes 'got sake'. At the top of the page, beneath 'S. Liz', Williams adds the phrase 'Panda Panda'. When Dorothy Pound saw this page she wrote to Williams to ask what those pandas were for. 'The *Panda Panda*, I'm sorry to say, has no meaning,' he replied, and explained it as 'a nonsense value in order not to reveal anything that might identify the work in question'. This is disingenuous. While Pound's name does not appear on the page, the 'S. Liz' clearly identifies the author. But this is not to say that the pandas add nothing. They are a profligate madness, eccentric beyond bounds, and they cast the whole as a cartoon of laughable raving.

We might think of suitable metaphors to explain the encounters between these two poets, conducted on the page as much as in person: that Williams dreams of springing Pound from the hospital grounds and into the rival custody of the poem; that the loose lines of *Paterson* are kinder walls than those of Cedar Ward. I prefer to return to Williams's own metaphor for poetic creation and here to see not walls but waves. Here is a sea, washing back and rushing forth, and the swell is thickening, tugging at the feet of the swimmers. Pound's voice is in Williams's poem, and Williams is spoofing Pound's *Cantos*, as if their poems were porous. Pound and Williams are joint swimmers in a larger tide of the poetry of American invention. In January 1950 Pound at last read *Paterson*, and he noticed the parody. He wrote to Williams, quoting the lines, and Williams, in turn, includes this letter – Williams quoting Pound quoting Williams quoting Pound – in Book IV of *Paterson*.

Paterson was not Williams's only avenue of response to visiting Pound. In 1951 he published his elaborate, defensive autobiography, including the chapter 'Ezra Pound at St Elizabeth's'. It is a wary double-telling. Pound is kept, he begins, in 'a gray stone building, designed and constructed not more recently than before the turn of the century, I am sure,' and he mentions the 'high, barred windows and long, broad halls' of the hospital and the 'parklike grounds' which surround it. He then tells of his first trip out to the hospital: the taxi out there after the recording session, the arrival to find Pound sitting beneath the trees among a group of other patients, as Dorothy reads aloud, and his walk across the lawn towards them. As he approaches, Pound turns and stands and embraces his old friend, but it is Dorothy who speaks. 'Well,' she says, 'it's Bill Williams. Isn't it?'

There is apparently so much detail in this account that it takes a moment to realize quite how total its silences are. Williams does not give the date, but suggests it was in the early days, during 'Ezra's first weeks or months of close confinement', but this is not right. Pound is sitting outside Center Building and Williams did not visit until October 1947, when Pound had been at the hospital for close to two years. 'We talked at random for an hour,' Williams continues, but 'All I could do was listen,' for Pound was a bore that day and would not stop speaking of 'the international gang' and FDR the criminal, and what really goes on in governments. After two pages of summary, Williams adds: 'I don't say that Ez *said* this, but from his halting broken jabs and ripostes of conversation, it is what I inferred.' These are not Pound's words but Williams's pastiche of them; in the piece, Pound does not speak at all, for Williams does not transcribe a single phrase of his. Williams returns to the city as he came, in a taxi, and on the way back he falls into small talk with his driver. The driver is suffering from a bad back and Williams gives him medical advice. Careful phrase by phrase, for two pages, Williams reports each word that the driver says.

This is the first half of the chapter. The second half tells of a later visit, in February of a year that is not given, but must be 1949 or 1950, and because it is winter Pound is inside the ward. Williams's account of this visit is elliptic and he only mentions Pound in passing. Instead, he dwells upon the details of his arrival at and departure from the hospital, for on his way up the circular stairway he climbed two flights instead of one and entered at the wrong floor. He was shocked by what he found. 'All about me were the inmates, lining the walls on both sides, some standing, some sitting, some lying on the stones,' he writes, in horror at the squalor and – less charitably – at finding himself in it. Back outside, and on his way home, he walks through the mud of the grounds and the cold of the day, and as he looks back up to the high windows of another ward he sees a naked male patient inside, 'The white flesh like a slug's white belly separated from the outside world, without frenzy, stuck silent on the glass.'

This squeamishness is oddly undoctorish, but it is in the service of a particular argument which runs beneath the chapter and beneath their friendship as a whole. It is a point about sensitivity and attention. 'Pound seems about as he has always been,' Williams wrote to Overholser, the week after his first visit, and in his autobiography he elaborates the point. 'I can't understand how Pound has been so apparently unmoved by his incarceration, guilty or essentially innocent as he may be,' he writes, and: 'His mind has not budged a hair's breadth from his basic position, he has even entrenched himself more securely in it.' Where Williams's delicate horror is the outward sign that he does not belong in this place, Pound's fixity of mind is in turn proof that he deserves his place, his position. The accusation follows. Dr Williams is finding Pound insane in the old-fashioned way, insensible to place. He is diagnosing, that is, against the spirit of St Elizabeths. Throughout the chapter, Williams refers to the hospital population as 'inmates', never 'patients'.

Noticing is humanity; sensitivity is grace, is salvation, is the blessed capacity to let one's mind be changed by what one looks upon. Yet Williams throughout this chapter of his autobiography is engaged in a studious practice of not paying attention. He spells the name of the hospital wrong – 'St Elizabeth's', where there should be no apostrophe – and he describes Center Building as made from 'gray stone'. Center Building is built from red bricks, but Williams's vision of this landscape is flat and grey and vague. The great missing is, of course, the silent Pound, who appears to talk, but is only ever spoken for, made loudly mute.

What makes this study in inattention remarkable is that Williams's poems are perhaps the finest acts of noticing in American literature. 'So much depends / upon // a red wheel / barrow,' he wrote in his most famous poem, and in miniature it pricks out the shining particularity of the noticed world. In another, called 'Between Walls', Williams finds in the trash of an alley 'cinders // in which shine / the broken // pieces of a green / bottle'. Looking hard at a tiny thing makes it glow with meaning, and the poet is he who looks hardest. The critic Adam Kirsch has called Williams's poem 'The Crimson Cyclamen', which lingers upon each precious speck of a single flower, 'one of the most sustained acts of attention in poetry', but at St Elizabeths he will not bestow this graceful, imaginative notice upon Pound. Rather, he casts his old friend and rival out into the silence of the unnoticed world, down into the blank beneath the horizon of care, and this is how he fixes him in place.

On my day at St Elizabeths, after seeing Overholser's quarters, Carter Wormeley and I return to the staircase and climb one more flight. At the top, we emerge into a wide, light room: a gymnasium, with nets set up for basketball. There are bars on the windows, but the sunshine washes in, across the court and the walls painted toothpaste green, hospital green. Carter jokes, we don't know if Ezra Pound ever played here. We stand for a while in the pale green light, just beneath the roof, and not for the first time I wonder what I'm looking for here, in an abandoned gymnasium, in a ruined hospital, in a poet's memory. I'm fairly sure, however, that Pound never played basketball here, for tennis was his game: un-American tennis, not a team sport.

The morning is waning by now, but before we go downstairs and out into the gardens again I take a right from the gymnasium into Cedar Ward. It is laid out like the ward beneath, but it is lighter, and I stop at the alcove halfway along the hall. There is a mural on one wall which might have been painted by a patient: of a cowboy, leaning on a pine, looking out over a lake ringed by trees. It is a fantasia of the Northern American clean life, so pure that it could only be Canada. The cowboy gazes at the lake and dreams his cowboy dreams, and needles never fall from the pine trees, and these skies never cloud, and on the floor beneath is paint in dry, flat folds.

At Cedar Ward Ezra Pound came home. It was not the home he had wished for, nor the homecoming. He had dreamed of a glorious return to America, where he would be listened to; instead he found himself in Amurika, a broken parody of his plans. At Howard Hall he lost his name, but at Cedar Ward, in his second year at St Elizabeths, he was given his own room with a typewriter and a view: west, out to the Potomac, over the grounds and trees. 'Stays in his room most of the time,' runs an entry in the nursing notes from his first years at Center Building, and: 'At times thru the night will have a light in his room.' Slightly puzzled, the nurses often note that as he works he hums an unknown tune, and even 'Appears at times to be singing.'

At Howard Hall Pound had begun drafting translations from the *Book of Odes*, or 'Shih King', an anthology of ancient Chinese poems collected by Confucius, and these first versions were what Kavka noticed. Pound worked from a decorous, late nineteenth-century bilingual edition by James Legge, but in early 1947 he got hold of a set of glosses of the sounds and each word of the Odes by a Swedish sinologist called Bernhard Karlgren. At Cedar Ward in May 1947 Pound transliterated all 300 of the Odes into what he called a 'singing key': instructions on how they were to be sung aloud. In June, when he was almost done, he wrote a short rhyme on the back of a notebook. 'Nobody thinks but grandpa,' it begins:

> He sits round all day
> Whistling in the bughouse
> Just to pass the time away.

Humming, whistling, singing: these 2,000-year-old Chinese songs were returning to life.

Pound had been thinking about Confucius for years. The opening poem in his volume *Cathay* – published in 1915 and arguably the book which invents modernist poetry – is a version of a Confucian Ode. At the end of January 1942, in his first broadcast after America's entry into the Second World War, Pound had spoken of his work on a translation of 'The Great Learning', which is one of the four prose classics, and of seeing that these ancient Chinese texts were not so distant. Confucius, he said in the broadcast, had 'been up against similar problems' and 'had seen empires fallin''. When the Italian soldiers came for him in May 1945, he hid his worn copy of

Confucius in his pocket; these were the books to which he turned in times of trouble. It was Confucius who taught him that historians used to leave blank pages in the history books, and in the first years at St Elizabeths, Pound stood in what might have been a bare white page of his personal history. When William Carlos Williams looked at the hospital, he saw only a field of grey. Now Pound resolved to fill those blanks with song.

After the noise of the *Cantos* and the furies of the broadcasts, his versions of the Confucian Odes appear a smaller music. They sing of worship and lament, of the sorrows of exile and the celebration of a fair prince, and we can hear Pound singing them still, for he recorded them at Spoleto in 1970. He was ancient by then, and the Odes sound so too, and as he chants with his cracked, half-American voice and distinctive rolling Irish 'r' it is impossible to avoid two complex sensations. First, to feel how old these songs are: how they touch upon myth or curses out of time, how they sit at the far, formal edge of what we now term poetry. And second, equally to be struck by how much they sound like the blues: those sweet songs of American longing, sung by working men often far away. 'Yaller bird, let my corn alone,' sings Pound:

> Yaller bird, let my crawps alone,
> These folks here won't let me eat,
> I wanna go back whaar I can meet
> the folks I used to know at home.

He is only almost singing, in that husky half-chant of the blues, when full song might be too much joy, but the rhyme forces you into lilt, and what makes them most like the blues is not their sound but their sad certainty that trouble rhymes, repeats across time. In Pound's voice these songs sound like precisely what they are: which is both classical Chinese Odes and American laments written in the American South in the middle of the twentieth century.

Perhaps what he found in these ancient poems was his own land-scape, turned a little in the light, tuned a little by time. In one, he writes:

> I wanted to go to the plains
> where the thick grain is.
> I would have asked aid of great states,
> their kings and great potentates.

It is hard to avoid the temptation to read this biographically: that is, to recall here another poet who travelled and wished to speak with leaders, who dreamed of economic fairness, but who in all this was thwarted. If it is hard for us, it must have been harder still for Pound, for all this detail was waiting in the original. He is not confessing; he is translating the words of another. The fourth Ode describes the faraway scene. 'In the South be drooping trees, / long the bough, thick the vine,' it runs, and these words for parts of trees and plants are in the version by James Legge from which Pound was working. But Pound wrote these lines in the South, in Washington, and from his window he looked out upon the drooping branches of a cedar, and climbing up the front of Center Building were thick vines.

He was in a room on Cedar Ward and looked out upon a drooping cedar tree. This is not coincidence. The wards of Center Building were named for the trees growing in the grounds – Chestnut, Cherry, Elm, Oak and more – and each was finished with decorative trim from the same wood. Cedar Ward was finished in cedar and Oak Ward in oak, as if the wards were only an extension of the gardens. On my day at St Elizabeths I saw maples, beech and a cherry in blossom, but many of the trees that stood here in Pound's years have since died; there are no elms any longer after the outbreak of Dutch Elm Disease in the 1960s, and without its trees only half the hospital remains. But the roads across the campus are still named on maps and the occasional street sign – Cedar Drive, Plum Street,

Sweetgum Lane – so when we drove across the site we drove through the memory of trees. They are remembered, too, in the *Confucian Odes*. In the Odes the chestnuts, elms, pines and pear trees that once were on the hospital grounds still stand, so Pound at St Elizabeths found his own present landscape inventoried in an ancient poem. In writing new versions he made the description true again: the ancient trees are still living in his translations, and in this writing Pound therefore keeps faith with both the original poems and the facts of the scene before him. He does not, that is, betray the present for the sake of the past.

The moral theory of treatment is a sweet pastoral poem and it relies upon a creative act of recognition: the patient looks upon a deliberate landscape whose artifice in turn remakes his or her restless mind. Place can be healing. With the *Confucian Odes* Pound internalized the hospital's original theory of care. He learned to look anew. In both versions of the thirteenth Ode that Pound consulted a particular plant is named as 'Southernwood'. This is a sharp-smelling European herb used in tea or to preserve clothes from insects, but in his version Pound has 'quince', a fruit. Perhaps this gives him a rhyme he needs, for 'prince'; perhaps this is because the southernwood did not grow at St Elizabeths, whereas quinces did and were preserved as jam. James Joyce boasted that if the city of Dublin were destroyed it could be rebuilt from the evidence laid out in his novel *Ulysses*. Should you wish to resurrect St Elizabeths as it stood in the green spring of 1947, you would have to start with the trees, and to reach those trees you might begin with Pound's versions of Confucius.

In the most famous of the *Analects* – the collection of his sayings – Confucius advises what must first be done when setting up a state. 'Settle the names,' he declared, and in his translation, made during the war, Pound adds an explanation: 'determine a precise vocabulary'. A little later another saying instructs: 'Remember the names of many birds, animals, plants and trees.' The names of things tell stories. In the first of the Odes, a bird cries out. In the ornate translation by James Legge, this is an 'osprey' and it cries 'guan guan'. In his version, Bernhard Karlgren does not translate the names of birds and identifies this as 'the t s'u-kin bird', but he glosses its sound: '*kwankwan*'. Now, there are ospreys in America, along the coasts and rivers of the eastern seaboard, but they sometimes go by a different name. There, they are 'fish-hawks', and when Pound came to this line he gave the bird its local name. The first Ode now begins:

'Hid! Hid!' the fish-hawk saith.

Pound, whose room looked out over the Potomac where the fish-hawks breed, is writing not of distant Chinese birds but those he sees before him. If he sees them, he has heard them, too. It is highly unlikely that Legge and Karlgren ever heard an osprey in the wild, for by the end of the nineteenth century these birds were almost extinct in Europe. Their versions, therefore, were working from the handed-down and corrupted gloss of a forgotten sound. Pound, in contrast, was following the evidence of his ears. The cry of the osprey is now conventionally transliterated by ornithologists as a 'cheep cheep' or 'yewk yewk', which rises in pitch if the ospreys panic to something close to 'Hid! Hid!' At St Elizabeths Pound heard the ospreys cry, and he quietly corrected the earlier gloss.

After I came across the osprey and his shifting cry, I tried to find the code behind Pound's reworkings of the Odes. I spent an afternoon with handbooks of North American birds and guides to trees of the Capitol region. At times it seemed too easy. 'Great horned owl, thieved my young!' begins Pound's version of Ode 155, and I turned back to Legge and Karlgren to find they had simply 'owl'. The Great Horned Owl is a uniquely American species and Pound is here bringing home the Confucian aviary. Elsewhere, Confucian 'insects' become Poundian 'boll-weevils', which are a particular American weevil and famous enough to be the subject of an old blues song. In all these, Pound is taking translation as the art of looking not at someone else's past, but at his own present, and his Odes encode the sensations of the hospital.

In Karlgren's gloss, Ode 26 opens with an emblem of the failure of a mind to find consolation in its place. 'Drifting is the cypress-wood boat, drifting in its floating,' it begins, and elaborates: 'I am wide awake and do not sleep, as if I had a painful grief.' Pound picked upon this image and from it spun the most moving of his *Confucian Odes*. 'Pine boat a-shift / on drift of tide,' begins Pound's version, and elaborates:

> sleep riven,
> driven; rift of the heart in dark
> no wine will clear
> nor have I will to playe.

The gloss implies that it is night-time, but does not specify, and suggests also that the pain suffered is only a metaphor: 'as if I had a painful grief'. Pound renders this suffering concrete. Now there is an actual 'rift of the heart', and now there is actual 'dark', and he is singing his actual grief. In the original – in both Legge and Karlgren – grief is compared to 'an unwashed dress', one that hangs loosely upon us, uncomfortable, a little shaming. Pound turns this into 'sorrow about the heart like an unwashed shirt'. In the hospital he was not wearing a dress but a shirt, and this is how translation becomes autobiography. He is speaking in the words of another. He is clothing himself in them.

The poem exists beautifully in its different versions for it is a tiny drama of exactly this: of the slight mismatch which falls between a feeling and its telling or between the mind and those images in which it tries to display itself. It is a dance of hide-and-reveal, and across its shifting versions it asks whether the damage in the heart can ever be read by another. This is the question of St Elizabeths and of its poet. In Karlgren's version the speaker promises: 'my heart is a mirror, you cannot scrutinize it.' This hints at reserve and dignity, at the impropriety of looking too intimately, and suggests that perhaps when we look hard we see only ourselves. Pound turns this, too, for he was a patient now, under the scrutiny of doctors. 'Mind that's no mirror to gulp down all's seen,' he writes in his version, and this shifts the stress to the inscrutable work that takes place as a watching mind transmutes the evidence it draws from the day.

The *Confucian Odes* are not simple evidence, but they richly testify. The last section contains the 'Odes of the Temple and Altar', and in Ode 278 dignitaries come to perform a rite. Legge pictures them as birds:

> A flock of egrets is flying,
> About the marsh there in the west.
> My visitors came,
> With an elegant carriage like those birds.

Pound sees this quiet scene, and one word in it: 'visitors'. He clips the image, by removing the 'like', and in so doing transforms the whole. He writes:

> Egrets to fly
> to this West Moat,
> guests at my portal
> be such cause for joy.

He translates the poem to the place in which he finds himself: for what was a marsh is now a moat, and 'the Moat' was the nickname for the area immediately around Howard Hall, just beneath the high wall. But he is also translating the place into the poem, for the visitors now become guests and now hospital visiting hours are an ancient ceremony. At Howard Hall his visitors were permitted fifteen minutes and only inside the visiting room, three days each week. After he moved to Center Building they came to him between two and four on weekday afternoons and over the weekend, and even walked outside with him, beneath the Confucian trees.

This poem is less a translation than an act of rendition, of bringing home from a faraway place, and it all depends upon the word that Pound leaves out: 'like'. Similes appear to show proximity between two things, but only ever reveal that those things are not the same: the bird-like visitors are not birds. Without the 'like' this becomes not a metaphor but a transformation. The birds are his visitors, and the visitors are birds, and both are helping him to remake the place, to turn it into home.

In the last months of 1947 Dorothy Pound and Julien Cornell prepared to submit a petition for habeas corpus with the District Court. They argued that since Pound was apparently permanently insane and could never be brought to trial, his liberty had, in effect, been taken from him without due process of law, which was unconstitutional; he should be released into Dorothy's care. As they discussed the petition, they were confident of its success. 'I believe we have a very good chance of securing your husband's release,' Cornell wrote, and Pound and Dorothy spoke of moving somewhere warm until the spring, to Virginia or North Carolina, and then perhaps Spain. In January 1948 Pound was moved from Cedar Ward, which is on the third floor of Center Building, to Chestnut Ward, which is directly beneath. He seems to have liked his new setting. On 11 February Cornell filed the petition with the District Court and, although it was denied, he had anticipated this and prepared an appeal. On 13 March Dorothy writes to Cornell. 'Please withdraw this appeal at once,' she instructs him. 'My husband is not fit to appear in court and must still be kept as quiet as possible.' Surprised, Cornell withdrew the appeal and Pound remained at Chestnut Ward for the next decade.

Dorothy's letter does not quite say this, but she is suggesting that the hospital is now a better place for Pound: a place in which he could work, and write, a quiet in which to sing. Although she signed the letter to Cornell, this was not in her interest. The instruction must have come from Pound. In the year of 1947 so many gave their rival versions of where Pound belonged: William Carlos Williams, in his attempts to contain; the doctors, lawyers, judges, all deciding upon his place. But Pound with the *Confucian Odes* sang his own America into being. In Center Building he made his home. Now the place was his.

4

The Bughouse

It is a little after three – Saturday, hot afternoon, 21 June 1952 – when the young Chinese student arrives at the hospital. Pound had asked her to come this day, for he wanted her assistance with a matter of translation, but when she reaches Center Building the attendants in their white dresses tell her that Mr Pound is out on the tennis court. She walks over and when she turns the fringe of trees she sees two men. There is Pound in loose khaki shorts with frayed edges, like an old soldier in a deckchair, and another man, tall, in a dark suit. He is sitting on a bench and his feet are perfectly parallel. He does not look quite like what he is, which is the most famous poet in the world.

On the tennis court Ezra Pound and T. S. Eliot are laughing about the past. 'We were just reminiscing about our London days,' Pound says as the student approaches, and he turns to tease Eliot once more. 'To think that you called that warmonger Rupert Brooke the best of the Georgians,' Pound says, and Eliot crinkles with laughter. It has been a good visit, this time, and soon the two men stand to leave. Pound folds his deckchair and extends his hand to his old friend. Eliot takes Pound's hand in his, and bows his head.

*

In the afternoon, after my visit to Center Building and west campus, Carter drops me at the new St Elizabeths. It sits on what they call the east campus, just across Nichols Avenue, and has much glass and a wide lobby. Where the old asylum was a castle, grand and apart, the new hospital is an office block, square and small. At its height the old St Elizabeths had 10,000 beds. The new St Elizabeths has 300.

At reception I meet a thin, gentle doctor called Jogues Prandoni. He takes me first to the small museum kept in a glass-walled room at the right side of the lobby. Inside the door is a panel about Dorothea Dix and how she founded the hospital to provide the most humane care for sufferers. There is a list of the earliest patients. The seventh to be taken in was Charles J. Guiteau, who assassinated President James A. Garfield in 1881. The superintendent of the hospital testified in court that Guiteau was insane, but the jury found him guilty and hanged him anyway. Later, an autopsy on his brain revealed the spread of syphilis, which causes general paresis and can in turn lead to delusions and psychotic behaviour. Dr Prandoni tells me that he has read Guiteau's writings. He says they show Guiteau had a – he pauses – a different world view.

In the cabinets are displays of tableware and china from the old hospital. Beneath the sign 'Art at St Elizabeths' and the slogan 'Their Creativity and Talents Endure' are lopsided figurines in glazed clay, a teddy bear, a bus, a sunken house. They are marked 'favourite places', 'favourite animals' and 'trusted people'. The patients were encouraged in this, for the activity of making was held to be curative, and what is celebrated here is not the objects but that activity, long ago, and the effort to return to the cities of the sane. These are what art historians call outsider art: artworks which do not follow the conventions, because they were made by someone outside the artistic community. Next to this is a cabinet of therapies: hydrotherapy, treatment in baths and showers, a photograph of lines of patients swaddled like infants, others discreetly naked. The moral theory of treatment held that what these patients needed was seclusion, rest and cleaning, in a place apart from the world. This was the founding principle of the old hospital, and it is by now an idea which belongs in a museum.

High on one wall is a portrait of Winfred Overholser, lit so that he has a halo. He worked at the hospital for twenty-five years and was the last superintendent to live in Center Building. There are red Chinese plates from his dinner set, in a cabinet now, and after we leave the small museum we walk through the halls past pieces of furniture from his quarters: heavy wood, stuffed, uncomfortable. On the walls above are photographs of Overholser, smiling gravely, shaking hands with President Nixon, receiving a medal. He is of another world. In the middle of the 1950s, Dr Prandoni tells me, the first psychotropic medications arrived. There was more pharmacology in treatment, he says, and the community mental health movement got started. These new drugs meant that patients might live stable lives in their own homes, and the hospital no longer needed to be separate, with a superintendent living in and eating from red Chinese dinnerware. The new hospital is designed to mirror life in the wider world. They no longer use the word 'ward', Dr Prandoni tells me, for the sections are called 'houses'. He mentions a therapeutic mall, anger management, dealing with stress, and when patients do stay in the new hospital they stay for only a short time, rarely more than ninety days.

Before my trip to the hospital, I had asked about Pound's medical records, and particularly those which might detail any treatment he received. Really, I wanted to know if the doctors had cut into him and touched his brain, but I was told that while the patient files from the old hospital are indeed kept in the new hospital, there were limits on what I could see. Specific patient files are protected under the Health Insurance Portability and Accountability Act (HIPAA), and open only to the next of kin. I ask Dr Prandoni if there are any records I might be able to see today, and he tells me that he has retrieved the annual reports of the hospital, for the years when Pound was here. He takes me up a flight of stairs to the library. At the far end, behind a wall of glass, is the locked archive, and he opens the door, hands me a pair of white gloves, and points me to a chair before a low desk. On the desk are pale boxes of the annual reports, lined up by year, some tied with string.

I sit, and behind me Dr Prandoni pauses and says, call me when you are done. He turns and as he leaves he locks the door behind him. I look up at the wall of shelves before me, and just above eye level there is a black archive box marked with a white note: Patients N, O, P.

Later, I will rationalize my decision about what I do next in this way: that I would have looked at the confidential patient records if I could be certain of finding only Pound's file, and because I cannot guarantee this – because I risk seeing the secrets of others – then I will not look at any. So, locked into the closed archive in the library of the new hospital, while above me waits the boxed-up life of Ezra Pound, I read instead the annual reports.

The Annual Reports of the Federal Security Agency, Section Six (St Elizabeths Hospital) are thin pamphlets and the story they tell is of hard work and repetition. I begin with 1945. 'It has been a difficult year,' records an anonymous doctor or attendant, who explains: 'The effects of the last stage of the war were felt in many ways. The intake of patients has broken all records.' On 30 June there were 7,466 patients on the rolls. That December Pound entered the hospital. I knew that I would probably not find his name here, but I pause, despite myself, when the report passes over Pound's arrival at the turn of a page. 'The psychiatric department has continued to provide every form of therapy, new and old,' the report goes on. This year, electroshock replaced Metrazol – a drug which induces convulsions – and there were hydrotherapy, music and art sessions, as well as rhythmic dance classes. In occupational therapy the patients made a total of 895 items and for the first time there were pottery classes, where patients worked with clay from the hospital grounds.

The tone is practical, humane, not fooled by history. I warm to these anonymous authors, how unfussy they were, how uninterested in the self. The doctors keep their heads down and their names out of the reports, and like waves through the hospital the patients come and go. In 1946 almost 2,000 patients were admitted and 2,500 were discharged. There were 400 deaths and the use of electroshock was 'extensive', in the nice phrase of the report, particularly for the depressives and schizophrenics. Occupational therapy was big – 1,279 pieces of clothing made in the sewing room, and another 9,000 mended – and on the farm, production was up. In the recreation room on the third floor of Center Building there were moving pictures screened in the evenings, and this year the patients' library suddenly grew as a thousand books were added to the shelves. The following year, eighteen patients were assigned to work as librarians, and they took to the work. The annual report proudly notes that at the end of the year, 'Fourteen sessions were held in the library at which book reviews were given, most of them by patients.'

The patients' library had opened in 1907 in a hallway in Center Building, but in 1930 the construction of a new pathology lab on the east campus freed up some space on the west campus. The former pathology lab and morgue were redecorated with armchairs, maps on the walls, and books and journals. This was a privilege for patients, and the hospital had a second library, known as the Medical Library, for the doctors. After the annual reports, Dr Prandoni has left out another book for me. It is stamped as item 13,565 from the St Elizabeths Medical Library, and it is a copy of the 1949 New Directions edition of *The Selected Poems of Ezra Pound*. This copy was presented to the hospital on 1 November 1949 and signed by the author. I look at the dedication – he has misspelt the name of the hospital – and the swirling signature. His 'E' is a mountain range and his 'P' a face in profile.

Since giving away the power of attorney in late 1946, Pound was not supposed to be signing any documents, but here is a defiant gesture. He is claiming ownership over his works and his person, and he has given the book to the doctors and not to his fellow patients. I turn from the title page past several blanks to the first full printed page. 'AUTOBIOGRAPHY' it says at the top, and there follows, in a list, a partial account of Pound's life. 'Born, Hailey, Idaho, Oct. 1885,' it begins, and beneath this Pound has handwritten two small corrections: to the formal title of his undergraduate degree and to the year he left London. The boldest change is to the top of the page, where he has struck through with a wavy line the first four letters of the title, so it now reads 'BIOGRAPHY'.

There are no other handwritten marks in this book: simply a dedication, a signature and the editorial scribble. But this is in miniature the history of so much trouble. The difference between autobiography and biography is the difference between Pound telling his own story and the versions told by others. It is the distinction between listening to and speaking for, and Pound's gesture is double. Even as he claims power over the facts of his life by correcting the dates, he surrenders control over the story of that life by cancelling those simple four letters.

With this specific edition, Pound was spoken for. The 1949 New Directions *Selected Poems* was, writes the Pound scholar Hugh Witemeyer, 'part of an initiative to counteract the notoriety of Pound's broadcasts on Rome Radio during World War II, his indictment by the United States government for treason, and his commitment to St Elizabeths Hospital'. The book was published in October and with it James Laughlin – Pound's long-suffering friend and publisher – sought to focus attention once more upon Pound's poetry and away from his troublesome recent history. Here was a selection from Pound's beautiful early works, along with palatable excerpts from the recent cantos. Laughlin had commissioned two introductions – one from a poet, the other from a critic – but neither was quite satisfactory. Neither, that is, managed the balance required to re-introduce Pound after so much scandal, so the volume was published without an introduction. Selection makes an argument about what it includes, as well as silently about what it leaves out. In the absence of an introduction, the reader is confronted even more radically with the proposition that the life and questions circling that life – questions of treason, madness, disrepute – are irrelevant to the poetry. Other than the brief, fragmented list of 'AUTOBIOGRAPHY' inside the cover, there are only the poems.

This edition's argument lies in excision; in the case of Pound, there was much to be left out. As the literary historian Gregory Barnhisel observes in his book *James Laughlin, New Directions, and the Remaking of Ezra Pound*, Pound's adherence to Fascist politics had been, from the perspective of his publishers, a commercial disaster. 'Faced with a poet whose books had almost entirely stopped selling,' Barnhisel writes, 'Laughlin decided to eliminate any mention of the political or social context of Pound's works from New Directions publicity materials, and began to focus solely on the aesthetic quality of these works.' In this version, Pound was only a poet and what a publicity note described as an American of 'egalitarian, *democratic* sympathies'. In 1946, when Pound was at his lowest, Laughlin commented publically upon the case of Pound. 'A poem is a thing in itself,' he insisted: 'You judge it by itself, for itself and of itself – not by the politics of the man who wrote it.' This is a particular way of understanding art: by quarantining the poet from his words, and the poems from their world. In signing this volume, and in cutting those first four letters from the title 'AUTOBIOGRAPHY', Pound is acknowledging – and beginning to resist – those artful separations taking place around him.

The history of modernism is a history of cutting up. The modernists made editing into art, raised excision to an aesthetic and philosophical principle, and a question central to all modernist art, as true for poetry as for painting, is: what has been left out, and what therefore are the relations between what remains on the page? Editing in all its forms – selecting, shaping, choosing between the pieces – was also the activity which formed the long friendship between T. S. Eliot and Pound.

They met in London a month after the outbreak of the First World War. Pound had read Eliot's poem 'The Love Song of J. Alfred Prufrock' and was immediately enthusiastic about this new young poet and his work. He sent the poem to a magazine in Chicago, with instructions to the editor that she must publish it, and this set the tone of their friendship. In 1917 Eliot wrote the first critical study of Pound's poetry. *Ezra Pound and His Metric and Poetry* is the title, and Eliot's name does not appear on the title page or anywhere in the volume, for they were already so associated that Pound feared this might look like bias. In the pamphlet, Eliot begins by noting that Pound has already achieved some notoriety, but that he will address himself only to the poems and keep away from what he delicately calls 'other phases of Mr Pound's activity during these ten years'. He instead treats technique and metre: gives praise for this sestina, for that graceful handling of alliterative verse.

In 1922, in Paris, Eliot hands Pound the baggy manuscript of his new long poem, and Pound runs through it in pencil, cutting confidently. This is *The Waste Land*, or at least it will be, once Pound has finished with it, for the version Eliot first showed to Pound is very different from the clipped, shard-like poem that is famous today. Much of the manuscript was pastiche, long stretches of verse designed to sound like something else, and Pound objected chiefly to those moments where the phrases sounded as though they had been used before. 'Blake,' he wrote, or 'J.J.' (for James Joyce); 'Too often used,' Pound noted, and cut the lines. A little later he scrawled in the margin 'georgian', which was what all these young men hated: the patterns and pomp of those decorous, pre-war poets. In the manuscript, section IV – 'Death by Water' – is ninety-two lines of occasionally rhyming blank verse, which describes a fishing expedition; in Pound's hands, this became ten lines about a drowned Phoenician merchant. He is cutting to make it new, and this is a kind of violence. In a self-congratulatory letter to Eliot, while they were going back and forth, Pound described the process as 'the caesarian Operation'. This is surgery, pulling the new from the body of the old.

Pound's editing of *The Waste Land* is one of the most resonant anecdotes of twentieth-century literary history. It is also a perfect emblem of their friendship. When they spoke to one another, they spoke of poetry; when they spoke about poetry they were really speaking of each other. 'Mature poets steal,' wrote Eliot in a much-quoted pronouncement: 'bad poets deface what they take, and good poets make it into something better.' Eliot and Pound edited one another's works, saw them into print, praised them in public, and occasionally this teamwork bled into theft, as if the lines between the poets were not fixed or firm; as if where Eliot ended and Pound began remained an open question. Pound spent the spring and summer of 1922 acting as Eliot's agent, negotiating with little magazines, and *The Waste Land* was published in the autumn. In the first draft of the closing lines, Eliot wrote 'These fragments I have spelt into my ruins,' and then, immediately above this, as a second thought: 'shored against'. This is how it was published, as the famous, aching claim: 'These fragments I have shored against my ruins.'

Spelt into or shored against: *The Waste Land* is Eliot's masterpiece, and conventionally described as the most important poem of the twentieth century, and its achievement lies in its dense patterning of fragments drawn from elsewhere. Eliot borrows clippings from Shakespeare and Christian proverbs, birdsong, Sanskrit and voices overheard in a pub. In July 1922 Pound returned to writing his own cantos, and he stole one line from Eliot. His Canto 8 begins: 'These fragments you have shelved (shored).' When he read this, Eliot objected. 'People are inclined to think that we write our verses in collaboration as it is, or else that you write mine & I write yours,' he scolded his old friend. Pound agreed to remove the line from the first printing of the canto in a magazine in the summer of 1923, but in 1925 when these cantos were published as a book this first line had returned, and remains in all subsequent editions.

There are three possibilities. Shelved, spelt, shored: these are different ways of thinking about how to make a poem, whether it is an account of ruin or a defence against that ruin, and Pound's 'shelved' is the most aware that this is really library work, a work of moving words around, of rearranging books. In 1928 Eliot selected Pound's poetry for a new edition. He followed closely the contents of the volume just published in the United States as *Personae*, but added a critical introduction, which explained to readers how to understand Pound and most of all how to place him. 'The poem which is absolutely original is absolutely bad,' he writes, and argues that Pound's works belong in the tradition of great poems, not as a digression from it: 'Pound's originality is genuine in that his versification is a *logical* development of the verse of his English predecessors.' This is a working-out of Eliot's own ideas more than it is any honest account of Pound's method, and Eliot had made this argument before. 'It is not in his personal emotions, the emotions provoked by particular events in his life, that the poet is in any way remarkable or interesting,' Eliot had instructed about poetry in general in his essay 'Tradition and the Individual Talent', written shortly before *The Waste Land*. In that essay, Eliot sets out his counter-intuitive and strangely brilliant idea that each new work of art takes its place in the whole artistic tradition and that therefore a new poem changes every poem written before it. So we must read our poets not for their lives, but instead as if they were already dead:

His significance, his appreciation is the appreciation of his relation to the dead poets and artists. You cannot value him alone; you must set him, for contrast and comparison, among the dead.

These are Eliot's two famous principles of poetic impersonality and tradition, and they are rules about all poetry, but we might hear inside them the example of one particular man.

The trouble is that Pound was never like Eliot, and that Eliotic modernism – cold, impersonal – was never quite Pound's style. He was a natural propagandist, one who spoke his mind. 'The critic who doesn't make a personal statement,' he wrote, 'is not a measurer but a repeater of other men's results,' and 'The serious artist must be as open as nature.' He committed to his ideas, put his passions on display, and this is why Pound's refitting as an Eliotic modernist was also a kind of death. In September 1946 Eliot wrote to Pound and told him: 'I think the thing at the moment is to push the poetry and hold back the prose.' This was good advice. The economic prose was incendiary, marked by Pound's Fascist enthusiasms, and contaminated by the aborted treason trial and the still-felt scars of the war. The poetry, on the other hand, looked just enough like it didn't quite belong in the world, and it might – given the right presentation, the right publicity materials – be sold this way. This was a saving strategy, devised by Eliot and Laughlin, but it was hard. Pound later described the selections made by Eliot as the 'Ezpurgation of Ez'.

In the spring of 1948 Pound's publishers in England – Faber and Faber, where Eliot worked as director – reissued the 1928 *Selected Poems of Ezra Pound*, with its introduction by Eliot. They brought this twenty-year-old volume back into print in preparation for the publication that summer of a new volume of cantos: *The Pisan Cantos*. These had been written in the prison camp at Pisa and proofread at Howard Hall, and are perhaps the volume of poetry with the most idiosyncratic, institutionalized publishing history of all time. They were published first in America, in July, and then in England, and they were a success: a new departure for the old poet, mournful, nostalgic, each one a memory palace. At the end of February 1949 a group of judges gathered by the Library of Congress – the group included Eliot and Robert Lowell – announced the award of the Bollingen Prize for the best volume of poetry published in the United States in 1948. The prize, the judges declared, would go to Ezra Pound for *The Pisan Cantos*.

This was always going to be a controversial choice, and anticipating objections, the judges issued a statement. 'To permit other considerations than that of poetic achievement to sway the decision would be to destroy the significance of the award,' it insisted, 'and would in principle deny the validity of that objective perception on which any civilized society must rest.' Only poetry; nothing else. This is perfect separation, and those who objected did so precisely by refusing to split poetry from politics or the man from his works. The conservative poet Robert Hillyer wrote two histrionic articles in the *Saturday Review of Literature* under the title 'Treason's Strange Fruit'. He accused Pound of serving 'the enemy in direct poetical and propaganda activities against the United States', and he pointed the finger at Eliot as a poetry mobster behind the scenes, 'a foreigner' and crypto-Nazi in possession of 'a stranglehold on American poetry'. In the *New York Times* the headline was 'POUND, IN MENTAL CLINIC, WINS PRIZE FOR POETRY PENNED IN TREASON CELL', and inside all this noise a serious critical point was under debate. Pound, as ever, responded differently. He prepared a statement of his own, although in the end he never issued it. 'No comment from the bughouse,' it said.

At the start of 1948 Pound was moved into his new cell in Chestnut Ward, on the second floor of Center Building, with a view to the west over the Potomac. This year begins the long last phase of his Elizabethan years, for he will remain in this cell until his release a decade from now. This year, also, his visitors begin to arrive in greater and greater numbers: poets, students, onlookers and tourists. In April 1948 the hospital superintendent Overholser wrote to Dorothy to express his concern that Pound had too many visitors, and of different types, as if this were not a hospital but a circus. 'Visitors do not fatigue him,' she insisted to the doctor, and they continued to come. 'Patient does no work, causes no trouble, visited by his wife everyday, has a awful lot of company,' note the doctors in June 1948, and a few days later they are puzzled that one 'Mrs W. R. Winslow' painted Pound's portrait. Visiting Pound became a social event and a literary moment, and by the following summer the doctors gave up control over the quixotic literary salon cropping up inside their hospital. On 12 July 1949 a note, in red ink, in the ward log: 'Mr Pound has the following privilege,' it instructs: 'When the ward does not go out, his wife may take him out on the lawn under her custody, but only in the vicinity of Locust and Chestnut Center and in view of the ward.' This is the tree-ringed triangle in front of the tower, and now he may roam, although not too far. The note concludes: 'Time limits are – 1 to 4 PM afternoons, during weekdays and on Sunday 9 to 11 AM and 1 to 4 PM in the afternoon.' His time is still bound but it is for a span his own.

The period when Pound's visitors are beginning to arrive is the period of Pound's return to renown. With the publication of his *Selected Poems* and the celebrated *Pisan Cantos* he was at last seizing back some of his former status as a poet and vital cultural force. The patient files are closed to me, but Pound's visitors were often young men who wished to be poets and writers. They were ambitious and sensitive to their own positions, and they therefore often wrote of what they saw. In poems, letters and memoirs they described their day in the bughouse, and while these accounts reveal few medical details of Pound's treatment, they give away instead a grander sense: of how the hospital felt, to those who walked its wards and sat beneath the trees. Like any set of literary works which tell a common story, these soon fell into a genre of their own. We might call this The Tale of the Bughouse Visit.

They begin with the journey out. In the first chapter of his memoir *The Mays of Ventadorn* the poet W. S. Merwin mentions the 'crowded bus' he took, and the pretty girl he flirted with on board, how she saw he was reading a book of poems and said she liked poetry too, smiling at him from beneath the dark fringe across her forehead. The young translator Michael Reck first went out to St Elizabeths in 1951, and he details this same journey in his biography of Pound. 'You board a bus among the Pennsylvania Avenue government buildings,' he writes, 'which careens along the right side of the Capitol building, then through the Negro slums, past gas-storage depots.' The literature professor Samuel Hynes was serving with the Marine Corps when in 1953 he wrote to Pound, and in his own long account of the visit published in *The New Yorker* Hynes describes at length the flight he took from his base in North Carolina to Anacostia Naval Air Station. Hynes flew himself in a small twin-engine Beechcraft plane whereas the poet Kathleen Raine recalls simply that 'I was taken by a friend of the Pounds who knew the way,' but all describe their journey to the hospital. This overture to the visit is redundant, for it matters not how they got there but that they went, yet it has a purpose. It establishes that the visitor is only this: that their admission is voluntary, and that they will therefore leave when they wish.

At the heart of each of the visitor accounts is a tension between visitor and patient. First there is sympathetic identification, as the visitor finds in this unexpected place some sign which says this is not so strange. 'It was like any old institution,' writes Hynes of his arrival: 'It looked pleasant enough, more like a small college than a hospital.' When he saw Center Building, W. S. Merwin was reminded of his high school: 'a large, broader, duller version of the brick neo-Gothic Abraham Lincoln School #14, between Academy and Division Streets in Scranton, Pennsylvania, which I attended for five years of my childhood'. For Kathleen Raine the place was a little rarer, but equally familiar. 'Immediately I recognized the place as Olympus,' she wrote, and here, in the home of the gods, 'Ezra Pound is a kindly Olympian.' The bughouse is somewhere you already know.

This first recognition suggests that you are welcome here, and hints that you might belong. The second step is the establishment of distance. Even as the visitor might feel much for Pound – and all go out of their way to record a kind impression – they insist that they categorically do not fit: that they are visitors not patients. Of all the architectural details they might choose, Pound's visitors fall again and again upon one. The door to the ward was, they recall, 'heavy black' or 'massive as a bank vault's' and 'iron-grilled, locked', and they emphasize the door, because this is what divides visitor from patient: what keeps him in, and what lets them out.

Next, the visitors insist that they cannot belong in the hospital, because they are sane. The visitor accounts make this claim implicitly, by the presentation of another patient. Every story of a visit includes somewhere in it a third man, a figure who is not the visitor and is not Pound, but instead plays the role of the generic madman. Merwin recalled how 'a man in pajamas wandered up and down the long room looking at the high discolored ceiling, pausing to reach up and pull some invisible object – a rope, a chain – and listen.' Raine describes 'a Chinese half-caste inmate who sat sometimes stock-still, or rose and stood, stick-still and rigid, gazing blankly in front of him.' William Carlos Williams, in his autobiography, saw a slug-like patient trapped against the glass, and sometimes these other inmates are disturbingly noisy or uncannily still, but they are always present and yet we never hear what they say. 'Who is the third who walks always beside you?' asks Eliot in *The Waste Land*. The third man is the true citizen of the bughouse. In all the troubling middle ground the encounter with Pound must raise, these obligatory madmen show that the visitor is the opposite of a patient.

This habit of separation stands behind another trait common in the accounts: the frequent mention of the exact visiting hours. Visiting hours are just as much for the visitor as they are for Pound, but they mean different things. To one, the sign of freedom; to the other, proof of restraint. The price of sympathetic identification with Pound is the confidence that this is temporary. Each account says in one breath two things. How strange and awful, they whisper: how like and unlike me.

A classic example of the bughouse visit is given by the pacifist and poet Ronald Duncan in his 1968 memoir *How to Make Enemies*. He visited Pound in 1951 and his account rehearses all the conventions of the genre, while also, in an odd twist, making explicit the fear that runs beneath. Upon arrival, Duncan first sees Pound and Dorothy out in the grounds, where they are sitting on deckchairs beneath the trees. Duncan found Pound 'leonine' and describes his outfit: 'a yellow sweater that gave him the appearance of a tennis coach.' They speak for a while, and then Pound leads him indoors to the ward, where Duncan is shocked by the noise from a television set and where Pound complains that he cannot write. Duncan observes another patient, close by them – 'a white-headed man beside us who was stroking the radiator and talking to it as if it were a cat' – and goes on to record fragments of Pound's monologue. Pound speaks about the price of gold and the crimes of Roosevelt, and serves Duncan a makeshift tea, with cream crackers.

So far, this merely obeys the rules of the genre, but when at last Duncan stands to leave, he finds they have been sitting for so long that the ward has closed for the day. He forgot that his freedom here was time-bound and that a visitor is only a visitor during visiting hours and, as in a fairy tale, some transformation takes place at the end of the allotted time. Pound and Duncan walk to the end of the ward. 'Together we examined the locked door,' Duncan writes, and Pound says: 'Two bullfinches in the same cage now.' While Duncan shouts 'I want to get out!' an attendant comes, and as Duncan explains, 'I'm only a visitor,' the attendant replies with a sense of humour undulled by the panic in Duncan's recall: 'Sure. Next time you'll tell me you're sane.'

The encounter between Pound and T. S. Eliot on the tennis court is one we can capture with unusual precision. Alone among the poets in this book, Eliot never wrote an account of his visits to Pound at

St Elizabeths, but they were glimpsed that day by the young Chinese student Veronica Sun, who was studying at the Catholic University in Washington, and helping Pound with his translations from Confucius, and she wrote it all down. She was the third at their meeting, silent, watching. For all the detail of their exchange – Eliot's dark suit and Pound's khaki shorts, their jokes and close handshake – perhaps the most resonant element of this resonant scene is not something either man said, but rather its setting: the tennis court.

By June 1952, when this specific visit took place, Eliot was famous. In May 1948 he had won the Légion d'honneur, and in the hospital Pound clipped a gossip item from his daily newspaper – 'I hear that T. S. Eliot (the most famous twentieth-century poet?) is to receive the Legion of Honour' – and sent it to Eliot along with a cartoon of an animal called a water opossum. 'Possum' was Pound's nickname for Eliot, and Eliot's name was known across the world. In 1948 a line from Eliot's new poem 'Burnt Norton' – 'Time future contained in time past' – was used in an ad for Esso petrol, and in November he won the Nobel Prize in Literature. With fame, Eliot's legendary discretion sharpened into something more like paranoia. He did not wish to be seen, and the tennis court was screened by a row of trees.

Pound and Eliot used to play tennis in London in the years immediately after the First World War, so this was also a return to the scene of the games of their youth – and they are laughing, now, at the past – but today they are sitting on the tennis court, not playing. Today they are old men. 'The "greatness" of a poet is not a question for critics of his own age to raise,' Eliot wrote in 1946, in an essay on Pound:

> it is only after he has been dead for a couple of generations that the term begins to have meaning. 'Greatness', when it means anything at all, is an attribute conferred by time.

By 1952, a couple of generations had passed since the first modernist poems: since Pound's translations from the Chinese, published in *Cathay* (1915), and since the startling first cantos; since Eliot's 'The Love Song of J. Alfred Prufrock', which inaugurated their friendship, and *The Waste Land*, which cemented it. Once these works had been shocking. Now they were literary history. In the spring of 1950 the *Hudson Review* published for the first time an exchange of letters between Eliot and Pound from 1921 and 1922, in which they discussed the editing of *The Waste Land*. In March 1952 Duke University Press wrote to Pound to offer him $150 for a critical commentary on *The Waste Land*. Pound turned down the offer, for all these were signs that the moment of modernism was long ago, and its materials were by now a topic of academic interest. Eliot and Pound had become the greying poets they had once rebelled against.

'I grow old,' moans J. Alfred Prufrock: 'I shall wear the bottoms of my trousers rolled.' He is a sweetly ridiculous figure, a young man dreaming of ageing, and of losing his hair, and the quick passage of time: worrying that, in the poem's celebrated phrase, 'I have measured out my life with coffee spoons.' There is a strain of mournfulness which runs through modernism. As the literary critic Frank Kermode explains, the modernist poets – he is writing about Eliot, Pound and Yeats – 'seek a historical period possessing the qualities they postulate for the image'. They dream of a historical moment which has the hard unity and clean lines of a poetic image, and yet, Kermode continues, these qualities 'though passionately desired, are, as they say, uniquely hard to come by in the modern world'. This is why Pound and Eliot's poems cast themselves back, again and again, upon the pieces of the past, but they find them unsatisfactory, only fragments and echoes. 'In the room the women come and go / Talking of Michelangelo,' runs the famous chorus of 'The Love Song of J. Alfred Prufrock', and inside the rhyme is the fear: the past is a museum we wander through, past the artworks, chatting, but one from which we are ultimately shut out.

Tennis is a perfect modernist symbol: a game played in the lost and longed-for past; a little unexpected; and the love of tennis shared by these two high modernist poets hints at history's resistance to any neat story we might wish to tell about what came before. In the biographies of Pound and in his letters, there are glimpses: London before the First World War, playing with Ford Madox Ford, who described Pound's style on the court as like 'an inebriated kangaroo'; 1921 in the south of France, exhausting himself by playing for five hours straight; the summer of 1938, in Rapallo, six or seven sets each day. Ronald Duncan said that Pound at St Elizabeths looked like a tennis coach, and the detail never quite fits with any sense of the seriousness of Pound. In May 1956 the doctors tested Pound's heart, and there is a curt note in the ward file under the heading 'Clinical Impression'. 'Wishes to play tennis,' runs the note: 'deemed inadvisable because of age.'

In the spring of 2013 I found, by chance, the telephone number of a woman who had once played tennis with Ezra Pound at St Elizabeths. I say 'by chance', but really there is no such thing any longer, and this was the obvious route: Facebook, teenage grand-children, an unusual family name. The chance was that I wasn't looking for Pound's tennis partner at all, but instead trying to find out what had happened to Winfred Overholser, the superintendent of the hospital. The more I read about Pound, and about St Elizabeths, the more it felt as though Overholser – the serene watchman of Pound's years there – was a major spider in the web I wanted to unravel. Google led me to his obituary, and I regretted that I'd never have the chance to speak to him, but it also led me to his son, who, it turned out, had brought his young fiancée to visit her future parents-in-law at the hospital. While they were there, one summer day in 1955, the superintendent suggested that she might like to play tennis with one of the patients. I called her and she invited me to tea at her apartment on New York's Upper East Side.

Annie Overholser was a Catholic girl from Belgium and in the early 1950s she met a handsome young doctor in Washington. This was Overholser's son, Winfred Jr., and the young couple went often out to the grand superintendent's quarters in Center Building, just outside the city. Dr Overholser wore a panama hat and white shoes, and on 4 July they sat out on the terrace and watched the fireworks. It was the best view in Washington, she says, and there were lunch parties for fourteen with filet mignon and stuffed mushrooms. She laughs as she recalls all this. I ask about the tennis. I have to tell you I am not an athlete, she says, and she begins the story with the pleasure of having told it before.

The summers are humid in Washington and she appeared, she says, properly dressed in tennis whites, and Pound was there, ready to go in his torn shorts and no shirt and a long white wool scarf. It was 100 degrees, and around his neck he had a leather cord and a big iron medal. As he played, it swung back and forth, and he was chatty. He was outgoing and he made funny remarks.

I ask if she let him win. I'm sure he won, she says, but I didn't let him. He was very gracious, and easy to talk to, and there was no standing on ceremony on the tennis court, but once he got back to his entourage, he was different. There, he was in control of his group, she says, and began expounding esoteric ideas. Mrs Overholser wasn't part of the gatherings beneath the trees. I only saw him for the tennis games, she says, and she doesn't know about what she calls all that fracas about traitorship. I ask if he was intimidating and she says, he was very tall, but he was very charming. Once, after one of their games, she met T. S. Eliot, and she was more intimidated by him, but she can't remember anything about that now. What she remembers is Pound on the tennis court: he is bare-chested, and the medallion is swinging, and they are playing tennis.

A few days after I met Mrs Overholser, I heard from her again. She was sorry, she said, that she had not been able to give anything of value to add to my portrait of Pound. I replied that this was not so, and that I had been delighted to speak with her, that it had been an honour and a privilege, and I meant all that, but what I really wanted to say was something that I didn't quite know how to. Following Eliot: in these rooms we come and go, talking of Michelangelo. Following Pound: the history books are composed of centuries-old gossip. Lives collide, and there are coincidences, and the old stories are told again, and beneath it all like a grand black river runs a single fear: that the past is unwilling ever to speak with us.

In 1948, as Pound took up residence in Chestnut Ward, there was a surprising uptick in literary activity across Center Building. At Christmas a book group met in the growing library, and in 1950 patients in occupational therapy acted in two short plays before an audience of other patients. This became a regular autumn activity. According to the 1952 report on the library, 'A very active program is being conducted not only in circulating books but in providing book reviews and informal readings and plays.' In 1954, from the occupational therapy record:

> patients gave two dramatic performances, one a Christmas pro-
> gram and the other a very clever and good-natured satire on the
> hospital entitled 'Hotel St Elizabeths'. This latter production
> [was] conceived, staged and acted by the patients. The perfor-
> mance was a remarkable one.

The plays were performed in the assembly room in Center Building, one floor above Chestnut Ward, the room that is now a basketball court. They were first conceived of as a strand of occupational ther-apy and a way of providing an activity to distract and soothe the patients, but soon these plays grew into something more than this. Upon the raised stage, framed by heavy curtains, the patients became performers and the hospital became a hotel, and for the first time a light distance was possible: between the words they said and the world they meant.

At the start of 1949, just as the patients of St Elizabeths were turning to drama, Pound decided to translate a play. He had been a translator for forty years and his work had long drawn inspiration from troubadour songs, Japanese Noh theatre and the wisdom of Confucius, but this year in the hospital he turned for the first time to one of the Greek classics: *Elektra* by Sophocles. This is a play about a character who returns to what was once his homeland and finds it strange; about the ways and impossibilities of saying our griefs aloud, and the threat of exile. In the spring Pound wrote a brief manifesto, which he sent out to ten classicists and academics for their signatures. His own name did not appear on it, but it is his voice. 'Alarmed by the neglect of the Greek and Latin classics,' it begins, and calls for a new attention to 'the literary arts which serve to maintain language in a healthy condition for civilized use'. The manifesto ends with a question for the student of those Greek and Latin works: 'What part of his discoveries is of use now, or is likely to be of use tomorrow, in maintaining the life of the mind here or elsewhere?' The classics are needed now.

Pound kept his *Elektra* secret – it was not published until 1989 – but in 1951 he began to assemble the contents of a new edition of his translations: the sonnets and songs of the troubadours Guido Cavalcanti and Arnaut Daniel, the Chinese poems from *Cathay*, and his versions of the Japanese Noh drama. In the summer of 1952 two young visitors recorded Pound reading aloud his Provençal poems on the lawn, with birds singing overhead and patients shouting in the background. The recording is now lost, but other songs remain. That year Pound began work on a second translation from Sophocles. The new volume, *The Translations of Ezra Pound*, was published in July 1953, and in January 1954 the *Hudson Review* published his version of Sophocles' *Women of Trachis*.

A lovely fiction sparkles here before us for a moment. In the first years of the 1950s, and culminating in the performance of 'Hotel St Elizabeths' in 1954, the patients of Center Building were busy reading plays and staging them; and this is precisely the period in which Pound is translating Sophocles; and all were joined in a minor literary renaissance. It is tempting to imagine the old poet as joining in with the amateur dramatics in the assembly room, and perhaps upon the stage with his fellow patients, and while I can see this story's lure I suspect that this coincidence of playwriting instead reveals a simpler lesson about translation, and tragedy, and our encounter with the past. Like the great classical tragedies, translations return us to the question of how, and whether, we may speak with all which came before.

Elektra begins with a return. 'Well,' it opens in Pound's version, 'here's where your father landed when he / got back from the Trojan war.' As always in classical tragedy, the setting is a short time after the end of a great war, and while the combat is over the aftershocks go on. Orestes is returning to the city of Argos. His mother Clytemnestra has conspired with her lover Aegisthus to murder his father Agamemnon, so Orestes returns in disguise, keeping his identity even from his sister Elektra. His disguise is also a story, which he describes as 'the yarn that I'm dead / and buried'. Late in the play, as Orestes sheds his disguise and confronts Aegisthus, he demands: 'Haven't you ever learned / That the DEAD don't DIE?'

In classical tragedy nothing simply dies, for the past remains troublingly present, and this is what makes them tragedies. These plays are distinctive also in their treatment of speech. Perhaps the strangest element of Pound's idiosyncratic version of this play is its mix of tones. The characters speak at times in elaborate formality, and at times in a flat, suburban voice; sometimes a teenage sarcasm, sometimes the hard noises of grief. They say 'You're blotto delirious,' and 'You're top dog' and 'the great mind in passing / Bears us together.' Sometimes they speak in English, sometimes American, and sometimes in Greek; sometimes they can say nothing more than 'Ajnn' and it is in this mash of voices that the play asks its central question: in times of woe how do we speak? As Elektra recalls the death of her father, she begins to describe 'the vilest of all days', but then breaks off, insisting that it was 'beyond speakable language / horrible', and this is one of the very few phrases Pound has added to the play.

Elektra's first line in the play is a cry from offstage. The poet Anne Carson has written of Elektra's cries, arguing that they are uniquely powerful and that in them 'Sophocles has invented for her a language of lament that is like listening to an X-ray.' She goes on, 'Elektra's cries are just bones of sound' and in her 2009 English translation of the play Carson renders Elektra's first line as a transliteration of the original Greek: 'IO MOI MOI DYSTENOS.' This is because, she explains in her preface, these long open vowels 'are as painful to listen to as they are to say', and in giving us the Greek again Carson makes the saying and the feeling equivalent. Whether or not we speak Greek does not matter; in hearing these sounds of woe we must, Carson insists, feel their depths, somehow beyond sense.

Pound offers no such equivalence between the saying and the feeling. In his version of the play, Elektra first says this: 'Oh, oh, I'm so unhappy.' This is wilfully insufficient and an almost comical failure of feeling, but as she enters she shifts register:

> OO PHAOS HAGNON
> Holy light
> Earth, air about us,
> THRENOON OODAS
> POLLAS D'ANTEREIS AESTHOU
> tearing my heart out
> when black night is over
> all night already horrible
> been with me.

The point is twofold. First: the gulf between the speech of the past and its speaking in the present is so wide that no translation can bridge it. Second: that shortfall is what makes it live. Carson keeps the Greek sounds, but makes them mean nothing, gives us a howl which sounds like grief. Pound does the opposite. He keeps the Greek because he believes that these ancient words are still talking in our age.

Tragedies arise in the mismatch between two forces: between sympathy and hate, civilization and wildness, honour and betrayal. In tragedies written before Sophocles – such as the early plays of Aeschylus – two characters spoke to one another on stage; the crucial innovation by Sophocles was to introduce a third character. This sounds like a minor matter of stage business, but, as the classicist F. E. Watling explains, it transforms the content of the play:

> The essence of the three-actor scene is that the turn of events will depend on whether A will side with B or with C; whether the combined efforts of B and C will change A's purpose; and so on. A choice is to be made, and the choice will be determined by the nature, as well as the situation of the person making it.

The presence of this third character moves the play from the presentation of action to the consideration of cause and choice. 'Character, not predestined event,' writes Watling, 'is now the focus of the drama.'

There is always a third man. Pound's Greek was not good enough for him to translate directly from the original, so he worked with a classicist called Rudd Fleming, who taught at the University of Maryland, north-east of Washington. Their method was in stages. Pound typed a first version, often at night, which the two men worked on together during visiting hours; Fleming then took the marked-up pages away with him and typed out a fair copy. Fleming is the extra figure at the visit and a reminder that there are always others present at – and perhaps interrupting – our encounters with the past. Within the play this third man is a minor character called Pylades – in Pound's version he is sometimes 'Mr Pilades' – who enters in the opening scene as Orestes' companion, and who is present when Orestes reveals himself to his sister Elektra. He is mentioned by other characters, but he never says a word. Pound turns this into a joke. 'Come on, Pylades,' he has Orestes say, 'cut the cackle.' But his role lies in silence: listening, marking, present.

In his turn to tragedy Pound was not alone. In February 1949 Arthur Miller's great American tragedy *Death of a Salesman* premiered in New York, and that month Miller wrote an essay for the *New York Times* in which he observes that the twentieth century had until now produced few tragedies. 'Our lack of tragedy may be partially accounted for by the turn which modern literature has taken toward the purely psychiatric view of life,' he speculates: 'If all our miseries, our indignities, are born and bred within our minds, then all action, let alone the heroic action, is obviously impossible.' Classical tragedy imagines our disasters as coming from outside our narrow selves – from the gods, the fates, an ancient family curse – and writing one now might involve a little resistance to the psychiatric view, which sees causes as coming from within. Each day the doctors looked at Pound; each medical evaluation insisted upon his limits; he was, they said, 'suffering from a paranoid state which renders him mentally unfit'. Pound's decision to translate tragedies is therefore a plea and an accusation. It insists that the causes of his trouble lie elsewhere, beyond his cell, outside Center Building.

Miller in New York and Pound in Washington were each writing tragedies; Eliot spent the autumn of 1948 at the Institute for Advanced Study at Princeton, where he wrote a modern-day tragedy, based loosely upon a Greek predecessor. *The Cocktail Party* was first performed in August 1949 and it is a reworking of *Alcestis* by Euripides. In the Greek original, as in Eliot's new version, a dead wife is brought back to life by the gods, and this choice of source might tell us much about Eliot's concerns, for his unhappy and separated first wife Vivienne had died at the start of 1947. Eliot followed this with *The Confidential Clerk*, which was first performed in the summer of 1953 and which is based upon *Ion* by Euripides, and then in 1958 *The Elder Statesman*, his new version of Sophocles' *Oedipus at Colonus*. In the post-war years, the two first modernist poets were looking back to ancient Greek tragedy.

In choosing to translate tragedy, Pound was speaking to the doctors, but he was also resuming his forty-year conversation with Eliot; and, as two old friends will often do, when they meet again, their talk turns to the past, to how they first set out. Both poets made their names through an art built from quotation, by taking voices from their natural contexts and assembling those phrases into odd new wholes. *The Waste Land* and Pound's early translations from the Chinese and his first cantos all follow this method, and this is how the poets most directly belong to the great art movement of their time. The primal form of modern art is collage, the process of sticking disparate pieces side by side, and it was invented by Braque and Picasso in the summer of 1912 as they began importing scraps of printed wallpaper into their canvases. The point of collage is that the sometimes surprising, sometimes shocking juxtapositions spark strange relations. Tragedy, modernism, translation, collage: all are concerned with the great action of drawing together. In taking fragments from the past they ask what fades and what remains, and imagine how our lives might come to fulfil the patterns set long before.

It helps to understand Pound's turn to tragedy in the context of a wider movement, by Miller and by Eliot, to think of what force these classical forms still hold in our modern world. But Pound's tragedies are also particular. Eliot – like Miller – borrows only the mechanics of plot from the Greeks. His plays have modern settings and happy endings, and suggest a kind of smooth translatability, where Pound's versions of Sophocles are obsessively concerned with blocks upon language. In 1953, after assembling the new volume of his collected translations, he returned to Sophocles and worked on a new play during the summer. *Women of Trachis* begins with a proverb that in Pound's version sounds like a cliché. 'No man knows his luck 'til he's dead,' Daysair says in the opening line. She is waiting for the return of her husband Herakles, and she hopes she may be able to outwit the omens which suggest that their endings will be violent. She hopes, that is, to be the exception to a general rule; she will be proven wrong, for all lives here fall into the same pattern. In the place of dialogue, characters trade in truisms. 'A good job's worth a bonus,' they say, and 'Don't get sun-burnt' and 'Keep out of drafts.' They break into quotation, or cockney, or French, for there are many ways to speak but all of them are equally unoriginal. All is second-hand.

The great tension of tragedy is that between the order set by fate or the gods and the specific bodies upon which the general rules must be played out; between the case of a single man and the law for all. By the end, Herakles is tricked into burning his own skin with a magic robe, and as he strips he demands that we look upon his ruined body. 'Without the wrappings,' he demands, 'look at it, all of you, / ever see a body in this condition?' He insists upon himself – this single pain, felt specially upon his flesh – apart from all else.

It is tempting to see Pound as Herakles, speaking to us in the words of the play. He is asking us to unravel the stories told around him – traitor, madman, genius – and to see him plain: to look upon the body of this single, unusual man. Look at it, all of you, he is saying: without the wrappings, without the names and prejudice. As the classicist Charles Segal explains: 'To be an individual in Sophocles is to have a special destiny apart from other men and to suffer a potentially dangerous, indeed fatal, isolation from the community and its secure values.' Pound's story presents all the materials of a classical tragedy, and his biographers and admirers have found this elegant old structure irresistible: often, they tell the life of Pound and particularly his years in the hospital as a story of apartness, isolation, and the punishment of the exceptional man, and in this they are unwittingly writing new Sophoclean tragedies. But the insistence upon Pound's specialness is a misconstruction. It misses all the ways in which St Elizabeths was for Pound and all its patients a place of terrible community just as much as beautiful isolation, and it confuses the hero of a tragedy with the man who writes them.

At St Elizabeths Pound was not imagining himself within a tragedy; he was trying to write himself out of one. He is not Herakles or Elektra; he is Sophocles. Like a modernist poem, the bughouse was a place where the past felt too sharply present, for it was precisely due to his past that he had been placed there. But in the years of 1948 and 1949, and into the beginning of the 1950s, Pound was reckoning with his past, and in doing so was coming to master it. In July 1953, once he had completed his two versions of Sophocles, and the same month that his new volume of old translations was published, Pound told the young writer Guy Davenport that he was returning to work on his unfinished, vast cantos. He had not written any new cantos for the previous eight years, since the prison camp at Pisa, but now he was ready. 'The poet looks forward to what is coming next in the poem,' he told Davenport, 'not backward to what has been accomplished.' Not backward: forward.

PART THREE

1954–58

Pity the monsters!

Pity the monsters!

Perhaps, one always took the wrong side –

Robert Lowell, 'Florence'

5

The Same Cellar

It is March 1954 and Robert Lowell is up again. Each time it is the same. He starts by reading *Mein Kampf* and talking, talking to anyone who will listen, about Hitler and the fascists. Then he leaves his wife and runs away with a younger woman. Then he writes to Ezra Pound, one monster to another.

His letter begins suddenly. 'I have been meaning to write you for some time, and it is better that I gabble on, and write badly, than that I say nothing,' he explains. He has just returned from Italy, where he went to collect his mother's body. She died in Rapallo, where Pound had lived before the war, and at the clinic where the corpse was kept he ran into Pound's old doctor. 'I was very close to you,' Lowell writes: 'And I think I know better now my old friend, the man under the masks.' He includes a new poem and Pound replies with a few kind words, and Lowell writes back. He has been thinking about Latin, and translations, and he asks whether Pound might send him his new book, *The Classic Anthology Defined by Confucius*, which has just been published. He cannot buy a copy, he announces in a lurching transition, because he is getting divorced. When he finishes typing this letter he has another thought and scrawls at the top of the page: 'Hardy & Browning are good company.' His best companions now are poets, dead and living.

The letters Lowell wrote to Pound in the spring of 1954 are a terror to read because they are so raw; you can feel how fast he is typing, can feel the speed and the fear. Five days later he writes again, this time without waiting for a reply. 'Uncle Ezra,' this next letter begins: 'Pardon this spate of letters, but for the moment you speak my language.' He announces a breakthrough. He is thirty-seven years old and he has always written poems in formal poetic measures, often iambic pentameter, but now he is going to abandon what he calls 'Jambics'. He includes a terrible poem he has just written, with the title 'Adolf Hitler von Linz', and what it says matters less than how he says it. Forty years before, the young Pound and Eliot had rebelled against the conventions of poetry by rejecting set formal measures. 'To break the pentameter, that was the first heave,' Pound wrote of this rebellion, and now Lowell is doing it again.

From the start their relationship was zigzag repetition. When Lowell was a freshman at Harvard in 1936 he met the glamorous older student James Laughlin, who told a story about how he had gone and studied under Pound in Rapallo, and Lowell decided he would like to do that too. In careful square handwriting he composed a long letter to Pound. 'I want to come to Italy and work under you and forge my way into reality,' he explained. There is something medieval about both his desire and the words in which he describes it. He wants to be an apprentice, and he writes 'I pray you to take me!' and he promises 'I will bring the steel and fire.' Pound's reply is dismissive; Lowell writes back immediately. 'Of course I don't actually know you,' he admits, 'but I have felt increasingly enthusiastic about you for some time.' He quotes Pound's poems alongside Shakespeare; he flatters. 'I have no delusions as to your bulk and my smallness,' he ends: 'I am only trying to show you more clearly why I wish to become your disciple.' Pound did not write back.

Their next exchange was in September 1947, and by then their roles had shifted. During the war Lowell had written a public letter to the president, in which he denounced the war and refused to be drafted into the army. He was put on trial and in October 1943 was sentenced to the Federal Correctional Center in Connecticut. He did mild manual labour for five months and spent the following summer mopping the floors of a hospital in Bridgeport for the remainder of his sentence, and in this curious paraphrase of Pound's own progress from prison to hospital Lowell also became a poet. His volume of poems *Lord Weary's Castle* was published in December 1946 and met with immediate praise and prizes, and the following June he was invited to Washington to become Consultant in Poetry at the Library of Congress. Once he arrived in Washington, Lowell wrote to Pound to tell him that he would visit. 'During the war, I spent a few months in jail as an objector,' he adds, 'so I suppose we have a little of that in common.'

During his year in Washington, Lowell often went out to St Elizabeths. He sometimes took other poets along – Elizabeth Bishop, John Berryman, Randall Jarrell – and something of the hospital stayed with him. After he left Washington he went to Yaddo, the writers' colony in Saratoga Springs, and he wrote to Pound that he felt he was in 'a sort of St Elizabeths without bars'. He imagined they were still sharing the same space. Jail time and scolding the president was not all they had in common. At the start of 1949 Lowell was beginning to crack up: seeing conspiracies and Communist spies, writing letters, drinking. In March, in Chicago, he was arrested for obscenity. A few days later he punched a policeman in Bloomington, Indiana, and he was tied up in a straitjacket and sent to a private hospital in Massachusetts, where they put him in a padded cell behind three locked doors and gave him electroshock treatment. In May, when he heard what had happened to Lowell, Pound suggested that he might like to come to St Elizabeths instead, and offered to make room on the ward.

There is a pattern here, even while Lowell was so wild. When he got his first divorce, in 1948, the lawyer he hired was Julien Cornell, and before he went to Europe in September 1950 he wrote to Pound to ask what he should see. He stayed in Europe for two years and reread the *Pisan Cantos*. Pound was, he wrote to a friend, a marvellous monster. Lowell spent the winter in Florence and in a poem he later wrote about the city he commands:

> Pity the monsters!
> Pity the monsters!
> Perhaps, one always took the wrong side –

and he confesses, 'My heart bleeds black blood for the monster.' Lowell's poems are marked by a radical and occasionally wretched sympathy. He imagines himself always to be elsewhere, in another place or another person, and he presents his feelings as too tenderly in touch with all around, as if it were too much for a sane man to handle in just one body. You can open his thousand-page *Collected Poems* almost at random and find the saddest intimacy. 'I want you to see me when I have one head / again, not many, like a bunch of grapes,' he wrote in a late poem about his hospital times:

> yet even on the steadiest day, dead noon,
> I have to brace my hand against a wall
> to keep myself from swaying – swaying wall,
> straitjacket, hypodermic, helmeted
> doctors, one crowd, white-smocked

When he got back from Europe in 1953 he went to Pound again. 'He's much fatter and healthier, jumps about, dances like a bear,' Lowell reported to his new wife Elizabeth Hardwick, and he is talking about both Pound and himself, as if the two were one. Lowell invented an alter ego who was a bear called 'Arms' or 'Arms of the Law', and when Lowell was manic then Arms would come out to play: roaring, wild hugging, dancing. This was Lowell's name for his madness, and he saw the bear in Pound.

Robert Lowell presents a different style of visit, for each time he went to jail, or hospital, or to write, he was always visiting a St Elizabeths of the mind. It was everywhere. 'You speak my language,' he told Pound, and years later, in 1963, when he heard that Pound had been depressed Lowell sent him a letter. 'I think there are times that cannot be softened or explained off,' he wrote: 'I sympathize and suppose I've lived in the same cellar for moments.' Down in the dark place they were all the same, a single twisting man.

Was Pound mad? In 1954 this became once more a question.

Until that year, the books appearing under Pound's name – *The Pisan Cantos*, the volumes of selected poems and essays, the letters – had been old work, written before his arrival at the hospital. This year, however, two new works by Pound arrived in print. In February the *Hudson Review* published his *Women of Trachis*, and this was followed in September by his versions of the Confucian Odes, with the title *The Classical Anthology Defined by Confucius*. To some, this was suspicious. After the publication of the Confucius anthology the US attorney general wrote to Overholser to ask, in a question that was not really a question, about this patient 'who seemingly is mentally capable of translating and publishing poetry but allegedly is not mentally capable of being brought to justice'. Until now Pound's poetry had been a useful proof of his insanity. But now it began to look like the opposite: proof of sanity or proof perhaps of a trick.

The same concern occurred to Pound's admirers, and it was put most firmly by the translator and poet Robert Fitzgerald, who in the early 1950s was beginning work on his version of Homer's *Odyssey*. He corresponded with Pound, asked his advice on the translation, and occasionally visited St Elizabeths, but by 1954 the contradictions had become too much. 'Can't you see the shadiness and absurdity you let your friends in for?' Fitzgerald wrote to Pound, and then, reaching for the harshest accusation he could, added:

You are in St Elizabeth's because you and your lawyer chose to plead insanity rather than stand up to a trial. If there was something you wanted to fight for aside from yourself you could have fought for it then. If your mind was sick then you belonged in St Elizabeth's. If it wasn't, then you were craven not to stand trial on your indictment.

Here was the knot: to sympathize with Pound one has to accept that he is insane, and yet to take his advice one must assume that he has real and sane things to say. To assume that he is sane is equally to assume that he is by extension a coward and a cheat, and therefore surely not a source of good advice on how to live or how to write.

In 1954 the contradictions buried inside Pound's insanity defence exploded into view. We can date his activity of this period with unusual precision, because Pound was writing a new volume of cantos and when he sent the manuscript to his Italian publisher Vanni Scheiwiller in December 1954 he included a note with the dates of their composition. He wrote Canto 91 between 26 June and 18 July 1954, and then Canto 92 in the second week of August; on 18 August he began work on Canto 93, which was complete by 14 September, and then he turned to Canto 94, which he wrote over the last two weeks of September. Canto 95 was written in the second half of October and the first days of November 1954. These cantos began to appear in magazines in April 1955 and the new collection – with the enigmatic title *Section: Rock-Drill de los cantares* – was published in Milan on 12 September 1955.

When the doctors looked at Pound they could not see that he was at work. 'Patient does no work, causes no trouble,' runs the note in Pound's case file from June 1948. In November 1949: 'He reads at night and hums in his room,' and then in May 1951, 'spends his time reading or writing'. In July 1953: 'Mr Pound does not do any work on the ward spends his time in his room reading & typing.' When the doctors think of 'work' they mean the occupational therapy in which the other patients engage: making brooms and mending clothes; stuffing mattresses and stitching quilts; filling muslin bags with Christmas gifts and jars with jam from the fruit of the orchards. Since the opening of the hospital, patients had assisted with landscaping its grounds – painting the benches, tending the trees – and during the expansion in the last years of the nineteenth century they had excavated sites for new buildings, so patient labour was literally the foundation of St Elizabeths. According to Philippe Pinel, the great pioneer of moral treatment in eighteenth century France, occupational therapy was 'the fundamental law of treatment of the insane', and this is why the doctors so often note their perplexity at Pound's apparent refusal to do any work at all. They could not force him into occupational therapy, since compulsion is opposed to the spirit of moral treatment. 'No work,' they write in the case file, again and again, even while the patient sits in his room typing, reading, humming.

What is the visible form of madness: its expression in the world? When Pound arrived at St Elizabeths, the diagnostic terms for the analysis and description of mental illness were in their infancy. This was the age of the first taxonomies of psychiatric terminology, and the language used by Pound's doctors was borrowed from manuals designed for army psychiatrists during the Second World War. It now appears crude. In December 1945 four doctors testified before the District Court that Pound was 'suffering from a paranoid state which renders him mentally unfit to advise properly with counsel', and this was as close as they came to a formal diagnosis. Paranoia is, according to the definition formulated by Overholser in his 1947 *Handbook of Psychiatry*, the condition of one who 'believes himself to be persecuted' by organizations or persons 'mixed up in plots against him' and the paranoid state is a temporary version of this, in which: 'The delusions are not so well systematized or worked out and are likely to have a bizarre nature about them that strikes laymen as "crazy".' That is, in a circular logic: one of the symptoms of this madness is the appearance of craziness.

In his January 1946 report on Pound's Rorschach test, Dr Kendig – who was not one of the four doctors who testified in court – came to a slightly different conclusion. He described Pound as 'a brilliant but pedantic individual with a marked personality disorder of long standing', narcissistic, egocentric, and prone to bursts of temper; he noted that the patient displayed contempt towards women, and added, 'While many of these qualities are schizoid and some of his attitudes paranoid, there is no evidence of psychosis.' The Rorschach test seeks its proofs in the pattern of a patient's response to inkblots on a page, and reading this report now it is hard to escape the impression that Pound was playing up. 'Abyssinians with whiskers,' he declares, when faced with one particularly spiky blotch, and the doctor notes: 'The hatred of women and other races, implied in his interpretations, is in line with Fascistic ideology.' At one point, Pound demands, 'Are these supposed to reveal profound sex perversions?' and the doctor notes, 'Perverse sexual trends are apparent throughout the protocol.' This is a little slapstick: the wisecracking patient and his credulous head-doctor, grappling over cartoons.

It is easy to poke holes in these early diagnoses, and to smirk at the slightly rusty old medical jargon. But the initial dispute over Pound's mental state – whether he is psychotic or not, and the duration of the condition – persisted in the diagnoses of the following years. In 1952 the American Psychiatric Association issued the first edition of the *Diagnostic and Statistical Manual of Mental Disorders*, known as the DSM. This was the first full compendium of criteria and titles for mental disorders, arranged by numbers, and it clarified the terms used by the doctors, but also sharpened their disagreement. In July 1953 Dr Bernard Cruvant – who had been Chief of Service while Pound was at Howard Hall, and also saw patients in Center Building – recorded a new diagnosis. Pound was, he proposed, a 'narcissistic personality type', following the typology set out in the DSM: '51.3 Personality Trait Disturbance, Other. Narcissistic Personality.' A little less than two years later, in May

1955, Overholser added a rival diagnosis to Pound's case notes. '24.2' this ran: 'Psychotic disorder, Undifferentiated.' The numerical code is simply translated. The first number is the classification, so 51 is 'Emotionally unstable personality' in the category of personality disorders while 24 is 'Schizophrenic reaction, paranoid type', within the larger category of psychotic disorders. The qualifying number after the period adds detail: 3 means 'with behavioural reaction' and 2 means 'with neurotic reaction'.

It matters less that these are differing diagnoses than that they fall into distinct categories. 'The basic division in this nomenclature,' runs a note at the start of the DSM, 'is into those mental disorders associated with organic brain disturbance, and those occurring without such primary disturbance of the brain.' Overholser found in Pound a psychotic disorder: in which, explains the DSM, 'the personality, in its struggle for adjustment to internal and external stresses, utilizes severe affective disturbance, profound autism and withdrawal from reality, and/or formation of delusions or hallucinations.' Its characteristics are unrealistic thinking, aggression and perhaps excessive religiosity or delusions of genius. Cruvant, by contrast, found Pound to suffer from a personality disorder. 'The disorder,' explains the DSM, 'is manifested by a lifelong pattern of action or behavior, rather than by mental or emotional symptoms,' and is displayed in the patient's reaction to stress, which falls into a repeated cycle: anxiety, feelings of guilt and strained relationships with others. We might understand the distinction as between two styles of a mind's response. In personality disorders the patient's actions refer to the external world. Psychosis is a break with that reality.

Madness might look like work or its absence; might show itself in seeming crazy or lazy or bold. Where diseases of the body are known by physical marks and external signs – of heat, colour and action – disorders of the mind are shown in more abstract symptoms: in dreams, delusions, the proofs of things that aren't there or are present only in an unusual form. Madness awaits representation and is therefore bound up with the ways in which a specific individual might display it, and this is the problem with the diagnoses of Pound: the doctors sound as though they are describing not his mental state but his poetry. 'His language is often esoteric, but does not represent condensation in a schizophrenic sense,' runs a note in his file from 1946. 'Condensation' is a symptom of schizophrenia: the condition when thoughts or feelings fuse into a single, repeated, often non-verbal expression. It is equally a poetic ideal for Pound. 'Dichten = condensare', he commanded in his *ABC of Reading*: to write is to condense. The doctorly vocabulary is also the poet's, and Pound was happy to borrow the language of psychiatry to describe his own ideas about writing. In his 1913 manifesto called 'A Few Don'ts' he defines the ideal image as 'that which presents an intellectual and emotional complex in an instant of time' and he had learned the keyword 'complex' from early Freudian psychiatrists in London.

According to the report from Pound's Rorschach test of January 1946: 'His handling of color is poor and he displays both color and shading shock.' This patient's responses to the coloured images revealed, the report goes on, 'poor adjustive capacity, egocentricity and narcism [*sic*], emotional instability and confusion'. In June 1955 this same patient imagined a perfect night-time scene. 'Moon's barge over milk-blue water,' he wrote in his new Canto 90, and while the poetic phrase might muddle apparently separate colours – the blue-ness of water and the cloudiness of milk, the whiteness of moon and the darkness of night – it is a dense, powerful image. It Is also rich with literary echo. F. Scott Fitzgerald's 1934 novel *Tender Is the Night* in one famous moment pictures 'a sea as mysteriously colored as the agates and cornelians of childhood, green as green milk, blue as laundry water, wine dark'. Pound has borrowed the metaphor, but doubled it by switching the green-milk sea for milk-blue water. This is condensation in both the schizophrenic and poetic senses.

Or perhaps he did not have Fitzgerald in mind. Pound's version of the classical Chinese song 'The Beautiful Toilet', published in

Cathay in 1915, begins with the line: 'Blue, blue is the grass about the river.' It is an arresting image, and the original has – of course – green grass; Pound has switched green for blue. This might be poetry and might be madness, but this specific shading, of green into blue and blue into green, was uncertain for him. In December 1918 Marianne Moore sent Pound a handful of her new poems, and he wrote back with a list of queries, one of which was about a particular colour she mentioned. 'It means peacock-green???' he asked: 'Or peacock-blue or p.b. green?' Peacocks are both blue and green – like the sea and the grass – and just like poets, their handling of colour is, in a diagnostic sense, confused.

'The day was green' writes Wallace Stevens in his 1936 poem 'The Man with the Blue Guitar':

> They said, 'You have a blue guitar,
> You do not play things as they are.'
>
> The man replied, 'Things as they are
> Are changed upon the blue guitar.'

Stevens is the great poet of the forms and shifts imagination may take, and here he records the accusation of those who demand a song 'Of things exactly as they are', and how he may only reply: 'I cannot bring a world quite round, / Although I patch it as I can.' The shift in colour is a sign of the poet at work. In his *Guide to Kulchur* Pound discussed colour as a fact of the world. 'Certain truth exists,' he declared:

> Certain colours exist in nature though great painters have striven vainly, and though the colour film is not yet perfected. Truth is not untrue'd by reason of our failing to fix it on paper.

We must not judge these works on paper – paintings, photographs, poems – by their fidelity to what Stevens calls 'things exactly as they are'. Instead, just like the doctors with the Rorschach test, we can find in them a record of the poet's responses. In this way, we might read Pound's *Cantos* as a great compendium of symptoms, and whenever in the *Cantos* he comes to describe colour, he is always seeing double. His colours are never primary. In Canto 2 the water runs from 'blue-deep' to 'green-ruddy', later stained by 'wine-red algæ', and later still is olive grey, 'colour of grape's pulp' and 'smoke grey of the rock-slide'. In Canto 4 he sees 'Crescent of blue-shot waters, green-gold in the shallows' and in Canto 5 he sees 'three sorts of blue', and it is not that there are too many colours here but that there is only one, and it is changing before his eyes.

His eyes: in November 1913 a writer in London described Pound's 'sharp red beard poised at a forward-downward angle and well-shaped features and deep-set blue eyes'. In late 1915 Pound was issued with an identity card by the American Embassy in London, and here he has green eyes and fair hair, and when in Paris in 1919 he applied for a new passport it lists his grey eyes and light brown hair. Perhaps his eyes were grey: in Canto 79 he appeals to Athena and follows it with the Greek epithet most often given by Homer to the goddess: 'glaukopis', which can mean 'grey-' or 'blue-eyed'. The eyes are changing colours.

The question of Pound's colours is not the same as that of Pound's sanity, but it suggests how slippery it is to measure a patient's mind through the pattern of his responses, and how the slipperiness is redoubled when that patient is also a poet: one whose work is defined by counter-intuitive recordings of the external world, or who renders the grass as blue. The madness of poets is an old Romantic idea and it became literal for a generation of Americans known as the Confessional poets in the 1950s. There was Anne Sexton, in long-term therapy at Glenside Hospital near Boston, and John Berryman, hospitalized for alcoholism; there was Delmore Schwartz, who suffered from many demons and died alone, his body unclaimed. Robert Lowell called them 'underseas fellows, nobly mad', and so many in this generation of poets were inhabitants of the same cellar: their lives marked by hospitals, their deaths in suicide.

To think of a poet as mad is another way to think about his place in society, and American poetry in the 1950s was in several senses institutionalized. Just as many of the Confessional poets spent time in mental hospitals, so too did they begin to take up other kinds of institutional posts: in universities, as lecturers or as students of creative writing; in writing colonies; and at the Library of Congress. What runs beneath the poems of this generation is a sense, sad and certain, that institutions are necessary magnets for the imagination, but that they are also only temporary. One grand square building is constantly dissolving into another. Anne Sexton was Lowell's student at Boston University and her poem 'You, Doctor Martin' is addressed to a psychiatrist who helped her. In her memories of treatment, its location keeps shifting: the initial 'antiseptic tunnel' of the hospital becomes first 'this summer hotel' and then the patients turn into children, who 'chew in rows, our plates / scratch and whine like chalk // in school'. Finally, at the poem's close, the place is named 'the madhouse'.

Pound's trajectory through institutions – military prison, courthouse, mental hospital – was echoed and exaggerated in Lowell's own career: from military prison to the Library of Congress and then mental clinic. He also lectured at universities; he was a man for all institutions. In 1957 Lowell wrote a short prose memoir called 'Near the Unbalanced Aquarium' about his crack-up of the spring of 1954. The aquarium of the title is nowhere mentioned in the piece, but it is a code for all the institutions Lowell has passed through, and in turn resurfaces more literally in one of his most famous poems, written three years later. 'For the Union Dead' describes a Civil War memorial on Boston Common, taking this unvisited monument to past glory as a symbol for the disappointments of the modern age, but its most powerful repeated motif is not the memorial but instead 'The old South Boston Aquarium'. He had visited the aquarium often as a child, but it is boarded-up now, closed and filled with dust. The poem ends:

> The Aquarium is gone. Everywhere,
> giant finned cars nose forward like fish.

The fish have become cars, swimming out into the world.

Behind the shifting institutions that shimmer through American poetry of the mid-1950s – behind the madhouses, schools, jails and universities, the writing colonies and the aquarium – is the grandest of them all. What joined Pound and Lowell most powerfully was the belief that poets belonged in Congress or the White House. In 1958, just as he was speeding up again, Lowell wrote to Pound to ask his advice. He was thinking about standing as a candidate for political office, he explained, and asked, 'Do you think a man who has been off his rocker as often as I have could run for elective office and win?' This was a curiously inelegant question to ask Pound, but the dream tied them close: a classical vision of poets as politicians, the moral authority of the prophesying, ruling bard. In January 1956 some young wag had the bright idea of printing bumper stickers. 'EZ for PREZ' they said. He sent one to Pound at St Elizabeths, and it sits today in the ragbag dusty Pound file held at the National Archives in Washington, DC. This is a joke, of course, and it depends upon an idea about the resilience of institutions. Pound couldn't be president, because everyone knows that Pound is mad. This is not his institution.

On a perfect spring break day I went to the National Archives in Washington. They are housed in a grand white cube in the heart of the neoclassical city and outside stand guards in white shirts with lapels and gold badges. They keep the Declaration of Independence here, and they cool the rooms against the morning heat. Each hour the files arrive in boxes on a squeaky cart from the vault beneath. The hush, the guards, the cart and the pillars: all confer dignity upon the treasures and the papers in the vault, and the section of the Pound case file which has been made public is held here among them. While I wait for the boxes to arrive I ask a plump affable librarian why some of Pound's files have been made open, while those of other patients are closed. Being a public figure he has less rights, the librarian tells me, and he pauses to chuckle. Then he adds: he's lucky he wasn't shot.

The holding for patient Number 58,102 is six green boxes, lightly dusty and in loose chronology, containing the non-confidential sections from the case file released by St Elizabeths. The first page I find upon opening it is a record of his weight. On the day he arrived at the hospital Pound weighed 167 pounds. By the following summer he had put on ten pounds, and then fifteen more by the start of 1948. These figures suggest how he is settling in, and he stays at a healthy 192 for the rest of his years here.

The section of the case file held at the National Archives is a litter of trivia such as this. There are Pound's dental records and the dates when his ears were cleaned. In April 1955 they gave him reading glasses – he was long-sighted, which is typical in a man his age, for he was almost seventy – and each spring he was tested for tuberculosis. There are fragments from the truculent and repetitive observations logged by the doctors on the ward, and occasionally his unlikely voice appears, as if preserved – a little warped – in amber. To a ward attendant who in December 1954 asks Pound to stop singing while others are trying to sleep, Pound smiles and replies: 'Does this happen often? I was completely unmindful, so absorbed in what I'm doing.'

The bulk of the file is the letters he received, from magazines and newspapers, from eccentrics and obsessives. There is a questionnaire from *Newsweek* – 'Do you consider yourself an "egghead"?' – and a request for an interview from the *New York Times*. His admirers send peach marmalade and apple candy, neckties, cigarettes, and two pounds of figs. Marianne Moore sends germicide.

What I was hoping to find was something I had read about: the visitors' book. In his 1972 study *The Pound Era* the critic Hugh Kenner – the most influential Pound scholar – recalled going to see Pound at Chestnut Ward, and how, on arrival at the hospital, he was asked to register his name 'in a book labelled "Ezra Pound's Company"'. The translator Michael Reck visited Pound often in the 1950s, and in his own account he remembers signing in slightly differently. 'At the office,' he wrote, 'a white-coated attendant asks your name and consults a card file.' A card file or a ledger: whatever it was, this is the document I had travelled to Washington to see.

The visitors' book is a handful of thin blue sheets torn from a pad stamped 'Nursing Notes Standard Form 510'. The attendants simply used what they had to hand, and in the column marked 'Medication-Treatment' they noted the names of visitors, while beneath the title 'Observations' is the visitors' address or place of work or some detail of who they are. They are 'artist, California' and 'Chinese culture student'; 'insurance examiner', 'Catholic priest' and 'schoolmaster, from England'. There are nine of these thin pages and the entries run from 28 July 1954 to 19 March 1955. The rest is lost or locked up in the hospital.

The most frequent visitor was Dorothy Pound, who came out to the hospital forty-eight times in these eight months. The next most frequent is Sheri – sometimes spelled 'Cheri' – Martinelli, who describes herself as 'artist friend' and who comes to see Pound twenty-three times. Some days there were many guests, and some weeks none at all. Robert Lowell is here on 6 January 1955, but otherwise this is a list of mostly forgotten names, of academics and fans who came a couple of times while they were in the city and never returned. It is an oddly lonely document. He had four visitors on 18 December, and then another four on 4 January. One person on the 6th; two people on the 8th; and there are many long and empty hours in between. They came sporadically, fickle like tourists, as one might visit the Washington Zoo or the museums along the grand avenues just outside.

The Pound file has 1,430 items and each one says: this man is special. He has been documented and therefore must be worth documenting. But the patient number stamped on the file insists that he was only ever one among many: 58,101 patients arrived before him, and tens of thousands would follow. The privacy laws protect patients for fifty years after their deaths, and therefore do not cover those patients who were at the hospital a little earlier in the century; and in the afternoon I worked out the reference code for the St Elizabeths files and called up some random case notes from the unprotected decades. This felt like a violation, but after all the slipperiness of Pound's warring diagnoses, I wanted to see how the more certifiably insane looked.

In November 1914 a St Elizabeths doctor interviewed a patient he describes as 'disoriented in all spheres'. The doctor asks the standard questions – 'Do you know where you are?' and 'Do you know today's date?' – and notes down the response, so the files are an odd composite of doctorly query and wayward syntax straying to the edge of the page and the edge of grammar. The doctor notes: 'Says this is castle Green or Old Ivy Castle. Says he has been here for seventeen years and came here in 1903. Does not know what he came here for. Says he is thirty-five years old and he was born way back in the 60s.' Another, from April 1913: 'Says this is Monday, 1918 or 1909.' Another 'Says he is insane because he bought a homestead in Kenya'. Another, when asked his age, gives it as about forty, but adds, 'I have been dead since I was 30.' These patients are lost in place and time and person. They arrive without knowing their own names, and instead of identities now all they have are unruly answers to standard questions. In November 1921 a doctor watches an unnamed patient walking three steps forward and then back. 'Will not tell why he does this,' the doctor records, and notes: 'A gray-eyed woman worries him by getting on his tongue and blowing bleached cans in his plate and will not let him eat.' A grey-eyed woman, like Athena, here in the old hospital: I wanted to read these files for hours, and when I looked up the light had lengthened and the guards were calling for the visitors to leave.

If these are the mad, Ezra Pound begins to look as if he belongs among the sane. In the boxes, during the afternoon, I found a test, dated 1910, given to patients to expose their state of mind upon admission to the hospital. This consists of a simple questionnaire on American history and geography. It asks the patient to name the Great Lakes and the cost of a postage stamp: 'Name two generals in the Civil War', 'What presidents were assassinated?' and 'Who is Mr Taft?' These were Pound's obsessions – military history, political figures and government fees – and after I left the archives I sat beneath the cherry trees that line Washington's grand boulevards and set myself the test. I knew the names of the presidents, but not of the lakes; I could list the American national holidays, but not the capital of Maryland. I knew the date and where I was sitting. There were tourists around me, in the shade of the hot pink blossoms, strolling upon the green, and for a moment everyone was a schoolchild and a patriot. I answered the questions as best as I could, and when I tallied up my score I found I had failed.

Perhaps the most resonant detail from Pound's case file is something that is not there. The file records that in January 1949 Pound is given the painkiller Novocaine, following a dental X-ray, and in April 1953 penicillin for an infected tooth. In April 1955 he sits an eye exam and he undergoes an ECG in May 1956. The doctors test his heart and eyes, and they clean his ears and teeth, but nowhere is there any mention of psychiatric treatment or therapy of any kind.

The treatment that Pound received sheds light upon the question of his sanity. For the obvious implication of the absence of treatment is that the doctors considered him to be sane; and yet because the file is incomplete, this silence is not in itself an answer. At the National Archives I called up pages from across the sprawling

St Elizabeths files, and these record the treatments given to other patients at the hospital. The 1940s was an age of enthusiasm for Electroconvulsive Therapy and I find its traces everywhere. In 1941, 80 per cent of federal hospitals were practising ECT. In December 1942 Overholser reported to a colleague that in the past eighteen months 100 patients had received ECT at St Elizabeths, particularly those suffering from schizophrenia, and in February 1945 he described the routine to a researcher. The patient undergoing ECT was treated with electric shocks three times a week. The day before, he or she is given no sedative and nothing to eat after midnight, and the treatment takes place in the morning. Afterwards, the patient stays in bed for two hours, and then has a shower and a light lunch. The most frequent complication was dislocation of the jaw, in perhaps a fifth of cases.

This is the treatment which might – or might not – have been administered to Pound. In 2005 Pound scholars and admirers assembled at Rapallo for the 21st Ezra Pound International Conference. It is a cheery gathering and that year an elderly Italian doctor named Dr Romolo Rossi addressed the opening session. Rossi had been working at the mental clinic attached to the Genoa University School of Medicine in the 1960s when Pound, now very late in life and living once more in Italy, came into the hospital. He had recently undergone prostate surgery and was suffering from depression, and in the course of examining Pound, Rossi explained, he was shown a report from St Elizabeths in which Pound's earlier treatment for depression was listed: ECT. Rossi prescribed an anti-depressant and Pound recovered, but Rossi added a diagnosis. Pound was suffering, he concluded – and told the conference – from 'manic-depressive illness (also called bipolar disorder)', and he went on to speculate that this condition might be behind Pound's rabid enthusiasms and antic behaviours throughout his life. The broadcasts and the *Cantos*, fascism and inspiration: all might be symptoms. Dr Rossi had not, however, kept a copy of the medical file.

In the vexed, slippery discussion of Pound's sanity, all are like children playing the old game: blindfolded and trying to pin the tail upon an imaginary donkey. Perhaps he was bipolar or manic depressive; perhaps he was psychotic, paranoid, schizophrenic or none; his madness is a question which can be answered only with reference to once-glimpsed, now-missing documents. The absent files and hidden truths invite the kind of hopped-up thinking we call conspiracy theory, and Pound's years at St Elizabeths have long attracted such excitable narrations. The conspiracy theories told about Ezra Pound at St Elizabeths run in two directions. In one, he is a traitor shielded by the hospital from the punishment which was his due; in the other, he is a fearless truth-teller punished for threatening to reveal all he knew. In one, Pound is the hero, wronged and justified. In the other, he is a trickster, mocking and weak. The two versions, however, agree upon their diagnosis: for in both, Pound is sane.

The most vivid telling of the first of these conspiracy theories is that given by E. Fuller Torrey, who was a physician on the wards at St Elizabeths in the late 1970s and early 1980s. While there he researched a book which boasted to expose what it describes in its colourful title as *The Roots of Treason: Ezra Pound and the Secrets of St Elizabeths* (1984). 'Reconstruction of the historical record, aided by recent release of files in the Department of Justice and his psychiatric hospital, has made it possible to understand Ezra Pound,' it promises on the first page. Torrey tells how Pound faked the symptoms of madness to escape the treason charge and relished his years in Center Building. Here he happily wrote, and when young women came to visit he pulled the screen and had sex with them on the ward. The doctors knew all this, of course, but Pound was shielded by Overholser. Often, the patient and the superintendent met to plan their great deception, and, cleverest of all, the two men conspired to leave no trail of evidence. 'There is reason to believe that Overholser destroyed all records of those meetings,' Torrey explains, and 'The destruction was deliberate.'

Destroyed files and secret sex: this is only the cartoonish extreme of a story that has bubbled along since the early years of Pound's confinement. In 1949, in an article in the *American Journal of Psychotherapy*, Dr Frederic Wertham described the Pound case as an example of 'the dangerous abuse of psychiatry'. Pound was not insane but simply the follower of outlandish economic theories, but the doctors who testified in court 'did not have enough acquaintance with either Pound's life or his work'. 'What is wrong with him,' Wertham declares, 'is not the disease of an individual but a symptom of social degeneration.' In 1963 Thomas Szasz – an academic and psychoanalyst, and libertarian critic of what he called the 'myth' of mental illness – agreed that this patient was a symbol of all the ills of wider society. 'The Pound case affords an example of the type of psychiatric participation in the criminal process which substitutes the Rule of Men for the Rule of Law,' he wrote in *Law, Liberty, and Psychiatry*, and the perfect proof that psychiatry is 'unregulated' and too subjective to play a role in the courts. The historian Stanley Kutler in 1982 set out to expose what he called 'the whole process of legal repression' he felt was dominating American political life. Pound's years at St Elizabeths demonstrated the troubling 'interaction between law and politics, public and private power alike, and the covert, as well as the overt, operations of power', he writes, and in Pound's suspended treason trial 'psychiatric testimony blocked and then aborted the legal process in his favor'. At last, with the familiar flourish of secret documents, Kutler concludes: 'as long-suppressed government files clearly demonstrate, Ezra Pound was not insane.' This secret has often been told, but is refreshed in each new telling.

The trouble is not that these secret documents do not exist; the trouble is that they might, and the documents which we can access permit this interpretation. As Torrey insisted, 'Dr Overholser did whatever he had to do to protect Pound,' and this first conspiracy theory always rests upon a specific psychological profile of Overholser. The superintendent, as we know, moved Pound into a room on Chestnut Ward which was next door to his own private quarters; there are friendly letters between the two men, as well as from Overholser to the celebrated literary figures who came to visit. Here is Overholser to T. S. Eliot in July 1946: 'I am looking forward to seeing you myself as well.' A portrait begins to suggest itself: of the superintendent as toad, flattered by grand writers, a snob in a white lab coat. Then there is the letter from Overholser to the Department of Justice in February 1955 in which he reports: 'So far as I am aware, Mr Pound has not done any recent writing of poetry,' while Pound had, in the previous years, translated two plays and a book of Chinese poems and written a new volume of cantos. Then there is Overholser's repeated refusal, recorded in the case files and court transcripts, to engage in any discussion of Pound's specific symptoms.

It is because this story remains so neatly tellable – because it offers an easy villain in the grander drama of the famous poet – that it persists beyond the more obviously conspiratorial accounts and finds its way into respectable biographies of Pound. Humphrey Carpenter's doorstep-sized life of Pound dismisses Overholser as an absurd figure. 'He had no flair as a therapist,' Carpenter writes, and 'reputation always concerned him'. He sought at all costs to keep 'his personal grip on Ezra'. Overholser appears equally undignified in the more recent three-volume biography by A. David Moody. Here he is simply weak, a doctor who reported to the Department of Justice 'what it wanted to hear', who 'blandly lied'.

This story works only so long as we imagine Pound to be the centre of our telling. If we shift the focus, it begins to stall. In the National Archives, the Pound file is in six boxes, but when I call up Overholser's papers they wheel them in on several carts. The Overholser file is thirty-six boxes of material, and these are an epic of bureaucracy and the measure of a truly public life. Overholser's career was a parade of institutions, from the US Army Medical Corps in the First World War to the presidency of the American

Psychiatric Association, and punctuated by honours: the Légion d'honneur from France, the President's Award for Distinguished Federal Civilian Service. His writings are stolid, optimistic, occasionally humourless. His files are kept in order. At the heart of the riddle of Pound's St Elizabeths sits this soft-faced enigma, this smiling bureaucracy man.

Overholser was a figure of great probity, and because he was so self-evidently right he was also accustomed to being misunderstood. Perhaps all psychiatrists feel this way. The first hero of modern psychotherapy is the French physician Philippe Pinel, who served at the Bicêtre asylum in Paris in the last years of the eighteenth century. When he explained his new methods to the prisons commissioner – he wished to treat the patients with kindness and to undo their chains – he was mocked. 'Why not proceed to the zoo and liberate the lions and tigers?' the prisons commissioner demanded, but Pinel persisted, and this story is recounted in a book called *Man Above Humanity: A History of Psychotherapy*, which was published in 1954 with a foreword by Overholser. This same gesture – of striking the shackles from the bodies of the distressed – reappears in the origin story often told about St Elizabeths. Dorothea Dix was visiting a jail in Massachusetts on a cold winter day and when she saw that the insane inmates were not provided with stoves to warm themselves or blankets at night, she resolved to found a new hospital for the mentally ill.

One story that psychiatrists might tell themselves goes something like this: the world is a hard and suspicious place, and the doctor's noble duty is to stand between the bodies of the distressed and those who would punish instead of trying to understand. This is their myth, and it was known to Overholser from the history books, and it can only have deepened his resolve to protect Pound from popular mistrust. To betray his patient would in effect have been to side with the prisons commissioner who compared patients to tigers, or the guard who froze his charges, and the history of psychiatry celebrates those who stand up to authority. Lecturing at Harvard in November 1952 Overholser treated precisely this discord between the institutions of psychiatry and the law. 'It is a fact that the law still proceeds on the basis of psychological assumptions which are not in line with prevailing psychiatric points of view,' he said, and noted that the two do not even share a common language, for the term 'insanity' is 'entirely a legal one, which is not used by physicians except on those relatively rare occasions when they have to answer questions about it in court.' Once you shift the perspective, Overholser is no longer the fraud who harboured Pound, but instead his noble guardian against an uncomprehending world.

The first conspiracy theory about Pound at St Elizabeths is a thriller of disguises and closed doors, and it centres upon Overholser. The second, rival theory is closer to a Western, with Pound as a lone gunslinger taking on the crooked system. This second story features a curious character named Eustace Mullins, who stalks around the edges of the Pound universe and who I came in time to think of as a representative sent from some dark Pound underground. But this, too, is part of the whole account of Pound's hospital years, and sheds some unexpected light upon the question of Pound's madness.

In the thin pages of the visitors' list the name 'Mr Mullins' appears twice. He is there on 7 August 1954 and again on 17 March 1955, and is described as a 'Financial writer'. Pound called him 'the Mulligator' or 'Useless Mullins', and the translator Michael Reck spotted him during a visit to the hospital. 'He seemed to have no spine,' he wrote, 'and floated rather than walked,' but this is perhaps unkind, and Mullins described his encounter with Pound as a religious conversion. 'The moment I entered the gloom of the insane ward,' Mullins later wrote:

> my former complaisance vanished, never to return. I suddenly realized that a great writer had been punished by being confined in a madhouse, solely for his political views. In an instant, Pound filled the ideological gap in my life. Never again would I remain silent in the face of injustice.

Pound offered this young zealot $10 a week and, more valuably, a purpose: to go to the Library of Congress and read up on the history of American banks. When Mullins returned to the hospital and presented his findings, Pound commanded – according to Mullins – 'You must work on it as a detective story.' In 1952 Mullins published *A Study of the Federal Reserve*, which reads like a whodunnit with a thousand footnotes and which recounts the dastardly founding of the Fed in a plot against the spirit of Jefferson and the principles of American democracy, but backed by the Rothschilds. The book includes as illustrations 'charts showing blood, marriage and business relationships', for all this evil is linked, and Mullins demands: 'Will we continue to be enslaved by the Babylonian debt money system which was set up by the Federal Reserve Act in 1913 to complete our total destruction?'

Mullins recounts his visits to the hospital in his next book *This Difficult Individual, Ezra Pound* (1961). He describes this as 'the only authorized biography of Ezra Pound', by which he means that Pound asked him to write it, and it is a deeply abject study. In it, Mullins explains how he smuggled a camera into the hospital to take a portrait of Pound, and he includes this with the caption: 'Pound considered this the best likeness ever made of him.' Among the illustrations Mullins also includes two photographs of himself. He describes the horrors of the hospital – 'a heart-breaking and appalling Bedlam' – and promises to bring justice: 'For the first time, the case *for* Ezra Pound, which should have been presented at the trial that the government refused him, is being presented in this book.' He invokes missing documents – 'in 1949, a souvenir-hunter on the staff absconded with a large part of [Pound's] case history' – and explains how instead of being an anti-Semite in Italy during the war, Pound in fact 'helped Jewish poets and shielded them from the death cars of the Gestapo'. The US government could not permit him to stand trial, for they feared what he might reveal in court: that the New Deal was a fascist idea, and the war had been a farce. 'Almost alone of western men, he has no blood on his conscience,' Mullins concludes, and 'Ezra Pound has been the most persecuted artist of our time.'

Mullins died in 2010, but he has a curiously vibrant, well-curated online afterlife. On his website his books are available to download for free, and there are links to other recommended sites. One, called 'whale.to', tells of fluoride in the water and how the American government stages school shootings as an excuse to take away the guns; and there are further links to ragged editions of Pound's works: a badly scanned copy of the text of Pound's broadcasts from Rome and an incoherent volume of the *Cantos* in which all the line breaks have been lost. One click: from Pound's broadcasts to white supremacist websites. Another click and I am told that vitamin B3 can cure

AIDS and acne and schizophrenia. One more click and I am back to Mullins and on through him to Pound.

These virtual networks are a genealogy of alternative and counter-cultural histories. The authors of these secret histories call themselves 'truthers', and they believe in lineage. Just as Mullins on his now out-dated website is introduced as 'the last living protégé of Ezra Pound', so too are there several characters claiming in turn to be disciples of Mullins. They helpfully list their names under a section titled 'protégés'. One of them, John Kaminski, runs a blog and lives in Florida and he lists a working email address. I write to him, explaining that I am interested in Mullins. John writes straight back and we agree upon a time to speak over Skype.

John's story began when he was working for a small newspaper in a college town in New Hampshire during the First Gulf War. He was just a dilettante back then, he tells me, until someone he describes as a suspicious character with a lot of Hitler memorabilia intro-duced him to *The Protocols of the Elders of Zion*, the *Tibetan Book of the Dead*, and the writings of Eustace Mullins. It was Mullins, he explains in his distinctive phrasing, who enabled him to put together the vision in his head that the ascendance of the Jews in the economic and political world began with Oliver Cromwell. Then a couple of decades later the Jewish menace started the Bank of England, which now basically runs the world.

Kaminski tells me about what he calls the odyssey of the last year of Mullins's life. Kaminski took him in and shepherded him around the country, making sure he ate his vegetables, and Mullins in his last days was in a state of ecstasy because he knew he had done the best he could. There was never any money, he says, because Mullins was such an independent guy and the big publishing houses wouldn't touch him. We think we're an independent country but we're not, he says, and now he fears what he calls a 360 degrees murder plot to cut down the population by various means, where the air is foul, the water is poison and the food is no good.

Finally I ask him: who is behind this? He pauses. I asked Mullins the same question once, he tells me, and he remembers that Mullins said: the Queen of England. At this, perhaps John hears the incredulity in my voice, and he adds: I don't know if he's right. He goes on, I don't think it is her, and I ask him again, who? He says: the Rothschilds are pushing all the buttons. But then he adds: there are 280 Jewish families, or Wasp families, and some elements of European royalty.

It is the Jews, one family or a few hundred; it is the Wasps and European royalty; and we can never come quite to the end of the secret. Conspiracy theorists are custodians of their mysteries, tending to them during the long nights, keeping them aflame. The last thing a conspiracy theorist desires is no more conspiracy. As we say our goodbyes I ask John how we can live freely, and he tells me that the world is too far gone.

St Elizabeths was from its beginnings home to those most suspicious of the American political order. On my day out there I had seen a sign someone had assembled from the letters of an old noticeboard. 'OBAMA THE GREATEST IDIOT,' it read, and whoever made this probably did not know about the hospital's tradition of admitting presidential assassins. The first criminal patient at the hospital was a man called Richard Lawrence, who had in 1835 been found not guilty by reason of insanity of the attempted assassination of President Andrew Jackson. There was Charles J. Guiteau, who succeeded in assassinating President James Garfield and was held here until his execution in 1882; when one hundred years later John Hinckley Jr shot Ronald Reagan in an attempt to impress the actress Jodie Foster, he was sent to the new hospital, where he remained as a patient until 2016. 'I think it might be a good thing to hang Roosevelt and a few hundred yidds IF you can do it by due legal process,' declared Ezra Pound on air in Rome in April 1943, and his broadcasts often turn upon the condemnation of that 'yaller hound Dawg' and 'chief war pimp' 'Frankie

Finkelstein Roosevelt'. Pound's anti-presidential attitude found an oddly fitting home here.

It is no coincidence that those most violent in their hatred of US presidents might end up at St Elizabeths, for the hospital's role as a federal asylum near Washington meant that it inevitably took in these federal prisoners. But its specific organizational structure, as well as its quasi-political role, mean that St Elizabeths has long been surrounded by suspicions and a hint of scandal. This was the case a century before Overholser's time. As the hospital's official historian Thomas Otto explains, the founding legislation instructed that while funds for the hospital came from Congress, a medical doctor must serve as the single, central authority in running the institution. This was the superintendent, and a figure granted this untrammelled power is bound to attract accusations of foul play. In December 1869 rumours began to spread through Washington that the patients at the hospital were being maltreated and badly fed, while in his grand quarters Superintendent Nichols lived it up with brandy and cigars. The superintendent was making a fortune, they whispered, by selling government land to crooked property dealers, and the story was soon picked up by the local newspaper. However, the newspaper went on to report, when Congress sent investigators to the hospital, 'the superintendent is so generous with his rare old liquors and good things whenever they visit the asylum that these amiable gentlemen cannot find it in their hearts to expose the skeleton in the official closet of the Insane Asylum.' Nichols was subsequently cleared of any untoward decadence.

In part because it was designed to be separate, and a place where the walls were meant to keep people out, and in part because authority here lay in the hands of a single doctor, St Elizabeths long offered the perfect conditions for distrustful imagining. What the Washington papers had called in Nichols's day 'the skeleton in the official closet' never quite went away. In December 1955 the academic Samuel Hynes – who had visited St Elizabeths a few years before – wrote an article called 'The Case of Ezra Pound' for the *Commonweal* journal. It was prompted by the recent publication of Pound's new cantos and the tenth anniversary of his incarceration in St Elizabeths, and Hynes in his cautious piece observes the confusions which the Pound case is perhaps always bound to provoke. 'The fact of Pound in Bedlam has been disquieting,' he writes, and 'a reflection of an apparently insoluble modern dilemma, of the way in which individual freedom and the common good have come to be seen as antithetical.' We must pay attention, he insists, and adds: 'It is only prudent that we Americans should from time to time remind ourselves that one room at St Elizabeths is a closet which contains a national skeleton.'

To recover the whole of Pound's years in the bughouse means at times these detours through the Pound underground. We must sift the dust and swirl of fantasies, and trace the shapes of older patterns through the tales spun about him. Those conspiracy theories which flock to Pound suggest the tenacity of secrets, and their persistent pull upon all of our imaginations, but they equally hint at another sadder truth. The pieces do not fit, however hard we try. This was the problem of the Pound case, and in 1954 and 1955, under the pressure of the new science and taxonomies of mental illness, it suddenly became more visible. He is the skeleton in the closet, the only sane man in the madhouse, a rational lunatic, a victim and a villain, and all these at the same time. Perhaps this is precisely why he keeps the power to make paranoiacs of us all.

In February 1949 Robert Lowell saw a plot. He was at Yaddo and he woke one morning to the belief that the writing retreat had become a shelter for Communists and spies. He wrote to friends to warn and then to marshal them into action, and when the board of Yaddo assembled to hear his accusations against the director, he harangued them with wild claims and conspiracies. In March 1949 he had an ecstatic vision of purgation and the saints and was diagnosed with 'Psychotic reaction, paranoid type'.

There is a legibility to Lowell's mad behaviour. In contrast to the obscurity around Pound's treatment and condition, Lowell displays the symptoms neatly, and he suffers the cures in orderly sequence. His psyche appears bright, knowable; and in this his story feels like one from a more modern age. In June 1949, at Baldpate hospital in Massachusetts, he was given ECT, and later that year at Payne Whitney in New York he was diagnosed with manic depression and began psychotherapy. Back at Payne Whitney in 1954 the diagnosis was revised: first as hypomania and then acute schizophrenia. He was given Thorazine, which is a derivative of chlorpromazine. In 1967 lithium carbonate arrived on the market and he started taking it. Lowell's biography is a shopping list of drugs and treatments, and his writing career was formed not only by mental illness, but also by the specific science of its treatment.

In 1955, to mark one hundred years since its founding, St Elizabeths commissioned a slim, dark red volume of essays and reminiscences by doctors. This was called *Centennial Papers*, and in his introduction to the volume Overholser observed that in this year of 1955 the world of medicine was changing. 'It may not be impossible that we are on the verge of a new era in the treatment of mental disorder,' he cautiously suggests, and names this 'a pharmacological era, which seems to be succeeding to some extent the physiological era of electro-shock and insulin shock'. This was also the year in which the world of treatments turned: from the days of ECT to the increasing use of psychotropic drugs, among which Overholser specifically names chlorpromazine and reserpine. We can see this shift of eras in the record of Lowell's treatments: he was treated with ECT and then became an early patient of chlorpromazine.

This succession of eras, from the physiological to the pharmacological, signalled a huge change in the treatment and conception of mental illness, and, on a much smaller scale, it marks Lowell's writings. His poetry emerges directly from the experience of suffering and then being cured from mental illness. This is not the old Romantic story about madness as poetic inspiration, but instead a scientifically specific, mid-twentieth-century psychotherapeutic literary career. To understand the poetry, we might begin with the drugs; and to understand the drugs, we might turn to the poetry. 'I keep no rank nor station,' he wrote in 'Home After Three Months Away' – perhaps the greatest poem about mental illness of the twentieth century – 'Cured, I am frizzled, stale and small.' The development of Lowell's poetic style mirrors the development of the clinical treatments for mental illness, and we can therefore read his poems as medical documents or a kind of poetical case file of notes upon a patient. They are equally a sequence of engagements with the most maddening poet of them all: Ezra Pound.

The first break of Lowell's development through styles is between the very wrought early poems of his book *Lord Weary's Castle* (1946) and the poems for which he is perhaps most celebrated: the confessional and intimate *Life Studies* (1959). This is the movement from a poetry marked by what his biographer Ian Hamilton describes as 'the thumping, unstoppable iambic line, the piled-up alliteration, the onomatopoeic consonants', to one 'refreshed by a direct, almost wide-eyed attentiveness to objects, places, personal experience'. In 'Home After Three Months Away', from *Life Studies*, he writes with an aching, tender grace of a simple domestic scene. He is shaving one morning at home and by his side his young daughter plays with the shaving brush and touches her nose to his, and he chides her quietly: 'Dearest, I cannot loiter here / in lather like a polar bear.'

Here, the style is loose and open, but the poem's freedom is always constrained, for it follows the simplest of all poetic decorums: rhyme. Rhyme is return, is rules: it is always a limitation. William Carlos Williams once compared Lowell's rhymes to 'a tiger behind bars', just like the prisons commissioner who feared his mentally ill patients were tigers to be locked securely in the zoo, and Lowell's rhymes remind us that this poet is a patient. He began this poem on the weekend of his forty-first birthday, which fell on 1 March 1958, while he was home on his first weekend release from a psychiatric clinic near Boston called McLean Hospital. He had been held there in the locked ward since the start of January, but in the new pharmacological era patients were permitted home visits, once the most severe episodes had passed. 'The time I put away / was child's-play,' he writes, but once the weekend is done he must return to the hospital for the week. It is the inevitable return at the end of the weekend which is the poem's deepest rhyme, but it is equally this inevitable return that gives the weekend its pleasure; and gives the poem its force.

The madness makes itself felt in something deeper, too, in something as transient as the poems' sensibility: their awful brightness, their wounded noticing, and their intimate, wretched sense that – to echo Wordsworth – the world is too much with us. In 'Sailing Home from Rapallo' he describes going to Italy to collect his mother's body, and the poem begins:

> Your nurse could only speak Italian,
>   but after twenty minutes I could imagine your final week,
>   and tears ran down my cheeks . . .

In 'Waking in the Blue' he evokes a night in the hospital:

> Absence! My heart grows tense
>   as though a harpoon were sparring for the kill.
>   (This is the house for the 'mentally ill'.)

Everything here is a little raw and worn by all that it has had to go through. 'I want to come to Italy and work under you and forge my way into reality,' Lowell had written in that first letter to Pound, and that is precisely the achievement of *Life Studies*. These poems forge reality. They give the effect and feel of naked, confessional truth, while at the same time doing so within carefully polished, perfect poems.

Two things make *Life Studies* such a remarkable book: its looser, open forms; and its intimate, autobiographical materials. Both – surprisingly – lead back to Pound. As an undergraduate, Lowell had wanted to go to Pound in Rapallo and was denied, but he finally reached Rapallo in February 1954, when he went to collect his mother's body. This trip in turn prompted – or was echoed in – a breakdown during the following months. In the early spring of 1954, as the mania once more returned to Lowell, he was also beginning to write the poems that would become *Life Studies*. It was in this moment of crisis that he reached for Pound, and in March began to write to 'Uncle Ezra' those rambling, personal letters. As much as we can date it, this is the start of *Life Studies*.

Later that year, once Lowell had returned to treatment at Payne Whitney, he wrote again to Pound. 'Please forget the personal nonsense I wrote to you last spring,' he apologized, and his abjection and oddly formal manners mask the true breakthrough. For it was then, as his writing became increasingly personal, that he remade his style. He spent 1955 writing not poems but autobiographical prose, and this gave way in 1957 to free-verse poems, many of them, very fast. He was moving through styles and arranging ways of approach: breaking the form, introducing increasingly autobiographical elements. At the start of 1958 he began to rumble once more into the by-now-familiar smash, and, as before, he turned to Pound. In the third week of January he wrote to Pound to ask if he would send him a portrait. Pound joked back: 'Wait till you can get it on a postage stamp.'

In the narrow terms sometimes set by literary critics to chart influence between poets, Lowell is nothing like Pound. Pound is sprawling, prosy, loud; Lowell is sharp, shiny, raw. But in his times of crisis Lowell needed Pound. Pound waited until March – until Lowell was emerging and beginning to write 'Home After Three Months Away' – and then sent him two large drawings by Sheri Martinelli, his young visitor and artist friend. Lowell wrote back to thank him – 'Soon you will be hanging above my hearth like a Chinese ancestor' – and he kept one portrait in the room where he liked to write. It was glimpsed here in March 1960 by the young poet Frederick Seidel, who had been sent by the *Paris Review* to interview Lowell. So while Lowell was finishing *Life Studies*, in the huge productive recovery years of 1958 to 1960, he sat beneath the face of Pound. This might be one way to understand Lowell's breakthrough in this volume. He took the mania and ordered it; he put Pound in a frame.

The second break in Lowell's career came at the close of the 1960s and is an exaggerated recapitulation of the glories of the first. In 1967, when he started taking lithium carbonate to cool the mania, he also began writing sonnets, fast. He handed out these fourteen-liners by the bucketload, perhaps four in a week, and his biographer Ian Hamilton suggests that this late bursting of sonnets was prompted by the new drug. Perhaps so; but these hundreds of sonnets are marked by a devouring sense that all the world might end up as a sonnet. He includes in them the voice of his dentist and tender letters from his wife Elizabeth Hardwick. He publishes one set in the volume *Notebook 1967–68* (1969), and then rewrites the same sonnets and includes them in the later volumes *History*, *For Lizzie and Harriet*, and *The Dolphin*, all published in 1973. All can be revised, can be told in what he called 'a litter of variants'; everything is the same, again and different, as if there is only one poem but a million ways to write it. Lowell drew many figures and voices into his new sonnet universe, and among them he turned once more to Pound.

In *Notebook 1967–68* the poem called simply 'Ezra Pound' recalls a familiar scene.

> Horizontal in a deckchair on the bleak ward
> some feeble-minded felon in pajamas, clawing
> a Social Credit broadside from your table,

it begins, and Pound is on the ward, speaking to Lowell, while beside them another patient – that 'feeble-minded felon' – tries to seize Pound's papers. Then Pound is released – 'sprung' – and returns to Italy. He is now, in Lowell's recollection, a penitent figure, and conscious of his own absurdity. In the poem, Lowell asks, 'Who else has been in Purgatory?' and Pound replies, 'To begin with a swelled head and end with swelled feet,' for he has aged.

In *History* (1973) Lowell included a new version of this same poem. What this second version reveals is that here is a poem – or two – about the dynamic of sameness and difference which underpinned all the encounters between Pound and Lowell. The change lies in the pronouns, and what pronouns do is arrange people and their relations to one another. The earlier version changes pronoun in the middle. In the first half Lowell is talking to Pound, addressed as 'you'; in the second half the poem speaks about Pound, and now he is 'he'; and this little distance is safe and Pound is in his frame. In the later version, however, Lowell and Pound are speaking only to one another. In the first version there is someone else with them, for Pound 'showed us his blotched, bent hands'. But in the later version 'You showed me your blotched, bent hands' and we are getting close now, close enough to touch. Where earlier he was safely 'in' his deckchair, now he is oddly suspended 'on' it, as if floating free. In the earlier version the setting had been given an extra adjective – 'the bleak ward' – but later it is simply 'the ward', because we are inside it, now, inevitable. The first poem leaves Pound behind; the second carries him with it. Reading the two poems side by side we see that Lowell is approaching Pound. He is moving into the asylum with him.

American poetry in the twentieth century is a cycle of encounters with Ezra Pound. The poets come and go, and they play their variations upon the game of same or different, nearing or retreating. For nobody is the dance more wrought or more intimate than for Robert Lowell. There is a photograph of Lowell and Pound meeting in the period of these late sonnets, after Pound's release from the hospital. They are standing side by side, in Italy: two poets, nothing alike. One tall, just middle aged; the other ancient, out of time. One has his hand perched elegantly at the button of a lightweight, grey summer suit. He looks like a mannequin with cropped dark hair; his whole rig is pure preppy. The other stands with his hands loose, awkward in a too-big shirt. His hair is wild about his thin face in a white halo. But: in their eyes, the same expression.

Perhaps Pound was his own best doctor. According to Dr Kavka he was 'an exquisite diagnostician of his own state of narcissistic regression', and his notes record Pound's repeated stabs at a rough self-analysis. Inside his head he said it felt like 'splinters', and at a session a few days later Pound turned to his writings. 'Two of my early poems,' he said, 'are poems of madness,' and added: 'Literature approximates science.' This is defiant. He is saying: I can measure myself as much as the doctors can and my poems are truer documents than all your questionnaires. In reading the cantos written in 1954, and published the following year as *Section: Rock-Drill*, we might take this idea literally. Here, the poet is an exquisite diagnostician: an artist of his maladies, shaping the madness. Here, the poems are both a symptom and a cure.

Section: Rock-Drill opens with a Chinese ideogram: a tree of wide black strokes growing out of three fat boxes. It bristles upon the page. Canto 85 is filled with thickets of these Chinese signs: there are 104 of them in the 17 pages of the canto. This is beautiful and bold, but it is also, as the critic Donald Davie writes, 'unreadable'. This is the point. Pound had long dreamed of a poetic image which flamed beyond the conventions and inconveniences of written language. 'The image is itself the speech,' he wrote in a 1914 essay: 'The image is the word beyond formulated language.' Now he has left behind the possibility of content legible in words. In these cantos, writes Davie, 'Pound aimed to express, not "ideas" [. . .] but rather a state of mind in which ideas tremble as it were upon the edge of expression.' Davie's 1964 study of

Pound – from which these lines are taken – is titled *Poet as Sculptor*, and these poems are made, solid things, to be looked upon more than read. The volume's title alludes to a famous work by the sculptor Jacob Epstein: *Rock Drill*, in which a sharp, stone man sits astride a pneumatic rock drill, breaking into the earth. The poem is a sculpture.

The ideogram which opens Canto 85 is named on the page as 'LING²', and this is conventionally translated as 'sensibility'. Ideograms are built from root components, and as the scholar Thomas Grieve explains, the

CANTO 85

LING²

Our dynasty came in because of a great sensibility.

All there by the time of Y Yin

All roots by the time of Y Yin.

Galileo index'd 1616,

Wellington's peace after Vaterloo

chih³

a gnomon,

Our science is from the watching of shadows;

That Queen Bess translated Ovid,

Cleopatra wrote of the currency,

Versus who scatter old records

ignoring the hsien form

root components present in this ideogram are 'Rain falling on the open mouths of figures dancing in order to induce the descent of the spirits'. This puzzling image in turn suggests, according to Grieve, 'the spirit of a being, which acts upon others', and so – the theory runs – we see the ideogram's meaning without needing to read or interpret it. The cantos in this volume aim for such immediacy: for a religious knowing of things as they are, transcendent, glowing. 'In nature are signatures / needing no verbal tradition,' he writes in Canto 87, 'oak leaf never plane leaf.' The images – the many scattered ideograms and, on one page, the designs of the four suits of playing cards, in black and red – combine into what Grieve calls 'a visionary order of fruition, renewal and plenitude'.

This, at least, is the theory behind Pound's ideogrammatic cantos. It has two problems. The first is that Chinese ideograms are not – as Pound wilfully assumed – purely visual. A few are, but the majority have a phonetic component. That is: Pound believed that even if one knows no Chinese, one could stare at an ideogram and intuit its meanings, but this is not so. The second problem is related. A work which so wholly disregards its reader becomes in the end not a poem but something more like a secret, constantly kept. The cantos in this volume are marked by the same attitudes inside conspiracy theories, and within the clinical condition of paranoia.

These poems are a document of madness. In 1952 the DSM defined paranoia as a style of thinking 'characterized by an intricate, complex and slowly developing [. . .] system, often logically elaborated after a false interpretation of an actual occurrence'. This was the style of Pound's broadcasts. On 30 March 1942 he demanded of his listeners: 'When are the American and English people going to take note of the pattern, the pattern in which wars are made, not one war, but wars, in the plural?' This pattern began, he goes on, in 1696, following the founding of the Bank of England, and since then all wars have been fought for gold. 'Whoever died at Dunkirk died for gold,' he said, and 'Whoever was shot at Dakar died for gold.' This is an extreme example, but the same habit recurs in *Section: Rock-Drill.* Canto 86 looks like a companion to this broadcast, phrased in a more poetic key. 'Bellum cano perenne . . . ' this canto ends – 'I sing perpetual war . . .' – and the war he sings is of the Rothschilds tricking the British government in 1857, and the later heroism of the Nazi sympathizer Edward VIII, later the Duke of Windsor; of how the professors 'falsify history', and how Fascist economics might come to save us. These are all Pound's rusty, clanking systems and medieval libels, corralled once more into a plot.

It is possible to follow Pound's echoes and allusions here, and many scholars have done so, but a sadness remains: one may decipher his fragments only to find that when they do cohere they make something scarcely worth the effort. This is a mind speaking only to itself, in a language of one, and the agents he names behind these dark plots are never satisfactory. At the start of *Section: Rock-Drill* he mentions one voice silenced by political gangsters: 'Galileo index'd 1616'. Galileo tried to speak the truth and yet his works were banned by the Catholic Church, and Pound's source for this phrase is a book called *Unconditional Hatred* (1953) by a naval officer and military historian called Russell Grenfell. The argument of the book – and by extension, the suggestion of Canto 85 – is that the British involvement in the Second World War was motivated by a quasi-racist plot, devised by Churchill, to kill Germans. This is one of history's hidden schemes, and in this canto Pound draws a dozen lines again from Grenfell's book. Canto 93 includes the line: 'Grenfell's death was (like some others) / suspiciously sudden.' Grenfell died in 1954 and Pound implies – with no basis – that this must have been murder, perhaps for telling inconvenient truths. This is bad history – Galileo's works were not placed on the Index of banned works in 1616 and Grenfell was not murdered – but also tendentious, as many would deny that British and American racism were major causes of the Second World War. But it is neat and therefore attractive to one style of thinking.

In these late cantos there are plots and feverish gestures towards dark and total schemes. But there is also – blessedly – the opposite:

a gentle observation of life on the ward. In a cryptic phrase in Canto 95, he introduces another character:

> Elder Lightfoot is not downhearted,
> Elder Lightfoot is cert'nly
>   not
>   downhearted,
> He observes a design in the Process.

Elder Lightfoot Solomon Michaux was an African-American evangelist preacher whose sermons were aired on Saturday evening radio broadcasts, as well as local Washington television, and Pound heard these playing on the ward of St Elizabeths. Lightfoot was nicknamed the 'Happy Am I' preacher, because this cheery hymn was the theme music for his radio show, and because he preached the good news of the gospels, so there is a joke here, for he was not a downhearted man. He was, like Pound, a radio presenter, who saw a design in the process, but one whose upbeat broadcasts brought him fame and popularity, and invitations to the White House. Pound was far from Lightfoot, but close enough to see some instructive echoes, and in these cantos Pound also quotes a joke told by a fellow patient, and names the squirrels and the birds he sees out on the lawns.

Michael Reck was a frequent visitor in these years, and is mentioned in one of these cantos. In his memoir, Reck records another image used by Pound to explain the mechanism inside his mind. 'He said it seemed as though a movie film were running through his head and that suddenly the film would jam and break,' writes Reck, 'and then there would be only a white light.' It is a fine image. For Pound loved going to the movies in Italy, before the war: he loved to put his feet up on the seat in front and eat popcorn and laugh along at the funnies, and, seen this way, his madness cuts through the simple pleasure with a shocking clarity. It is also a perfectly modernist epiphany, of the sort that the novels of Joyce and Woolf are filled with, as their characters break from daily routines into a moment of clarity, and perhaps it is the best answer to the old question: was Pound mad? Inside his head, it felt like a break and shock, both familiar and strange, and sometimes, at his best, it felt like the truth. He was paranoid; he wrote impossible poems, which keep their secrets and yet let some parts slip. The cantos of *Section: Rock-Drill* make madness visible.

In early May 1955 the patients and staff of the dance therapy group at St Elizabeths prepared a play. It was called *Cry of Humanity* and in choreographed dance routines it presented the life of the hospital's founder Dorothea Dix in her struggle to bring humane care to the mentally ill. It included, too, a section on daily life at the hospital, from the perspective of the patients, and it was performed – running for three hours – in Hitchcock Hall as part of the hospital's centenary celebrations, which took place throughout this year.

A photograph survives of the performance: the dancers, who were patients, dressed in tight-fitting black suits, and standing with their arms raised into the light shining in one spot upon the darkened stage. They run through the routines of their day: waking on the ward and the rush to breakfast; then into group therapy or to one of their occupations, woodwork or rug-making; and later a walk in the gardens. In one scene, these patients upon the stage undergo hydrotherapy, and in another they are woken at night to take their medication. There is no record of whether Pound was in the audience for *Cry of Humanity*, but this was his own pursuit. The actors playing patients are also patients playing actors, and they are turning their madness and their place into a performance: into a kind of poem.

6

CasaPound

It is Thanksgiving 1953 and a freshman at Harvard has taken the Greyhound bus all the way from Boston to visit Ezra Pound. He is seventeen, so young and sure, this Frederick Seidel. This is the great American family holiday, but this sure young man has gone to see Pound instead. He wants Pound to tell him to leave Harvard and go to Rome, to be more serious. On the ward, Pound sings ancient poems in a strange language and, late in the afternoon, another visitor arrives. He is a surly figure, thin, not a poet at all. This rival for Pound's attention is another young man fresh from university; his name is John Kasper. On that first day Seidel tells Pound that he will not share his time, this visit, and Pound sends Kasper away. In triumph, Seidel stays in Washington for the weekend, returning to the ward on Friday, Saturday and again on Sunday, and then on Monday he goes back to college, just as Pound told him to.

Sixty years later: it is raining in Manhattan and I take the train uptown to make my own visit. Frederick Seidel opens the door and his every move is charming. We sit on comfortable chairs beneath a window looking down on to the city and the rain, and as I begin to ask my questions I ready myself for repetition. I tell him I have read the accounts and ask him what else he might remember. I say, I'm looking for the details that were left out before. When Seidel begins to speak I am surprised. I remember going in, he says, and the first thing that happens is another patient drops to his knees and prays to me, right there on the ward.

Seidel took several things from Pound. He took Pound's advice, to stay at Harvard, and also what he calls the sense that it was important to carry on. Pound told Seidel to go and see T. S. Eliot, and Seidel took this introduction too, and he took what Pound would call a 'boost', a little prompt to his confidence. For, Seidel recalls, before he went, he took a crash course in Chinese. It was sweet nonsense, he laughs, and he showed up at St Elizabeths with the suggestion that Pound should change a phrase in his translation of *The Great Digest*. In his version, Pound's Confucius advises that a ruler must 'love what the people love and hate what is bad for the people'. But, Seidel objected, what if the people love the wrong things? Seidel laughs as he recalls his bravado, and I ask how Pound responded. Seidel says: the glory of my visit was that a few days later he handed me a rewrite of that passage in Confucius. He had followed Seidel's advice and emended the phrase, so that it read 'Respect the people's creative urge'. I ask Seidel why he tried to correct Pound. First of all I was right, Seidel says, and I was taking the matter seriously. He adds: of course, one might see in this an assertion that I am a poet.

There are two parts to each visit: you have to walk towards Pound, and then you have to walk away. Seidel recalls how on his way out Pound escorted him as far as the locked gate, and then, after he got back to his university, he found in the mail a note from Pound. 'Only you,' it said, 'can save Harvard from that kikesucking Pusey.' As he tells this Seidel laughs, for Pusey was the President of Harvard and, he says, a very Presbyterian fellow of appalling rectitude. It was sad to see the note, he says, and after this silly slur, he did not see Pound again.

Later, Seidel became a great poet of possessions and renunciations: of what we hold on to and what we deny, and the trouble of loving the wrong things. His poems list beautiful things: bespoke suits and motorbikes, expensive meals in chic restaurants, and the hollow man dressed in such wealth. Of a Parisian jeweller, he writes:

> Joel has designed a watch
> In platinum.
> This watch is the sequel
> To anyone you have ever lost

and his poems work on the edge between love and loss, between banishment and desire. Almost as if Pound were for him another possession, Seidel often in interviews and in poems returns to this encounter in Center Building. 'I was a freshman,' he writes in 'School Days' from his collection *Nice Weather* (2012): 'When I visited Ezra Pound / At St Elizabeths'. Another poem from the same collection recalls: 'Ezra Pound channeling the great troubadour poet Arnaut Daniel / In St Elizabeths Hospital for the criminally insane', and how it 'sounded like he / Was warbling words of birdsong'. Meeting Pound made Seidel a poet. In 'Poem by the Bridge at Ten-Shin' – its title borrowed from Pound – Seidel pictures himself sitting in his apartment, high-up on the Upper West Side. 'I came here from St Louis in a covered wagon overland,' he writes, 'Behind the matchless prancing pair of Eliot and Ezra Pound.' This was his exile and his beginning.

The fullest telling of Seidel's visit is in his earlier collection *My Tokyo* (1993). 'I was seventeen / Every terrifying hungover sunrise that fall,' he writes in the poem 'Glory':

Thanksgiving weekend 1953 I made my pilgrimage to Pound,
Who said, Kike-sucking Pusey will destroy Harvard unless you
  save it.
I persuaded him two words in his translation of Confucius
  should change.

He recalls both the slur and his challenge to the master, but what matters from the meeting is the holy violence here, the great heat at the beginning of things, and most of all the beauty of this figure. 'Pound reciting with his eyes closed filled the alcove with glory,' he writes, close to the end of this poem, for this is what remains. Some parts we keep and some we send away. It is by choosing between the two that we get to glory.

John Kasper was banished from St Elizabeths in November 1953 but he did not stay away for long, for on 21 September 1954 he appears on the fragment of the visitors' list. Where the attendant usually registered the visitor, Kasper that day signed his own name. His handwriting is deliberate and a little bold, as if he is just learning to join it up for the first time.

Kasper first went to see Pound in June 1950, as soon as he had finished college at Columbia in New York, and since then he had been a sporadic but devoted visitor. In 1953 he opened a small bookstore called Make It New at 169 Bleecker Street in New York City. This was Greenwich Village: one block away was the San Remo Café, where the Beat poets drank, and that summer Charlie Parker was playing at the Open Door. Kasper's FBI file includes a description of him during this bohemian period: he is wearing high-waisted riding pants and a dark green shirt, 'in a manner similar to the late Nazi Storm Troopers'. Coming and going from the bookstore were, the witness adds, 'quite a few colored and Chinese homosexuals'. It is a curious mix: part-counter-culture, part-fascist, pure underworld.

Outside St Elizabeths, the world was turning. In May 1954 the Supreme Court issued their decision in the case of *Brown v. Board of Education of Topeka*. It ruled that 'separate educational facilities are inherently unequal' and therefore that the segregation by race of high-school students was anti-constitutional. Integration was not immediate, but over the following eighteen months, as previously white high schools planned to admit their first African-American students, right-wing groups rallied in opposition: states' rightists, white supremacists, Southern conservatives. Kasper travelled down to Alabama, where he worked on the senate primaries campaign of the white supremacist Rear Admiral John G. Crommelin. In June 1956 Kasper was back in Washington, where he announced the establishment of what he called a 'White Citizens' Council', and at the end of August he went down to Clinton, Tennessee, where he gathered crowds to protest the start of the academic year at a desegregated high school. There was a riot and Kasper was arrested. He spent the following year in and out of jail in Tennessee. In September 1957 a bomb went off at a high school in Nashville and Kasper was suspected, but never convicted. In November he was finally sentenced for conspiracy and sent to the federal prison in Tallahassee, Florida. Journalists who covered the trial reported that, as he left the courtroom, Kasper held a copy of *Mein Kampf* in one hand.

In early April 1956 Kasper wrote to Pound. 'Dear Gramp,' his letter begins, and it goes on to ask for help. Kasper was trying to think up 'some short quotable slogans' for use in the primaries campaign of Rear Admiral Crommelin, and suggests possible themes, such as 'Separation of Races' and 'Mongrelization'. He then adds, as a prompt: 'The kike behind the nigger.' These seem extreme, but they are precisely the phrases used by Pound himself in the journalistic writing he had recently turned to. Between late 1955 and the start of 1957 he contributed perhaps 200 short opinion pieces to small-press, right-wing journals and newspapers in America and Australia. Pound kept his name off these many scraps of journalism and signed others under a range of pseudonyms. He is 'an American student' and 'A traveller in the United States', and sometimes he gives a name and sometimes initials: 'J.T.' from Pittsburgh, 'José Boler' from Mexico City. But thanks to the extensive detective work of Pound's bibliographer Donald Gallup, as well as the account given by Noel Stock, who edited a newspaper called *New Times* in Melbourne, Australia, in which Pound published the most virulent of his pieces, we have a rough picture of these writings. There were eighty or more items in this period published in the *New Times*, as well as fifty more in a journal called *Strike* and forty-four in the magazines *Edge* and *Voice*.

These quasi-anonymous journalistic pieces are often ugly, and ugliest, perhaps, for what they never quite say, but only imply. Pound never calls for violence, but preaches brutality in code. In early April 1956, in *New Times*, an item signed 'M.V.', but written by Pound, observes: 'Our Victorian forebears would have been greatly scandalized at the idea that one might not be free to study inherited racial characteristics.' In the same journal, two weeks later: 'Some races are retentive, mainly of the least desirable bits of their barbaric past.' Two weeks after this, an unsigned item by Pound compares the 'Jewish-Communist plot' to 'syphilis', and on 1 June another item dismisses 'anti-biological nonsense about "equality"'. In June he mocks 'The jew managed sob-stuff in the jew-run agitations against "race prejudice".' On 10 August 1956 a piece headed 'De-Segregation' begins: 'It is perfectly well known that the fuss about "de-segregation" in the United States has been started by Jews,' and what America needs, it concludes, is 'race pride'. Just as much as the later cantos or his versions of Confucius, these are Pound's Elizabethan writings.

We can glimpse him in this period. The week after Thanksgiving 1956 a doctor made a note in Pound's medical file. 'Mr Pound conducts himself in orderly manner always, has many visitors and seems to have plenty of things to occupy his time,' he wrote, and he observes Pound's scruffy clothes and messy room before adding: 'Altho he is of high intellect I have noticed a slight difficulty in explaining some subjects, using "I mean" and clearing his throat repeatedly and figiting around before it finally comes out.' It is a sad image and a reminder that Pound is ageing now, but his confusions and particular habit of speaking by implication and repetition are evident also in his journalism. He never quite says what he means.

Pound's voice and words circulate in unexpected ways. Noel Stock suggests that in addition to his journalism, Pound may have ghost-written some of the pamphlets published under Kasper's name, and it is at times hard to tell between the two men's writings. And yet, in a curious irony, division was always their chief theme. In 1957 Kasper wrote a pamphlet called 'Segregation or Death' in which he claims that 'Any man who fails to distinguish between this thing and that thing may be called ignorant and lacking in reverence,' and the arch and oddly Old Testament tone is Pound's own style. The idea, too, might have come straight from Pound. In his *ABC of Reading*, published more than twenty years before, Pound began with what he called 'the anecdote of Agassiz and the fish'. Agassiz was a nineteenth-century biologist whose work was motivated by the Victorian rage for classifications of knowledge, and in this anecdote he instructs his students to look and look again at the specimen before them, even until the fish has begun to rot. 'A general statement is valuable only in REFERENCE to the known objects or facts,' Pound glossed, for we must specify between types. We might put the same point a different way, as Pound did in June 1956: 'It is unscientific to stop studying racial characteristics.' Science is segregation; knowledge is, he insists, a division between races.

In the last months of 1956 John Kasper's association with Pound was becoming increasingly public. On Wednesday 30 January 1957 the *New York Herald Tribune* ran the first of four splashy articles about Kasper. These were written by a journalist called Robert S. Bird, who signed the byline from Washington. The first appeared on the front page beneath the headline: 'Segregationist Kasper Is Ezra Pound Disciple'. The lead paragraph establishes the accusation. 'Former social intimate and confidante of Negro literary aspirants in Greenwich Village, he became overnight in Clinton, Tenn., last September one of the most reckless and dangerous segregationist rabble-rousers in the south,' it announced, and Bird goes on to explain this wild young man's genealogy:

> Inquiry by the *New York Herald Tribune* reveals that it was, curiously, right here in this government mental asylum that the mad poet has personally dispensed over the years inspiration, counsel and ideology to his young votary, Kasper.

Alongside this are photographs: of the lawn outside Center Building, in the summer; of the windows of Chestnut Ward, seen from outside, and a white arrow marks 'Where Pound Lives'. Bird next describes the process of visiting Pound: how any new visitor must first write to the superintendent and then, with Pound's permission, travel out to the old hospital. In 1956 a visit to St Elizabeths turned from a colourful literary ritual into a toxic political act.

These articles in the *New York Herald Tribune* tell a story of entanglement. On the cover of the next issue, the headline ran: 'Kasper Looks Like College Boy, Uses the Language of Ezra Pound'. Here, the article quotes phrases from Kasper's own writings – 'DAMN all race-mixers' and 'HATE mongrelizers' – in which, it claims, 'The language, references, manner of phraseology are patently derived from Pound.' These lines sound a little like discount Pound or a cardboard copy, and the article goes on to report an interview with one of Kasper's college professors. In a literature class this professor advised Kasper to write an essay on Pound's poetry, and Kasper replied that 'he didn't like Pound's poetry but did like his politics'. In the third article, Kasper's college classmates reminiscence about this quiet student from New Jersey: 'Why, I used to share my Greek grammar with him,' marvels one. He was, they say, so quiet, this 'soul-searching youth', until he graduated and 'made a pilgrimage to St Elizabeths to meet the insane poet'. Just like Seidel, a pilgrim to the poet, but this one turned to rot.

It is tempting to discount this alliance between Pound and Kasper and to banish that which we do not like from our history. Pound knew well this dividing urge, and when he thought of it, he imagined it as a segregation between literary forms. 'Most good prose arises, perhaps, from an instinct of negation; is the detailed, convincing analysis of something detestable; of something one wants to eliminate,' he wrote in 1918, and explained, as the opposite: 'Poetry is the assertion of a positive, i.e., of desire.' When Kasper looked, he saw a prose Pound: a man of hate, whose blood ran hot with the instinct of negation.

Some things, once adhered, will not come unstuck. Pound welcomed Kasper in and never denied his association. He stayed loyal to that which damaged him. In December 1957, a month after Kasper had been jailed and after all the newspaper noise, a journalist from the *Village Voice* wrote to Pound to ask him what he really felt about his troublesome young disciple. Pound replied with a brief postcard upon which he had typewritten a question: 'Have you ever asked yourself why Kasper gets so much publicity and Agassiz and Confucius get so little?' This is what Pound liked in Kasper: when he spoke, he spoke loudly and the crowds listened. In his bookshop in Greenwich Village, Kasper began a small imprint of cheap paperbacks called the 'Square $ Series'. These included Pound's own works, which other publishers were unwilling to put into print, and he promoted other titles on Poundian themes or with Poundian connections: a dollar edition of the American Constitution, Eustace Mullins's study of the Federal Reserve, and the anti-Semitic forgery *The Protocols of the Elders of Zion*. Kasper was another microphone for Pound.

The two men shared also an idea of what politics might be and who it might be for. John Kasper believed in white blood and American earth, and he promised his audiences that he could ennoble their grievances. At his final trial, one character witness described him as 'an intellectual Robin Hood', who steals from the rich and gives back to the poor. At another of Kasper's many trials, a journalist observed the following:

> 'We didn't have no education, no way to let those city folks know how we felt,' one lean weather-bitten woman said outside the courtroom at Kasper's trial in Knoxville last year, 'but now John can speak up for us and tell them about the colored and all that. He's been to college, but he's for us.'

What Kasper sold to white, working-class America was a very powerful illusion: that hate might be translated into an ideal and that history might teach us to be pure. When Pound at the microphone in Rome roused his listeners with the cry, 'Back to the old constitution, old betrayed constitution,' and when he encouraged his supporters to call him 'Grampaw' and put on a folksy, Southern voice, he was appealing to this same paternalistic fantasia, about the land, and freedom, and America's white history. Kasper embodied Pound's idea of himself and here is the crux: he did it better than Pound ever could.

Some might argue that Pound cannot be held responsible for how others interpret or misrepresent his views. But these foot soldiers of the Poundian dreamwork can by their refracted, violent light lead us back into the labyrinth of St Elizabeths in 1956 and 1957.

I began this book in a New York winter, in days as sharp as a new haircut, and very early on I went to speak with an esteemed Poundian, a wise translator and essayist, in his perfect writer's house in the West Village. This was, I later realized, just seven short blocks from the corner where Kasper used to have his bookstore, but that bookstore is now long gone, and in its place is a bar called Thunder Jackson's. The writer's house was another world: there were bookshelves and tulips in vases and in the study one of those half-reclining chairs you see in TV shows about therapists. As we talked, I asked about

Pound's political afterlife and about the groups who have since his death adopted his name and his words. He said to me, flat: there is no connection between Ezra Pound and the Italian neo-fascists. That was the day I decided to go to Rome.

It was spring when the plane landed. In the city, early in the morning, I turned a corner past a woman begging in a black velour hat and a man selling handbags. Across the street was a building, grey and brown, seven storeys tall. In front hung a tattered flag, red and black, and on the ground floor were Chinese boutiques selling bejewelled phone cases and neon scarves. Above the shops was a sign, in letters three feet tall: CASAPOVND.

The hallway into the house of Pound is filled with names painted bright upon the walls. Here are soldiers and philosophers, novelists and Communists and cartoon characters. It is a contradictory set. George Orwell is next to Oswald Mosley, the founder of the British Union of Fascists; Kerouac is next to Wagner. Spengler, T. S. Eliot, Saint-Exupéry; Yeats, Clausewitz, Ian Stuart, who was the lead singer of the English white power rock group Skrewdriver. Evita is in red, Dante is in orange. Plato, J. G. Ballard, Corto Maltese.

My meeting that morning was with the militant in charge of culture, which is a grand and alarming title, but Adriano Scianca turned out to be a nicely rumpled man. He opened the door and walked me up the stairs to the office. It was macho and unkempt, with slightly too much furniture and a Tibetan flag over the door. We sat on mismatched chairs at a conference table full of holes, beneath a poster saying 'Your Friendly Bank Betrays You' and another of blood-spattered gladiators. They are occupying the building, he told me, and upstairs are twenty homeless families who have nowhere else to go.

We began in Italian, but my Italian is not good enough, nor was his English, so the cultural militant called for a translator, who came to us down the stairs. Let's say his name is Seb. He spoke with a slight French lilt and his haircut was that of a matinee idol, spit curl and side parting. His features were delicate against the hard outfit of cargo shorts and a sweater, but his shoulders were broad.

Adriano told me that he once went to a conference about Ezra Pound and there were five people there. The curators of the memory of Pound, he called them, and he said, if you are a lover of Pound, then you will agree it is a pity his work is so unknown. He said: our aim is to make his work better known. He went on: if you go to Google today and you type in 'Pound', then you will find things mostly about CasaPound. We put him back on the table. Later, he told me: we might be the only Poundian organization in the world.

They call themselves 'i ragazzi di Ezra' – Ezra's boys – and they speak in a collective 'we'. When I emailed them to set up the meeting or to follow up after, their replies were always unsigned and the addresses generic. They speak like the chorus in an ancient play, and as Adriano told me their history it sounded like a modern myth. They began by printing 15,000 stickers with the word ZETAZEROALFA in block black letters, and they stuck them on walls all across Rome. This was, Adriano explained, to make the people wonder. Could this be a new brand of car, a TV show? It was a punk rock band, who play concerts in abandoned train stations and whose audiences beat themselves in a dance they call the 'cinghiamattanza', the belt massacre.

On the day after Christmas 2003 a few of the boys began to squat in an abandoned government building not far from Rome's main train station, and this is where we met that day. When they arrived, they found that the lights had been left on for a decade, Adriano told me, with a shrug at the waste of governments. They had occupied buildings before, but this was the first one inside the city of Rome, and with it came a new name and a new purpose. Soon they began to arrange conferences. Since the start of the occupation there have been a hundred of these, Adriano explained: four or five on Pound, and others on themes dear to Pound, such as money, housing and the sovereignty of nations. They ran one on Jack Kerouac to mark the forty years since his death, and another on Japanese tattoos. They opened thirty-three new places across Italy last year, Adriano told me: bookshops, gyms, pubs. Here they conduct what he calls meta-political activity. He added: in those places we pay the rent.

Adriano is good with slogans and careful with language. We want to be effective 360 degrees, he said, and several times he reminded me, we do not call ourselves a political party, but a movement. If I tell you that we are a political party, he said, you will not imagine that we have a theatre, an art gallery and evenings where people dance. He likes this idea of movement. He was not so much answering my questions as defining terms, and when I once described the group as 'right wing', he corrected me. In one of his letters, he reminded me, Pound describes himself as a fascist of the Left, and this is how our conversation proceeded: in triplicate, robotic, as if by rote.

The Ezra Pound of CasaPound is a man of many things. On their website is a short biography in which he is introduced as 'Poet, essayist, economist, translator, cultural agitator, a free man', and in their eyes this variety is precisely what gives him value. He rolled up all these disparate pursuits into a single life and they treasure him for his struggle. The biography lists his literary friendships with Eliot and Joyce, and his horror at the First World War, and then it tells how he was 'declared insane and imprisoned in the criminal hospital of St Elizabeths in Washington. He passes the first year in complete isolation, in a cell with no windows, with no contact with the outside world. He remained there for thirteen years.' This is not wholly accurate, but the black and white of their telling has a purpose.

These young men have turned Pound's trouble into strength and have built a mythology from his life. In the stairwell outside the office are three photographs of an ancient Pound in Venice, frail inside a tweed jacket. He looks as though his skin is set to fall softly from him, so otherworldly is he, but here in the house of Pound he lives again as a promiscuously fertile symbol: a poet punished by foolish capitalism; a seer and a time traveller. His biography is a parable and his writings are scripture. There is a contradiction, Adriano told me. People say he was the best poet of the twentieth century, a genius, and when you raise the subject of his political involvement, they say he was a child, he was stupid. We see the contradiction, he said, and he quoted Pound to me: 'With usura hath no man a house of good stone.' This is from Canto 45, which continues:

with usura the line grows thick
with usura is no clear demarcation
and no man can find site for his dwelling.

From the beginning, Adriano explained, CasaPound was concerned with the question of housing, how Rome is full of empty buildings and yet so many are homeless. In Pound's name, and with reference to the *Cantos*, they have developed a policy proposal which they claim might restore these houses of good stone to Italian families. They call it the Social Mortgage. Italian families with limited income are, in this scheme, granted an interest-free mortgage on a newly built house. The repayment rate on the mortgage is limited to one fifth of the family's income and the house cannot be repossessed, nor can it be resold. It is only a living space and it is, of course, restricted to Italian citizens.

As if he were another empty building, Pound has been occupied by these strong young men: we might call it theft or we might call it resurrection, but it is also an act of literary criticism. 'With usura is no clear demarcation,' Pound wrote, 'and no man can find site for his dwelling,' and the canto's biblical repetitions continue to echo. The poem ennobles the politics, and the politics fill out the poem, and in the hands of CasaPound all is entwined, even the unlikeliest things: difficult poetry and simple policy; the promise of a home and scorn for such bourgeois tastes. To celebrate Pound's birthday in November 2013 – he would have been 128 – the boys of CasaPound hung posters in fifty Italian towns and cities. 'Il tempio è sacro perché non è in vendita,' their slogan ran, in a quotation from the *Cantos*: the temple is holy because it is not for sale.

At the end of my morning at CasaPound I asked Adriano what he is writing now. He is writing not a biography and not something ideological, he told me, not another book trying to see Pound strictly as a fascist. His book is called *Ezra Fa Surf* – 'Ezra Surfs' – after a line in one of his favourite films. In *Apocalypse Now* the psychopathic Colonel Kilgore declares of the Viet Cong he is about to napalm: 'Charlie don't surf.' Adriano wants to say the opposite of Pound. He wants to say, Pound is cool, Pound is iconic, a pop figure who has come to save us from the global financial crisis and the shadowy bankers behind the European Union. As we parted, Adriano and I warmly shook hands and agreed to exchange copies of our books, once we are finished. We're both Poundians, now, and this is common courtesy.

What happened next has stayed with me since. The interview ends and, as Adriano and I are saying our goodbyes, the interpreter, Seb, offers to take me to lunch at a restaurant nearby. This restaurant is, he explains, friendly to CasaPound. Before we go, we lean out of the window and smoke cigarettes. He tells me about the *atelier*, using the French word, where artists can use studio space in return for a few hours' work as nightwatchmen. Last year, they projected a huge image of Mussolini's head on to the side of a building.

On our way out he takes me upstairs, along tiled and dusty halls and into the hostel. People pay a few euros a night, he says, and there are flags on the walls and bunk beds. I ask where the people who stay here come from. They come from Quebec, he says, but not English Canada. They come from Ireland, but not England, and they come from Mediterranean countries, from Latin America. Seb lives here with his wife. He tells me that he worked for ten years in an office in Quebec, a good job with a pension, and one day he came here, to live in a building with no heating.

We walk to lunch through colonnades and dashes of sunshine, past carts selling underwear and CasaPound posters on the walls, each showing their logo of a sharp geometric tortoise, red and white and black. At a corner we meet a couple of other men – beards, clipped hair, grins – and we duck into the shade of an open-fronted restaurant. It looks like any other in Rome – white tablecloths, photos of minor celebrities who have eaten here – except all the waiters have tattoos up their forearms, and except that at the end, after cold antipasti, a heavy tagliatelle all'Amatriciana with fat nuggets of bacon swimming in the sauce, red wine from a carafe, bitter brown digestivo, and coffee, no bill ever came. What we are doing, Seb tells me as we eat, is not connected to money.

In a pause between courses Seb shows me his tattoos. On his left forearm, the CasaPound tortoise, beneath a burning book and the number 451. This is for *Fahrenheit 451* by Ray Bradbury, which is one of Seb's favourite novels, because for these followers of Pound a burning book is a symbol of the worst danger of conformity and the system. On his left shin is a fleur-de-lis – from the flag of Quebec – and on his right arm a squared-off Futurist design. It is by Marinetti, he explains, the author of the Futurist Manifesto and early supporter of Mussolini. Seb tells me that he once went to a big exhibition of Marinetti's works in Paris, but there was no mention of his allegiance to Fascism. Seb was taken aback, for Marinetti is his hero, and he quotes Marinetti: there should be no police or prisons because every man should be able to beat up a wrongdoer. Seb adds: if someone called my wife a slut, I would slap him.

Before I went to Rome I expected many things. I had seen the photographs of the strong young men, their shaved heads, their beards; I had seen the symbol, the tortoise which is almost a swastika. I had read about how they collect used syringes from parks in poor neighbourhoods and how they clean bike paths; and I had also read about how in December 2011 a CasaPound supporter went on a shooting spree in a market in Florence and killed two Senegalese traders and wounded three more. I could have predicted that Italian neo-fascists would sit for an excellent lunch, and that their generosity, while narrow, would feel deep. I was ready for both the smile and the teeth.

What I wasn't quite expecting was their high-mindedness alongside the thuggery, and how these two traits might cohere into a single way of being in the world. At lunch Seb and I agreed that George Orwell was one of the great writers, and another young Poundian at the table recommended a book to me. It was Tim Redman's *Ezra Pound and Italian Fascism*, published by Cambridge University Press, and it is a serious, scholarly study, and indeed a book I do very much admire. I'm not a fool. I understand that these sons of Ezra saw in me that which they could agree with, and perhaps this works both ways. Whenever I interview people, I always dress up. Usually, I play the absent-minded poetry professor, knitted tie and bright socks, but the night before I went to Rome I clipped short my hair, because I wanted to look like them and because I wanted them to like me.

Historians have been understandably wary of acknowledging the appeal of extremist politics, and particularly of fascism. 'Fascists don't really have concepts,' notes the historian Tony Judt, 'they have attitudes,' and this light condescension is shared by liberal analysts and historians of fascism. They note the contradictions in fascism's alliances, and the endlessly negative character of its ideology, which has many things to dislike, but few to propose. 'Fascist policy was constructed from a wholesale borrowing of ideas,' writes Mussolini's biographer Denis Mack Smith, and those ideas changed often:

> Up to 1919 Mussolini had been a socialist [. . .] Subsequently he posed as a free-trade liberal. Then after 1925 he reversed this trend and proceeded through an exaggerated phase of monopoly capitalism to end up after 1938 reverting back to his original views as a class-conscious, revolutionary socialist.

If we wish for fixity in our politics, then this looks like hypocrisy or contradiction. Mack Smith concludes that any attraction fascism holds for intellectuals must be 'irrational'.

The parasitic, collage aspect of fascism – a movement that is always reactive, that lifts it symbols from elsewhere and is not led by any clear ideology – has made it easy to ridicule and easy to miss. But it is precisely in this hoarding up of disparate things that fascism finds power. In October 2012 the think tank Demos surveyed those who follow CasaPound on Facebook. The sample is not necessarily representative, for people have many reasons to click 'like' on the movement's well-tailored page – I have been following CasaPound for more than a year – but the report observes that CasaPound's supporters tend to be male and tend to distrust institutions. It notes the 'ambiguity' of the movement, and continues:

> What seems to be clear from our research is that CasaPound is appealing to a significant number of Italians – particularly young Italians – through a combination of right- and left-wing ideology, symbols and methods. A number of people view CasaPound's direct approach to politics – through street protests, occupying abandoned buildings and political stunts – and emphasis on culture and music as an exciting alternative to traditional politics.

There is no holy book of fascism, no manifesto or founding document. The temple is bare and upon finding this hollow space the boys of CasaPound have filled it with the figure of Ezra Pound. They have a militant in charge of culture. They paint the names of their heroes upon the walls.

When I asked Adriano which is for him the most important of Pound's works, he mentioned one I had not heard of: *Carta da Visita*, first published in Rome in 1942. It is not very long, Adriano added encouragingly, and when I was back in London, I went and found it in the British Library. *A Visiting Card* was translated into English in 1952 as part of a series called 'Money Pamphlets by £', and it is a summary of Pound's thinking on key issues in short chapters: 'The

History of Literature', 'Text-Books', 'Money' and so on. It begins directly, with a section called 'Fascio', and the complete text of this section is:

> A thousand candles together blaze with intense brightness. No one candle's light damages another's. So is the liberty of the individual in the ideal and fascist state.

This is a metaphor for the fascist belief that many individuals bound together are the origin of the strong state, and it works perfectly well as a metaphor, for many candles make much light. But it is not only a metaphor which describes fascism, for fascism is itself a metaphor. The name derives from the fasces, which was a bundle of rods around an axe, carried by magistrates in ancient Rome. Candles, rods: the pieces do not matter, for fascism is when each piece defers to the logic of the whole.

This is the first paradox of fascist style: these strong young men borrow power and pride from a gesture of submission. In tattered posters, under arches and on the yellow walls of buildings all round CasaPound I had seen their symbol: an angular black tortoise on a red background. At lunch I asked Seb, why a tortoise? I was unprepared for the ardour of his exegesis. Holding out his left hand in the attitude of a charismatic professor of art history, he begins. The animal carries his home on his back, he explains, and this means housing, and it is also a formation used by Roman legions: half your shield protects the soldier on your right, and now we have the concept of solidarity. He holds his right arm square in front of him, and goes on. The tortoise is an animal that lives for a long time, which we hope will bring us luck, and he walks slowly and makes little noise. Where politics is usually a dog that barks, we would rather have an animal who paces, one by one, he says. There is a crusader castle close to Bari in the south that has this same shape, ringed by an eight-sided wall, and the number eight has occult powers. He twists his fingers to show me how the number eight turned on its side becomes the mathematical symbol for eternity, and last upon the tortoise's back are four arrows converging towards the centre. This is the inverse of chaos, he says. This is the idea of order.

Their tattoos are as clear as black ink upon white skin, but their meaning is in code, which is why CasaPound is, despite its symbols and sharp shaven heads and purple tattoos, curiously invisible. In the restaurant Seb tells me that a couple of years ago this was ranked at number five among all the restaurants in Rome on the popular tourist website TripAdvisor. He is not sure how this happened – perhaps a glitch in the algorithm, perhaps a small number of disproportionately positive reviews – but it meant that people from Tel Aviv and Sydney called to book a table a year in advance. Seb laughs as he tells me this, how the boys had to pretend to have a reservations book while the gastronomic tourist waited on the other end of the line. The restaurant doesn't even have a freezer, he says. This is how we end our lunch. As we stand to leave I offer to shake hands with the waiter and he reaches out his right hand, with the tortoise on the forearm, and he grasps my arm just above the wrist, and smiles.

We are close, this waiter and I; and for that instant bound in a frozen gesture, and even as it was strange and abrupt, it was also familiar. This is the Roman handshake I had read about. 'My skin tensed between my shoulder blades and my wrist,' writes Pound in Canto 72:

> seized in such an iron grip
> That I could move neither wrist nor shoulder
> And I saw a fist grasping my wrist but saw no forearm.
> Holding me fast as a nail in the wall.

It is a curious, disembodied image – these grasping wrists apart from arms – and he adds: 'This sounds foolish to anyone who has not been thru it.' A little awkward, but sinister, for the phantom who here is grasping Pound finishes by promising: 'The regiments and the banners will return.'

Pound wrote Canto 72 – and its companion, Canto 73 – at the very end of 1944, as Italian Fascism was collapsing. Rome had fallen in June of that year, and as the Allied armies progressed up Italy, the Fascist state retreated to the Nazi-backed Republic of Salò in the north. By December British troops were in Ravenna, and Mussolini gave his last public speech, but the cantos written during this period promised eternity. 'If one begins to remember the dung war / certain facts will well up again' begins Canto 72, and Pound – ever the eager historian – recounts how a dead man comes to him. It is Marinetti, who died on 2 December 1944, but who wishes to fight on. 'I want to go on fighting / & I want your body to go on with the struggle,' the shade of Marinetti tells Pound. He cannot give his body, the poet replies – 'my body is already old, / I need it' – but he vows to preserve him nonetheless. 'I will give you a place in a Canto,' promises Pound, 'giving you voice.'

This is what Pound had always given. In the Republic of Salò he continued to write scripts for others to read on air, and here in the canto he is still broadcasting to the ruins and giving voice to Fascism's ghosts. Marinetti leaves with the cry 'PRESENTE!' – which is the slogan engraved upon the white marble statues set up across Italy in the 1930s to mark the martyrs to the Fascist cause – and Pound goes on to encounter a medieval despot, who lists the heroes of the Fascist movement and generals who have died during the war. They are now forgotten, but named again – Farinacci, Miele, Borsarelli, Volpini – and he calls them 'heroes'. The poet hands the canto over to these visions; he salutes the parade. This is less a poem than a bow.

Canto 72 is a poem of presence – of the modernist return of the dead and of the perpetuity of the Fascist dream – and yet it is also anxiously a poem of absence: of forgetting, and leaving out. At St Elizabeths, Pound told visitors that Cantos 72 and 73 were his 'ghost cantos', for they had been carefully left out of his published volumes. They look a little like splendid defiance; and yet in them, too, is an abashed silencing, and the awareness that this poet's best efforts have come to little, have ended in what the canto describes as 'Confusion of voices, as from several transmitters, broken phrases.' This is how Pound's broadcasts had been heard. They were confusion and broken speech, and if this poem is a Fascist monument it is also like all monuments acutely aware of the ease with which its history may be forgotten.

For the critic Robert Casillo, Canto 72 is 'the smoking gun' of 'the reality and centrality of Pound's fascism', and for Pound's biographer Humphrey Carpenter 'There is nothing even faintly ambiguous about the political stance of this canto.' I am not so sure. I have read this poem many times, and each time end in division. I see its ugly boasts and how it vows itself to the name and charge of an abhorrent politics; and I see its odd hesitations and its deep awkwardness, and then, in turn, I wonder whether I am by now only trying to forgive Pound by blessing him with indecisions he does not, in fact, display. In the Roman sunshine the poem looks different. Now it warns of the perils of complicity; now it whispers of the weakening body and the promised message, and beneath it all it knows that attachments must come at a cost. In the after-lunch sun on the street outside the restaurant, I say my goodbyes, and Seb says, when the book comes out, you can come back and give a talk at CasaPound. We invite you, he says, if you are courageous.

At St Elizabeths Pound liked to tell the story of his meeting with Mussolini. It was dusk, at the end of January 1933, at the square, red Palazzo Venezia in Rome, and as he crossed the street of black cobblestones and through the tall doorway into a hall of pitted white marble, he was carrying a book. It is the first volume of his *Cantos*, in a limited edition of 200 copies, which had been published in Paris two years before, and he took it up the wide marble stairs. As

Pound recounted to William McNaughton, who edited *Strike* and visited him often at the hospital, he entered the grand office on the first floor to find Mussolini with a large blonde woman. 'A real Valkyrie,' he laughed. Pound opened the *Cantos* and the dictator looked down at a page and said, 'But this is not English.' Pound explained, 'It's my idea of the way a continental Jew would speak English,' and Mussolini replied, 'This is entertaining.' Now Pound hands over a list of economic proposals and Mussolini looks over them, and at last he says, 'Now this third point, a man would have to think about that.'

This is the most baroque version of a story told and retold, and in each version, the details shift. In Canto 41, written not long after the meeting, Pound quotes Mussolini:

'MA QVESTO,'

said the Boss, 'è divertente.'

Pound's compliment follows: 'catching the point before the aesthetes had got there'. In letters, and to his visitors, Pound added that the dictator asked why he wrote poems, to which Pound replied that this was so he could put his ideas in order. To this Mussolini only asked another question – 'Why do you want to put your ideas in order?' – and this phrase surfaces in the cantos Pound was writing in 1955. 'Why do you want to / – perché si vuol mettere – / your ideas in order?' runs a fragment in Canto 87, and again in Canto 93: '"Perché" said the Boss / "vuol mettere le sue idee in ordine?"' It is a perfectly wretched symbol: the poet stoops to the politician, and hands over his poems.

The great challenge facing those who would write about fascism is the problem faced by historians of religion: how to understand a belief system if you do not share its beliefs. If you are barred from its dreamwork, then it is tempting to see it only as a set of odd, old rituals and symbols, external things, costumes, salutes, parades.

This turns the historian into a strange tourist, wandering among what looks like the scraps of a backward time, and in Rome I saw stalls selling mugs and postcards of yellow ruins and gladiators, and among them key rings decorated with Mussolini's stony head. One afternoon I took the train out to EUR. This is the suburb begun by Bottai, the Fascist governor of Rome under Mussolini, and it is an unfinished place, all laid out in lines.

I walked along straight white streets past the familiar tortoise poster to the Palazzo della Civiltà del Lavoro. This vast white cube is six arches high and nine arches wide, because of the number of letters in Mussolini's name, and great marble men stand in the arches. Its perfect edges shine and at the top, an inscription:

VN POPOLO DI POETI DI ARTISTI DI EROI
DI SANTI DI PENSATORI DI SCIENZIATI
DI NAVIGATORI DI TRANSMIGRATORI

Here are the glories of Rome: the artists, philosophers and saints; the adventurers and the heroes. Poets are first in the list.

This is the gift that Mussolini gave to Pound: a fantasy of resonance and of power in the world. It is a poet's dream, and here is the second paradox of fascist style. Its grand claims for eternity are founded upon squalor, and at its biggest it was always so small. This is the sadness of Pound's journalism of 1956 and 1957. It is so petty, so mean in the service of what it imagines to be a great cause. 'There were no gas ovens in Italy,' he notes in the *New Times* in April 1956, and in May he mentions in passing the 'fuss about Hitler'. 'All usurers are liberals,' he writes and, in a triumph of hypocrisy, he declares, 'The Enemy is the faceless voice, whining behind a partition,' in an item in the *New Times* which he then signs with the initials 'J.T.' He mocks newspapers most of all, along with universities, which he blames for the 'decay of mind', and then in turn mocks the treatment of mental illness and 'the psychiatric racket'.

He warns of the dangers of tobacco, which he hints can cause madness, and he comments on presidential candidates and the Supreme Court. After seeing an anthology of political essays by Swedish poets, Pound approvingly decrees: 'Poets in Sweden (some of them) are interested in the world around them; they see no special virtue in picking of daisies.' This is his vision of how a poet should be: actively engaged in the world's affairs, passing judgement, speaking out in words which deserve to be carved in stone. But he sounds like nothing more than an old crank in his chair by the fire, far out of touch, far from sense.

These journalistic scraps are in prose, but among them, very occasionally, are poems. On the front cover of a small magazine called *Nine* in April 1956, the following appeared under Pound's name:

> The pink
> Took to drink.
> Rather than think of le probleme monetaire
> He bought a monocle and dyed his hair.

This is best described as doggerel, and perfectly forgettable, except that at CasaPound Seb mentioned some of the slogans he had recently been writing, and among them was: 'Reds Don't Read.' This is unremarkable and a kind of lazy anti-liberalism, but it echoes oddly with Pound's ditty. The foolish, foppish leftist – a pink or a red – is common to both, and both rhyme. Adriano told me that Pound's importance for poets was that he brought politics into poetry, and this is Pound's fascist style: patterned language, mocking, barbed.

St Elizabeths was built as a place of healthy banishment: holy ground where the mind might be soothed by agreement and reason. But Pound's visitors came in and with them brought sweets, books and stories, and sometimes they brought trouble. Sometimes they were mirrors which reflected Pound's own worst impulses; and sometimes they were microphones, shouting out into America.

Pound at St Elizabeths could not stay apart from the world and its politics, and in a curious irony one fragment of the Fascist past was close to him here. After Mussolini was captured by Communist partisans in April 1945, he was shot and his body was strung up in a square in Milan alongside that of his mistress. Pound had memorialized this in the first of *The Pisan Cantos*, but he did not know that the dictator's corpse was then cut down and given an autopsy at the University of Milan. Two samples of his brain were boxed up and sent to the United States for further examination: one to the Army Institute of Pathology and the other to St Elizabeths. In 1955 a reporter from the Washington *Evening Star* newspaper heard this story and went to the hospital to investigate. According to his report, he was shown into Overholser's office and the superintendent opened up his safe and held out a jar containing a grey sample. It looked like chicken liver, the journalist wrote, and the superintendent put the sample back into the safe and it was never seen again.

7

Ezuversity

On Valentine's Day two poets make their way out to St Elizabeths to call on Ezra Pound. It is 1948 and the season of the first rush of Pound's visitors, and today Robert Lowell takes with him a friend. Lowell has been in Washington as Consultant in Poetry at the Library of Congress and his path ahead seems sure, but the prospects for the second man do not look so certain. This is John Berryman, and his first collection of poems is just about to be published, and he is worried about the reviews. Some days, he is flush with confidence; some days, with despair. Not long ago he began seeing a psychiatrist; he doubts that he has yet learned how to be himself on the page. Later, he will become the most idiosyncratic American poet of the second half of the twentieth century, but he is not that today. At the hospital he sits on the floor with his arms around his knees. He smiles and asks Pound to sing for them, and Pound's voice floats above the ward.

Half a year passes and Berryman returns to St Elizabeths. This time he goes alone and Pound offers to feed him: first a roll and then a banana, which Berryman refuses and Pound eats himself. Later, Berryman writes: 'the lunatic one / fidgeting with bananas'. Today, Pound tells Berryman the story he tells to all his visitors, about how the soldiers came with guns and how he held on to

Confucius and the Chinese dictionary, and he tells Berryman about the cage at Pisa too. Berryman goes away and writes it all down. He types it up like journalism: how Pound raced up the hall to him and the food he offered. He notes Pound's phrases and how he had put on weight, and how he had promised that there were only sixteen more cantos to write until he reached 100 in total, and then he would be done.

A few months later Berryman converts these prose notes into a poem. It is deliberately not in Pound's style. The poem is in careful four-line stanzas, and each holds to regular rhyme, and each of these are wholly unlike Pound's expansive, crabwise patterns. But its language is drawn from Pound's own phrases, as it quotes him on 'Bankers' and 'Yids' and 'a conspiracy', and it begins by telling again the story of the day the soldiers came with guns. Berryman's poem is a structure holding Pound's own words in place. The poem is a frame and its title is 'The Cage' and it ends by imagining the field at Pisa, empty now:

> And the empty cage
> Sings in the wringing winds where winds blow
> Backward and forward one door in its age
> And the great cage suffers nothing whatever no

In this poem, Berryman retells Pound's story as the tale not of a prisoner, but of his prison.

We have seen this before. A young man goes out to the bughouse and returns a poet. At the heart of the story of Pound's visitors is a knot of reverence and self-invention, of worship met with use, and a whole generation of American poets underwent this ritual. They became themselves by visiting Pound and then writing about it. This was their graduation. But in the case of Berryman it feels even more mercenary, even more pragmatic. From the start their relation was business. Pound had seen Berryman's name on an article in a magazine, and in February 1946, at Howard Hall, he asked his first visitor Charles Olson to contact him. 'Sez he,' wrote Olson to Berryman, 'now Berryman, 1 of 4, 5 serious,' but as Olson wrote, and wrote again, Berryman did not reply. By the start of 1947 Dorothy Pound takes up the pursuit. She sends Berryman a postcard; in May she asks Berryman if he could write to Pound once a month or each six weeks; and she follows this with an even more piteous plea. 'Ezra has said more than once, that he would so much like to see you,' she wrote to Berryman, and offered to pay him for his time, to buy him a train ticket or to put him up in a room at the YMCA.

What Pound wanted from Berryman was a feeling of outside. 'Dear B, No 1 write me all 2 often,' Pound wrote in February 1947, and added: 'I live vicariously in the OUT.' He asks often for news and in October pleads: 'Is there anything going on in that vast morass that surrounds this bug-house?' He wished to feel once more as if he were a part of that world elsewhere, still a player in the drama, and this is why he busied himself with introductions and suggestions for magazines, for books to publish, for meetings and alliances. From Berryman, Pound sought a version of release.

But this is not quite what Berryman was willing to give. In this spring of flattery and persuasion, and of postcards from Pound and his proxies, Berryman was teaching at Princeton, where he experimented with writing in new styles and began an affair with a married woman. He described the progress of the affair in a cycle of sonnets, and in one he mentions Pound and boasts, 'to whom I owe / three letters'. Another poem written in this time is addressed to Pound. 'Your letter came,' it begins, and in twisted sentences describes the frozen winter landscape and then 'the massive sorrow of the mental hospital'. He is writing of Pound, but he has not yet been to visit. Like a painter priming the canvas, he is readying the surface. In June 1947 James Laughlin wrote to Berryman to ask if he might be willing to prepare a selected poems of Ezra Pound and added that Pound had specifically requested him for the job. In the year before he first went out to St Elizabeths, Berryman was making Pound his subject, and he began to make pencil notes which he kept in a folder marked 'Pound biog'. Pound's life would be his literary property.

Berryman never wrote this biography of Pound, and the introduction he prepared for Pound's selected poems was rejected by New Directions. In the archives of Berryman's papers, now held in Minneapolis, there is another imagined then abandoned project: a short note, dated June 1951, which sketches a play Berryman thought he might like to write, about political traitors, including the names of the Cambridge spies Guy Burgess and Donald Maclean, but also Ezra Pound. Pound remained for Berryman a rich symbol. In the mid-1950s Berryman began to write the cycle of poems which would make him famous. These became his strange, mesmerizing *Dream Songs*, and in them he returned again to St Elizabeths. In Dream Song 21, published in 1964, Berryman surveys the many lost souls of his generation, and recalls:

> In a madhouse heard I an ancient man
> tube-fed who has not said for fifteen years
> (they said) one canny word,
> senile forever, who a heart might pierce,
> mutter 'O come on down. O come on down.'

Pound was not tube-fed, nor was he exactly ancient, for when Berryman went to St Elizabeths Pound was sixty-three, but the Dream Song presents him as adrift in time, and one whose speech has been judged no more than madness. The quoted lines echo Pound's own famous phrasing in *The Pisan Cantos*, where he wrote, 'Pull down thy vanity / I say pull down,' and Berryman's Pound is muttering half-inaudibly his own poems. He is a hollowed figure.

In his letters Pound had asked Berryman for a window onto the world, but when he came to rewrite his encounter Berryman put Pound behind walls. In the second volume of *Dream Songs*, however, published in 1968, Berryman returned to Pound, whom he glimpsed, but did not approach, at the memorial service for T. S. Eliot at Westminster Abbey in February 1965. Pound was leaning on his cane and throughout remained silent, and Berryman writes:

The Abbey rang with sound. Pound white as snow
bowed to them with his thoughts – it's hard to know them
    though
for the old man sang no word.

The singing, muttering Pound of the hospital is now a quietly monkish figure, and Berryman salutes him with a tender memory: 'The tennis is over.' But this is not quite all, for the silence leaves a space for speculation, and Berryman goes on to wonder: 'The last words are here? / What, in the world, will they be?' He means Pound's last words, but equally the closing lines of his unfinished *Cantos*. The man's death is also the end of his speaking and writing.

In Berryman's versions of and deferred encounters with Pound we see the working-out of the troubled and redoubled process by which Pound was finally released into the world. He will be freed, but it will not be simple. These will be the closing ironies of Pound's emancipation: to be freed he will be seen as – in Berryman's phrase – 'senile forever' and he will spend his declining years in silence. He will become a subject, eternally prey to the tellings preferred by others.

In February 1958 two young students wrote to Ezra Pound. 'Dear Mr Pound,' their letters begin, properly respectful; each explains that he is writing an essay on Pound's poetry for an English class, and asks if he might come and speak with Pound. These two students were at different high schools within a dozen miles of Washington, and they wrote to him separately, unknown to one another. That their letters arrived at the same time and are now held in the same manila folder among the hundred-box mass of Pound's papers is simply a chance. But the coincidence is revealing. By 1958 Pound's poetry was a subject for high-school study and although this might at first appear to be an honour, he did not welcome it. To one of the students he replied by standard form letter: 'he regrets that he will be unable . . .' To the other he sent a card upon which he or Dorothy had typed: 'Mr Pound has not the energy to see strangers in cold weather. Nor to do pupils work for them.' He signed it with a red flourish, EP.

The oddity of his response is that Pound had long dreamed of educating the world. On the ward and on the lawns at St Elizabeths in the middle years of the 1950s this old ambition blossomed. Until now the hospital has assumed many guises: it has seemed a prison, a circus, a place of judgement, a green world and a tragic scene, and now it takes its last shape: a classroom. In October 1952 the nurse supervisor on Chestnut Ward filed a worried report with the ward's medical officer. Some days, she reported, there were six or more visitors with Pound simultaneously, and they often brought books and briefcases with them. She added: 'Mr Pound assumes the role of a professor lecturing to his pupils, rather than an ill patient receiving comforting visits from loved ones.' After madman and traitor, patriot and poet, professor was one more role for him, and this is why he had to turn the two high-school students away. They presented themselves not as disciples coming to the master, but as young scholars looking at their homework. Their letters imply that he is not the teacher but the subject.

In Pound's last years at St Elizabeths the hospital authorities relaxed their rules and widened his terrain. From August 1955 Pound was permitted to sit out on the lawn directly in front of Center Building until eight in the evening, unaccompanied; on 1 June 1956 this was extended until 9 p.m.; and in all this we see his growing universe. Although his visitors were supposed to leave promptly at four, they stayed on, until half-past. He is reaching later and stretching wider. On 21 September 1956 he was granted further freedom of the grounds, to wander beyond the lawn during daylight hours, and this same month a young graduate student from Texas called Marcella Spann first visited the hospital. During the spring and summer of the following year, she and three or four other regular visitors enrolled in what she later called a class in 'post-Texan Ezrology'. They came out to the hospital, usually on Saturdays and Sundays, to sit with Pound on the lawn, to eat with him and listen, and to improvise around him a rough classroom.

None of the Ezrologists were really poets, although several of them dabbled, and this is perhaps what made them such fine disciples: none needed to rebel. Each was set a task. The would-be young writer John Chatel was to follow on from the work of Henry James and write the great American novel. David Gordon was studying basic Chinese at a local university and had come to ask Pound for advice on how to translate poetry; this, in turn, became his duty. David Horton, who had worked with John Kasper on a Poundian publishing series a few years earlier and was now employed at a naval laboratory in Washington, was expected to spread the word of Pound's economic teachings. The model and already infamous Beat generation muse Sheri Martinelli was also one of the group, and Pound praised her painting wildly, comparing her to Giotto. Marcella Spann was put to work on an anthology of poetry, which Pound hoped would contain in a single paperback all that a student might need. It was finally published in 1964 as *Confucius to Cummings* and is a chronological compendium of excerpts, some briefly introduced with a comment by Pound, and at the end includes appendices of 'Questions for Classroom Use' and 'Suggestions for Teachers'.

It was in Spann's account a wonderful time: part ivory tower, part pastoral dream. The students spent the summer of 1957 sitting beneath the giant elms while around them played squirrels and blue jays and Pound read to them the whole of Ovid's *Metamorphoses* in a sixteenth-century English translation. These are tales of wondrous escape and the shifting forms of things, stories of transfusion and flow, and he read the *Cantos*, too, but he would never explain what they meant. 'At St Elizabeths, introduction to the *Cantos* simply meant Pound reading the poem aloud,' Spann later recalled. 'He never told us what we were to understand from the reading.' This was perhaps Pound's holiest belief about poetry: that to appreciate even works this knotty, all you must do is look at it, listen to it. The teacher is the one who hands you the right materials.

In return, they brought him treats: fudge brownies, blue cheese and cookies. This was the kind of disposable, American food he liked. His visitors recall being handed mayonnaise on bread or a BLT wrapped in brown paper, a banana or a plain roll, but what he craved was luxuries for children: ice cream, apple candy, maple syrup, peanut butter. With the leftovers he fed the birds on the lawns and sometimes the squirrels, too, with a nut tied to the end of a string, which he would whisk away when the squirrel came too close.

He wished to be the teacher, not the subject. There is a slight confusion here, and it is reflected in the nickname Spann gave – perhaps copied from Pound – to her disciple work. For they were working on his projects, sent out like toy soldiers beneath his generalship, but she called it 'Ezrology', which is the study of Ezra. One may approach Pound as a scholar, seeking to learn about him, or as a disciple, wishing to learn from him: the two processes are parallel, but they are antagonistic, and in 1956 and 1957 the line between them is fading. The first full critical study of Pound's work was Hugh Kenner's *The Poetry of Ezra Pound*, published in 1951, and there was another scholarly essay on the *Cantos* published that spring. But in the middle years of the 1950s these isolated critical studies became a thicket. In April 1955 Robert Mayo of Northwestern University published a commentary on Canto 9, and in October 1956 John Berryman gave a talk on Pound at a symposium on criticism at the Institute of Contemporary Arts in Washington. In 1957 two graduate students in California published the *Annotated Index to the Cantos of Ezra*

Pound, while in 1958 Professor Clark Emery of the University of Miami published *Ideas Into Action*, his study of the *Cantos*.

There had been essays and reviews of Pound's poetry in magazines in London, Chicago, and New York since his poems first began to appear, half a century before. But these were the first specifically academic studies, prepared by students and professors in English departments at universities and aimed at a university audience, and another element unites them too. This first generation of Pound's academic critics was made up of his visitors. Kenner had first visited Pound in June 1948 and he had returned several times. He later wrote: 'My mind was principally formed on a few visits to St Liz.' Clark Emery went out to the hospital in July 1952, and a PhD student named Myles Slatin from Yale visited in January 1955, as did Guy Davenport, who was studying for his own PhD on Pound at Harvard. This was Ezrology: visitors turned students, scholars turned disciples, and up around the *Cantos* like a reef was growing an academic industry of interpretation, commentary and gloss. This was the direct product of Pound's teachings on the lawn and his improvised classroom behind the screen on the ward, yet it was a betrayal of the spirit of his ideas about teaching. Just as in the tales from Ovid he so adored and read aloud to his disciples beneath the elms, one thing becomes another.

Pound was conscious of this shift: of the winds which twisted around him and around his work. He was still working on the *Cantos* and was therefore in the curious position of composing a work which had already begun to be interpreted by others. In a canto drafted in the autumn of 1957, Pound quotes another inmate on Chestnut Ward, who went by the nickname Yo-Yo and who once asked him, 'What part ob yu iz deh poEM??'

Like confused migratory birds, the world's Poundian academics gather every two years in a different city. This is the Ezra Pound International Conference, known affectionately as EPIC, and the scholars fly in from universities across the globe. In 2013 they met in Dublin, a city to which Pound had almost no connection, so I boarded a cheap flight from London. My airline allows passengers 10kg of luggage, and in my case I have two large books: my paperback copy of the *Cantos*, 800 pages and 900g; and the first volume of the most recent and most thorough biography of Pound, at a whisker under 1kg.

Over the next three days I see an Italian Poundian in a camouflage dress give a paper she describes as 'a footnote upon a footnote', and an elderly German Poundian lengthily scold a hapless young scholar from Oxford for over-running the twenty-minute allocation for talks. I learn about bird imagery, the symbol of the rose, and the correct pronunciation of the name of the Romanian sculptor Brancusi. 'Brancooo-shh,' the Poundians coo, 'Braaaaancuu-sh.' I give a paper – bang on twenty minutes – and am, in turn, chided by an aquiline professor, who objects to my suggestion that a poet may have a murky psychological life. Like all the Poundians I look forward to chocolate cookies and coffee at 10.30 each morning. The Axis Powers of World War Two – Italy, Germany, Japan – are healthily represented among the delegates, but there are American Poundians, too, in chinos, and a Frenchman in red trousers. I watch Pound's Italian translator boast that his translation has an index, whereas the German translation does not; the German translator is sitting next to him, so this gets a big laugh. I hear 'versifier' used as a term of abuse, and an hour-long elucidation of three lines of a fragment. I hear an awful lot of gossip about long-dead literary editors. I hear no mention of fascism or anti-Semitism. I do not open my copy of the *Cantos*, not even once.

Pound hated universities: he called them 'Institutions for the obstruction of learning' and 'perverteries'. The trouble started at school and lasted throughout his life. At high school his classmates nicknamed him 'professor', because he was the only one wearing glasses. When he was fifteen he was sent to university at Penn, and soon after arriving he was invited to join a fraternity, but there was an upset during the initiation: he bit one of the brothers. He did not graduate from Penn, but instead transferred to Hamilton College in upstate New York, where he felt the cold and failed to find friends. The records of his grades survive. He receives an A followed by a C in a course in Old English and an A followed by a D in German; an A, a B and a C in French all in one year. This must be a symptom of something, but it is unclear what. It is as if the system cannot read him and he is, in these traces, illegible. After Hamilton he returned to Penn for graduate school, but he did not complete his studies here either. The university is not for the unusual man, one of his professors told him.

In June 1907, not long after Penn declined to renew his fellowship, Pound addressed a series of poems to the specialists in the 'inanities', who 'bow down in homage / to scholarship's zinc-plated bull'. He here begins a line of scorn that runs through his career. 'Literary instruction in our "institutions of learning" was, at the beginning of this century, cumbrous and inefficient,' Pound archly noted in 1920. 'I dare say it still is.' This is from the first part of his pamphlet 'How to Read': the title is an affront to all the business they get up to in the universities, and he expands this short pamphlet into the even more scornful *ABC of Reading* (1934), as if reading were a thing even children can do, needing no scholarly apparatus or advanced degree.

The problem is professors. Pound's *Guide to Kulchur* (1938) indexes all the ills of the world: usury, the misuse of words, paper money. 'Obviously the American University system is run by hirelings and boors in great part,' he writes, adding that they are 'in the main stuffed to the gills with parasites and bloated dullards'. On the Italian airwaves he ranted often against the 'professoriat' and found conspiracy in Oxford and Cambridge: 'Plenty of muckers down there sittin' pretty, and drawin' 5000 or ten thousand a year for not tellin'.' Writing anonymously from St Elizabeths in February 1956, he blasted 'the planned falsification and blackout of history, forwarded by the Regius

Professorships' in the *New Times*. In June 1956, while graduate students at Harvard and Yale were courteously visiting Pound, and another two in California were assembling an index to the references and allusions in his *Cantos*, he wrote another short item for the *New Times*. It is signed simply 'A traveller in the United States' and it observes: 'Two things that one notices are the high percent of illiteracy among writers, and the decay of curiosity in the universities, especially among faculty members.'

Each of these is a diagnosis of a particular ill: that the system has been corrupted does not mean that we must abandon faith in the possibility of its perfection. It is faith that sharpens Pound's scorn. His series of essays 'Patria Mia' of 1913 called for an American Renaissance begun by education. 'There should be a respectable college of arts in New York (or Chicago, or San Francisco, or in all three),' he instructed, and its members would be painters, sculptors, architects, musicians, poets and scholars. 'The important thing is that there should be a class of artist-workers free from necessity,' he insisted, and he dedicated 'How to Read' to the 'starters of ideal universities'. He is speaking not of quadrangles and dormitories, nor even libraries and studios, but of the dream which joins up all of these. As a young man, Pound's publisher James Laughlin had travelled to Italy to listen to and learn from Pound, and he had a joking name for the flow of talk and ideas in which Pound conversed. This was, he said, the Ezuversity.

Pound loved universities. He believed in them as a measure of value, as a man might believe in the carats of a diamond, and while he insisted that he had been happy to escape from Penn and postgraduate research in 1907, he continued to use the title. Lecturing at the London Polytechnic in January 1909 on 'The Development of Literature in Southern Europe', he announced himself as 'Ezra Pound, M.A. (sometime Fellow in the University of Pennsylvania)'. Later he wrote to his old university – in 1920 and again in 1931 – to ask if they would accept his books as fulfilment of the requirements for the PhD. Each time they refused, but in the summer of 1939 he was invited back up to Hamilton College, where he was awarded an honorary doctorate. 'Dr Ezra Pound': this is how he was introduced before his broadcasts from Rome.

In the cantos written during 1956 and 1957, and later published in the volume *Thrones* (1959), Pound addresses the scholars and academics who flock to him. An italicized note in the middle of Canto 96 observes: '*If we never write anything save what is already understood, the field of understanding will never be extended.*' Such explicit and defensive editorial comment is unusual in the *Cantos*, and Pound continues: '*One demands the right, now and again, to write for a few people with special interests and whose greater curiosity reaches into greater detail.*' This is the scholars' dream: the 'we' of a narrow yet expert community, bound by obsession and depth of expertise, working for an ephemeral reward. Cantos 98 and 99 gather phrases from the Sacred Edict, a seventeenth-century catalogue of Confucian principles, and in Pound's handling set out a vision of an ordered society, founded upon education. 'There can be equity in plowing and weeding,' he writes in Canto 99,

> when men of war know the Odes.
> Esteem sanity in curricula.
> You cannot leave out the classics . . .

Each man has his trade and the scholar's job is keeping the curriculum clean and full. 'Don't pester scholars,' he writes, 'nor lose life for bad temper,' and he celebrates a prefect of the Han dynasty who built schools. The canto ends:

> All I want is a generous spirit in customs
> 1st/ honest man's heart demands sane curricula

Scholarly analysis is the heartbeat of an ordered society. Perhaps his vision is a little medieval – a society arranged in trades – and perhaps it touches close upon the Fascist state, which was lined up in corporations. But this is the scholarly dreamworld, and few are trying harder to build it than those who choose to devote their careers to the study of Ezra Pound.

The academic study of literature tries to separate the reader from the reading. It resists the truth that when we read we do so only stumblingly, feelingly, personally; it seeks instead to present criticism as science, as something which can be known by all. In these cantos Pound proposes an alternative antidote to the limits of individual subjectivity. In his vision of a scholarly community, all are working together towards a larger knowledge. 'This is not a work of fiction,' he writes in Canto 99, 'nor yet of one man.' All are joined in this dream of a collective mind, and in Dublin I was struck by another kind of academic community. Poundian scholars are loving and occasionally irritated; they are bound to one another; they are fractious and in all this they are like a family, and among them in the concrete conference rooms and off-white hallways of the university buildings walk members of Pound's real family, too. Pound's daughter Mary, sparky and otherworldly, sits in on the panels; she blushes when the comments touch upon her, and she rarely speaks. Her daughter and son are present, too, and all are evident by the same strong profile. Pound scholars are like a family; and his family are scholars. Pound's grandson Walter gives a very learned paper on one allusion in the *Cantos*, and his granddaughter has also translated Pound's works into Dutch. 'The business of relatives is filiality,' writes Pound in Canto 99, and all are bound by these filial bonds, of duty, affection, love.

The cantos of *Thrones* celebrate this ivory-tower vision; and yet Pound's relation with the academic world was always fraught. He is conscious of the scholarly work being done upon him and upon his poem; he is also carefully apart from it, and these cantos play with the practices and methods of academic study. The great Pound scholar Hugh Kenner in his masterpiece *The Pound Era* (1971) has argued that each volume of the *Cantos* has a particular theme or core concern – what he calls its 'plane of attention' – and in *Thrones* this theme is 'philology'. This is the technical term for the scholarly study of language and literary works as historical: philology seeks to establish the origins and proper form of literary texts, as separate from the interpretation of those texts. As the critic Michael Davidson has noted in his essay 'From the Latin Speculum: The Modern Poet as Philologist', the habits of the philologist – selecting and displaying fragments of old literary texts, doing lexical research, using dictionaries to fix the shifting meanings of words – are central to modernist poetry, and particularly the poetry of Pound. When Pound in these cantos exhibits words – ideograms bristling upon the page, phrases in many languages – he is acting as a philologist.

These cantos adopt an academic method, and in them Pound poses as a scholar, but it is only a pose. For he draws attention to his own habits and in a flourish turns quiet study into loud performance. The central tool of the philologist is the dictionary, and here dictionaries are props or jokes. In Canto 98 he recalls the mocking comment made by his old friend Ford Madox Ford: 'And as Ford said: get a dictionary / and learn the meaning of words.' In the following canto he writes, next to one unlikely phrase: 'this is a mistranslation.' Nothing is fixed. The practices of philology are shown to be no more than empty gestures and in the place of sober academic study Pound's poem adopts a kind of sombre clowning, as if he were only spoofing the scholars, only dressing up in their borrowed robes. 'Secret of teaching is a bit theatrical,' Pound wrote to one of his many correspondents in 1933, 'Simply act the best prof you have known,' and John Berryman, a poet who spent his life posing as an academic, underlined this phrase in his copy of Pound's letters. In Dublin, as I walked between concrete seminar rooms and breaks for coffee and cookies, and as I made small talk with Pound scholars, I was painfully aware that my presence here was a sham, playing the role of a Poundian and yet taking my secret notes; and equally aware that he had anticipated this.

Here is the barb at the heart of Poundian study. A poetry this dense can only be apprehended intellectually, with glosses and commentaries open upon the desk, with the expense of diligence and care. It asks a certain style of attention, and scholars and academics have in turn lavished such attention upon it, compiling guides and giving papers upon the allusions and untangling the editions and the stages of composition. They have given Pound what he demands and yet this is precisely the style of reading that he scorned. 'Pay no attention to the criticism of men who have never themselves written a notable work,' he wrote, and 'For every reader of books on art, 1,000 people go to LOOK at the paintings. Thank heaven!' He needs us and does not want us.

The Ezuversity is not bound to any set of buildings, but wanders from place to place and we wander with it, carrying our *Cantos*, speaking of him. On the first morning in Dublin two Poundians disagree over whether Pound attended a reading by W. B. Yeats in Philadelphia in 1903, and archival evidence is marshalled to prove each side, without settlement. Another shows slides of Pound's last unpublished notebooks. Here, among the scribbles, in a child's exercise book, Pound asks himself: 'Have I seen the divine where it is not?' The morning wears on, and when one very informative paper on allusions to Byzantine church decoration threatens to spill over into lunch, there is a little shuffling in the seats. The speaker says, Pound has characteristically chosen a detail that is exactly right, and shows us a slide of a peacock. Her bow-tied companion pokes her gently. This is my last statement, she says, with a pause, and then shows another slide of a peacock.

On 27 July 1946, from his room in Howard Hall, Pound wrote to his old professor. 'Dear Bib,' he begins, 'It works for a few minutes daily.' This must be a reference to some question in the professor's now-lost letter to him, but time is on his mind today: time and attention, and the care a man may take. He continues: 'It is now nigh on to 43 years since you sd: "a man who has spent 40 years on an epic".' Perhaps to remind the elderly academic, he adds, 're/ Bentley'. Pound moves to end the letter here, but then he strikes across the page and scrawls, 'There are now 80 parts.'

A footnote: Pound met Joseph Darling Ibbotson at Hamilton College in 1903. Ibbotson – known as 'Bib' – was ordained as a Presbyterian minister, but worked as a professor of Old and Middle English from 1896 until his retirement in 1936. He taught *Beowulf* to Pound, as well as the Anglo-Saxon poem 'The Seafarer'. Later, Pound will return to these ancient poems, adopting their stuttery metres in the opening of the first canto, writing a free version of 'The Seafarer'. At Hamilton, Bib used to sit up late into the night, talking with his student, and one night they spoke of 'Bentley'. Richard Bentley was an early eighteenth-century editor of Horace and the master of a Cambridge college. He was the kind of man who should earn respect, yet is remembered chiefly for a monumental folly. Bentley claimed, on no particular evidence, that a mysterious 'Editor' had corrupted Milton's epic poem *Paradise Lost*, and decided to restore it to its intended glory by rewriting it. One example of his leaden technique: Milton's Satan in hell gazes upon 'darkness visible', but Bentley corrected this enigmatic, hellish phrase to the banal 'transpicuous gloom'.

A footnote upon the footnote: although it seems unlikely that Bentley really did work on his version of Milton for forty years, the number is mythical. Bib's own career lasted forty years, from his start at teaching in 1896 to his retirement in 1936, and just over forty years separate the ambitious and wayward young student from the famous poet in the madhouse. In his letter Pound compares himself to Bentley in one measure only: the devotion of time to a single subject. 'There are now 80 parts,' he scrawls, to complete the thought. Pound will always do this – place two things side by side and ask us to imagine what binds them – and in the first half of 1946 he was checking the proofs of his *Pisan Cantos*, which are the seventy-fourth to the eighty-fourth cantos. His forty-year work is the *Cantos*: the first mention of these is in a letter from 1915, when he reported to a friend that he had begun 'a cryselephantine poem of immeasurable length which will occupy me for the next four decades unless it becomes a bore'.

Forty days of Christ in the wilderness, forty years of Moses in the desert: at Howard Hall Pound is thinking back to how he began and to what the years between have held, and he remembered Bentley not for any goodness or badness of what he produced, but for the depth of care he poured into its production. In 1936 – the year of Bib's retirement – the magazine for Hamilton alumni interviewed Pound, and he told them to 'record that the CANTOS started in a talk with "BIB", and Bib's remarks on Bentley's attempts to "edit" Milton.' What is moving and important is the attempt and not the achievement. A man may step outside time if he will focus on one thing for long enough, and this is what is valuable: care, forty years of care. We might also call it love, ennobling that which it falls upon. 'J'ayme donc Je suis' runs the slogan at the top of the writing paper Pound had printed for his correspondence from St Elizabeths: I love therefore I am.

This is the academic world: balancing irrelevance and love, and believing the two to be equal. One night in the winter before the Dublin conference, I stopped in at a regular but casual reading group, dedicated to discussion of the *Cantos* and held at Senate House, the austere tower at the heart of London's universities. The group meets between six and eight on Friday evenings, hours that forbid those with families. In the other world this is cocktail hour. It is darkening outside in Bloomsbury and I walk quickly across the slip of marble, through art deco halls, past pale wood double swing doors.

A young man – he looks like a teenager – sits at one side of a square of tables, beneath a projector screen, with a boxy laptop. Around the three sides of the square are others, older, mostly men. There are hearing aids, worn faces. The light is hard and bad. There are jokes about Lytton Strachey. The men wear dark shirts and shiny jackets with sharp lapels. In front of each is a fat copy of the *Cantos*, some black, some bound in liturgical red.

The young man announces that he is going to use semiotic and linguistic theory as a way in to reading Pound's late cantos. This is the kind of thing that academics say, but what he means is that this evening's topic will be how to connect the words of the poem with their world and with ours; he will preach to us, this evening, of love. The text he has chosen is Canto 93, and he begins with one unexpected phrase from close to the end of it:

> You are tender as a marshmallow, my Love,
> I cannot use you as a fulcrum.

The marshmallow, he tells us, refers to Sheri Martinelli, the young painter and Ezrologist who several biographers have suggested was Pound's lover. He gave her nicknames; he called her 'La Martinelli' and here she is 'my Ondine', a water nymph from a fairy tale. Sheri was, the young scholar continues, a muse who failed, and he starts to tell us a love story that sounds like a myth: Pound loved a woman, who, because she was human and present, could not be the perfect classical muse, could not be Beatrice to his Dante. The shortfall between the present lover and the dreamed muse is held in the surprising word choice: she is as tender as a marshmallow, but no fulcrum.

He speaks so earnestly, this young apostle, and when he is done there is a pause, and then we clap, a little, and then an older man around the table says, 'But,' and we all laugh, for we know this is the ritual. We do a little footnote-skirmishing – who is the Ian Hamilton mentioned in the canto? A First World War general – but really the Poundians wish to speak about the love story. The young man has implied that this is a poem about loss and failure, but the older people see renewal. They wonder aloud whether or not Pound had sex with Martinelli – one woman points out that there were lots of shrubs behind which to hide in the gardens of St Elizabeths – and they blush a little. At the end of the day his friends had to leave, the woman says, and he could not have anyone with him in the night.

As we sit here, and the wine bottles pass, we can all feel that Pound is getting a little bigger. Pound is for richness, renewal, says a man close to the end of his days, and then: it's just my view. Now the comments change, and now in the place of answers the Poundians read aloud lines from the *Cantos*. Their voices dip and press at the stresses, roll over the ends of lines, thrilling on the foreign words, and in the place of debate there is only Pound, as if the truth were arriving now, coming into focus.

Later, the Poundians go for pizza in the Bloomsbury dark. I don't go with them. Instead, I walk home and look again at this evening's canto. As in many of the late cantos, an initial choke of detail gives way to a lyrical refrain, often in pieces, as a cloudy day may give way to scatters of sunlight. Canto 93 begins with hieroglyphs and references, Greek, quotations to challenge even the most dogged footnote – Yeats, Kati, 'the Boss' Mussolini – but all falls in time to a chorus. 'First petals   and then cool rain,' Pound writes, and repeats, 'First petals / and then cool rain.' When we read late Pound we wade through a river of allusion which runs hard upon a love story beneath.

This is the grand tension of this impossible poem. Capaciousness – the welcoming in of all sorts of voices, sources, modes and interference – is the *Cantos'* great gift to poetry, but it is equally its damage. It is so tempting to read only for those fine lyrical refrains, and to overlook the bitty, argumentative interference: to read, that is, as magpies, picking at the pieces; but we may not. For the *Cantos* do not permit a simple opposition between poetry and history, or beauty and politics, or between reading as a poet and reading as an academic. Instead, we must ferret out the footnotes, must consult the guides and speak with the scholars, before we can make any sense of them. The *Cantos* ask of us this care: that we expend our time in their unpacking.

This is, however, a trap. For the *Cantos* are an artwork which demands forty years of attention – many have devoted their working lives to precisely this – and once a reader has expended such care, he or she is bound to assume that its object has been worthwhile. It is the care which ennobles the subject, and this is how Pound converts literary critics into disciples. It is not possible to be a casual reader of the *Cantos*. It is, perhaps, not possible to read them as a poem. 'How shall philologers?' he asks in Canto 93, and then: 'A butcher's block for biographers.' The poem is a challenge, a block upon which we work and upon which we stumble. Philologers concern themselves with the state of the text, while biographers are concerned with the details of the poet's life, and in reading Pound's late cantos we are stranded in the wasteland between the two. What we are left with is a kind of gossip, wondering who he slept with, guessing at what took place behind the bushes out on the lawn.

To tell the story of Pound's years at St Elizabeths we must at times stoop to soap opera, and the diva of this plotline is Sheri Martinelli. She is a character of pure pink melodrama. She first wrote to Pound on the day after Christmas 1951. 'My circumstances,' she explained: 'A young poet here in Washington for several weeks.' She had no family and it was the holiday season, so Pound invited her to come and visit. Soon, she moved to Washington and took a job at a waffle shop, and soon Pound was helping to pay her rent. She had an oval, sometimes sad face. She was thirty-three and he was sixty-six. When she was in Washington, she sat on his knee, and when she was away, he wrote to her. He sent her flowers from the hospital grounds taped to his writing paper; he sent her jokes and Italian stamps, to show her paintings. He sent her a drawing of a little man in a boat and she sent him a photograph of herself in a bikini. In the cantos written in 1955, he quotes her laughing reply – 'My bikini is worth yr/ raft' – and adds, 'And if I see her not / No sight is worth the beauty of my thought.' She paints Pound's portrait: on a ceramic tile in blue; in pink and orange on the back of an envelope. In Canto 97 he mentions her 'russet-gold' hair and 'pale sea-green' eyes; in Canto 90 he calls her Sibylla and sings 'm'elevasti' ('you raised me').

June 1954 was the peak of this: eight letters in ten days, forty-seven pages from him to her, a waterfall of endearments, a tumble and a rush of baby talk and poems, prayers, commands. 'A cascade of people all the afternoon,' he writes to her on the 15th: 'a world of wooden ducks & mechanical Toys. They know not what they do.' Before sleep he returns to the letter. 'I will read to you when the brambles are cleared, benedetta,' he adds at one in the morning, and 'Holy mother of angels / protect her.' Before seven the next morning he is back, confessing his frustrations, and later in the day he sends another prayer. 'From the squalor of ignorance. Good Lord deliver us,' he writes. 'Stella di luce.' This is Pound in love. That month, Dorothy wrote to Overholser to ask if Martinelli could substitute for her as Pound's supervisor when he sits on the lawns. In this arrangement, she would not need to be always present when Martinelli was there. In the fragment of the visitors' record, the two women alternate. Sheri visits on 28 July 1954 and Dorothy on the 29th; Sheri is there on the 30th, and both on 1 August; Dorothy on the 2nd, Sheri on the 4th, Dorothy on the 5th.

In the *Cantos* Pound imagines a community of scholars and shared minds; yet some are always exiled from this bright and sunshine place. Some are always sent away or do not belong, and the spiritual love story is revealed to be a pettier affair of hurt feelings and small betrayals. One figure who scarcely visited Pound at St Elizabeths was Olga Rudge. She had been Pound's mistress for thirty years and was the mother of his daughter Mary, and later Pound will spend his final years living with her in Venice. She travelled to Washington from Italy in the summer of 1955 to see him. It was a hot day and she made her way out to the hospital to find that Martinelli was already there, sitting by Pound's side. Pound hardly acknowledged Olga; Sheri grinned; after that visit Olga returned to Italy. In time, Martinelli was dropped too. She is one among several favourites during 1957 and the summer of Ezrology, and by the end of the year Pound's attentions have wholly passed on to Marcella Spann. Later, in her letters and to interviewers, Martinelli will tell often of her closeness to Pound. From a 1981 note among her papers: 'taking EP out on the lawn was far more than a "weekend" it lasted from abt 1954 / – 1958.'

Just as Pound's poems were drafts and fragments, so too his family was improvised, tentative, a little loose at the edges. It was marked by collateral damage. In the mid-1950s Dorothy had been married to Pound for forty years and was living in a rented basement flat ten minutes' walk from the hospital. She stayed close to him during all his dozen years at St Elizabeths and was his most frequent visitor, yet it is precisely because she was so often present that she has left fewer traces in the records. Years later, Sheri Martinelli told an interviewer that Dorothy had liked having Pound held in St Elizabeths, because she could be certain of where he was sleeping every night. This might be proof of the most breathtaking cruelty or the most devoted care, or a little of each.

The true missing figure and sad silence of this story is Omar Pound. His birth certificate describes him as the son of Pound and Dorothy, but his father was an Egyptian army officer Dorothy met in Cairo very shortly after Olga Rudge gave birth to Mary. Omar was born in Paris in 1926 and soon sent away to nannies in London and then an English boarding school. He joined the US army at the very end of the war, and in April 1946 he wrote to Overholser to ask permission to come out to St Elizabeths. The superintendent denied his request. Later, he was permitted, but Omar remained an outsider. In time, however, he learned to copy the more successful approaches made by other young poets. After studying at Pound's old college, Hamilton, Omar became a translator, and he wrote to Pound at the hospital, seeking advice on a point in a Chinese translation. 'Is "justice" OK,' he asks about one pictogram in December 1949, 'or should it be "equality"?'

Like so many others, Omar is courting Pound not as a father but as a scholar; and like so many others in this story, he is wondering about the distinction between what is just and what is fair. Later, his translations from Persian and Arabic were privately printed in pamphlets, and each Christmas he would send a copy to Pound with a note of greeting. In one of these pamphlets, from 1971, is a poem translated from the Persian by Omar with the title 'Epigram'.

> I send you my verses
> Citing passion without passion:
> Three this week and two before

it begins, and continues:

> Perhaps you ignore the stuff
> Or blush. Your silence
> Gives me no excuse for more.

When Pound died in Venice in November 1972 Olga Rudge arranged his funeral. It took place only forty-eight hours after his death, which gave enough time for Mary, who lived in northern Italy, to travel to Venice, but not enough for Omar, who lived in England. He flew to Venice as soon as he heard, but arrived after the ceremony.

Omar's papers are now housed in the Pound archive at Yale University. It is an extraordinary collection. Here are Pound's drafts and manuscripts; here are his passports and the eighteen messy folders of his wayward correspondence with Sheri Martinelli, whose pages still crinkle with the pressed flowers stuck upon them; here are the receipts for the payments that Pound received for his broadcasts. It was such a random life, composed of so many discordant notes, and its million scraps have been tenderly indexed and are held in cool, archival air, as if his scrawls are orchids. Here is his will, which disinherits Omar in favour of Olga Rudge and, by extension, Mary, and here among the rest is a file marked 'YCAL MSS 53: Box 40, Folder 905'. Inside the folder is an envelope, and inside the envelope is a sheet of green tissue paper, and wrapped in the tissue paper are three small, off-white, almost orange chips. 'Mary 1st tooth' says a note on the envelope, and 'E.P. corner tooth'. He broke it when he bumped into a doorframe in the dark in his house in Rapallo in October 1942, and he kept it, and now its pieces are mingled with Mary's. 'What thou lovest well remains,' Pound wrote, in perhaps the most famous phrase from all the *Cantos*. What remains in the archive is a story of pieces: of teeth, and cantos, and a missing son and a daughter, and everything is a footnote upon a footnote.

'And the empty cage / Sings in the wringing winds,' wrote John Berryman, just after he met Ezra Pound, 'And the great cage suffers nothing whatever no.' The treason indictment against Pound was dismissed on 18 April 1958, and three weeks later he was officially discharged from St Elizabeths. He had spent close to 4,500 days in the hospital. He was sixty when he entered, and seventy-two when he left, and a grandfather.

Pound's release from St Elizabeths was long in coming and at last came about because of the confluence of several factors. By the middle of the 1950s Pound in the bughouse had become a point of shame for the Department of Justice. There seemed something squalid in the ongoing incarceration of this elderly, celebrated man, who was neither quite mad nor sane and had never been convicted of a crime. He had become with the passage of years too resonant a symbol: of the failure of American justice, or the disregard of American culture, or the perversion of American liberty. In 1954 Pound's old friend Ernest Hemingway – who had never visited Pound at the hospital – won the Nobel Prize in Literature, and in an interview with *Life* magazine he said, 'I believe this would be a good year to release poets.' As Pound turned seventy calls for his release grew. There were letters in the *New York Times*, petitions by famous writers, questions in Congress. Dag Hammarskjöld, the Secretary-General of the United Nations, commented on Pound in public. Frank Lloyd Wright offered Pound a house he had designed in Arizona; Igor Stravinsky and Jean Cocteau sent letters; and the beloved poet and national icon Robert Frost took up the cause, meeting with the Attorney General at the White House. In September 1957 the magazine *Esquire* ran a long and sympathetic article about Pound and in each of these we can feel the generations shifting. The war was long ago now and Pound was an old man. He looked like literary history. In both senses, he looked like he was out of time.

In tandem with this chorus of pleas from cultural celebrities, a legal process slowly took shape. In 1956 the poet and lawyer Archibald MacLeish – a good government man and solid American – arranged a series of petitions which called upon the Department of Justice to drop the indictment on the grounds that they would never prosecute Pound on the old charge of treason. At the start of 1958 the Attorney General acknowledged at a press conference that he was considering dropping the charges, depending upon the opinion of Pound's doctors, and in the middle of the month Pound's new lawyer Thurman Arnold filed a motion to dismiss the indictment. Pound was, the motion claimed, for ever mad. 'Defendant's condition is permanent and incurable,' it stated, and if they would never be able to prosecute him, then release was only charitable. On Friday 18 April 1958 Pound and his lawyers returned to the District Courthouse. His shirt was untucked and his pockets filled with papers, and he stayed silent as the motion was heard and the indictment dismissed. After, on the courthouse steps, he wrapped a long yellow scarf around his shoulders. Upon the scarf were embroidered Chinese characters, and as the reporters threw questions at him, and as the photographers clicked beneath, he pointed to one. It was the ideogram for 'sincerity' or 'a man of his word'.

In the following weeks, many will interview Pound, will ask him how he feels now that he is free, will await his scorn or his righteous fury. It never quite comes. Instead, he will comment: 'Few men of letters have had these opportunities' and, when asked how it is to at last be out of the mental hospital: 'All America is an insane asylum.'

Pound's biographers tend to tell his release as a heroic narrative of one man's victory. They assume that the stubborn government and greedy doctors all schemed to hold on to Pound, while against them struggled – and eventually won – Pound's famous friends. One of the great attractions of this story is that it plucks, against all the odds, a parable of the triumph of art from the long and messy saga of Pound's bughouse years. This is perhaps only partly true, however, for Pound's release was messier and more compromised than this. It is something a little sadder, and in the place of a triumphal Pound we find a smaller figure, once more reduced.

After the court hearing on 18 April Pound returned to the hospital and to his room on Chestnut Ward, where he stayed the night. Dorothy had attended the hearing and as soon as it was over she left Washington to stay with Omar in Boston. The next day a portly businessman and poetry fan called Harry Meacham drove out to St Elizabeths and took Pound into the city for Chinese food. Pound ate two portions of chicken chow mein and that night he stayed at Dorothy's vacant basement apartment near the hospital. In the following weeks Pound returned to the city and saw friends. The outside world looked strange to him and he was struck by the street signs, which he had not seen in a dozen years. He wrote to Eustace Mullins with a scheme for their improvement: in his ideal city, street names would be printed twelve inches high, and the numerals on corner houses would be illuminated at night. At the end of April he gave a talk to the Poetry Society of Virginia, and through these weeks he returned at night to the hospital, where, at his request, he was still enrolled as a patient. This was because he liked the dentists at the hospital and he wanted them to finish work on his teeth before his release.

I have spent many hours thinking about Ezra Pound's teeth and I am not alone in this. The most extensive medical notes in his hospital file concern his dental work, for at St Elizabeths his teeth were treated, cleaned and anaesthetized; they hurt and they were fixed. In April 1949 the doctors note 'Patient would like to have his teeth taking care of. He says they need attention,' and when they looked into his mouth they found that one of his cavities – in the mid-upper jaw, close to the back – had lost its filling. In July 1953 he was given penicillin for toothache and in March 1957, as he was writing Canto 99, his teeth were on his mind again. 'Tinkle, tinkle, two tongues? No,' he wrote, in a riddling phrase which suggests the double speaking of one who will not stand by his word, and answers with an instruction which combines the values of precision and oral hygiene:

> But down on the word with exactness,
>   against gnashing of teeth

Because he has been speaking with dentists, he knows the proper terms, and he adds in parentheses '(upper incisors)'. Pound dreamed of owning a powerful mouth and of speaking fire. He believed that the Chinese ideogram for 'to speak' showed a mouth with two words and a flame coming from it, and this dream of a heightened, dangerous language, composed of words which glow and flame, lay behind both his poetry and his politics. He longed for words with teeth, words which would bite and burn with all their meanings, and beneath the epic of Ezra Pound lies this unlikely symbol: teeth fixed and broken, blunted, pulled and kept. Now his teeth lie in a university archive and others speak for him.

As Berryman saw in his strange poem about caging which is also a cage, Pound cannot be simply set apart from his hospital. This is the story of a prisoner but it is equally the story of his prison, and if, for a moment, we shift our focus from the single individual and look instead at the records of daily operations at the hospital, then the melodrama of Pound's release looks a little different. In May 1958 there were 609 patients on the rolls of the West Side Service – which covers Center Building and Pound's own Chestnut Ward – and this month saw an unusually high number of court hearings, which required expert psychiatric testimony, so that patients were finding it hard to meet with senior physicians. Ten patients were discharged in March, and ten in April, and ten in May, and then eleven in June, followed by sixteen in July, and this increase was reflected across the hospital. From St Elizabeths, 884 patients were released in 1956, and 1,104 in 1957, and 1,076 in 1958. By 1959 they were releasing more than 1,500 patients a year, and the percentage of patients discharged in relation to admissions was also rising. The hospital was shrinking, and this is the context of Pound's release.

If we view history with Pound at the centre, then here we find a heroic drama about poets rescuing a poet. If we see the institution as the centre, then here is a case study of changing trends in psychiatry. Behind these statistics lies a generational shift in the treatment of the insane. By 1957 more than 2,000 patients – close to half the population of the hospital – were on tranquilizers and anti-psychotic drugs. Where once the hospital had been a castle, fortified and apart, now in an era of pharmacological cures and community treatment, its walls were dissolving. Now, patients in occupational therapy no longer make Christmas decorations and broom handles, but are sent out to work as clerks and stenographers at the Department of Health, Education and Welfare. The hospital files for the spring of 1958 note that ping-pong and television were popular in Center Building, and at half-past seven on the last Monday of each month the Catholic War Veterans Authority entertained patients with movies. There were jigsaw puzzles and miniature bowling on the wards, and softball on the lawns, but as if to mark the final triumph of psychiatry over poetry – or the victory of the hospital over the single patient – there is no mention of the release of Ezra Pound.

He was only one among so many, and in another, deeper sense, St Elizabeths kept Pound. On the day the charges against him were dismissed, Pound wrote to his daughter Mary. 'Officially I am crazy as a coot,' he reported to her, with grim humour, 'but not a peril to society or myself.' The motion for his release had, for the first time, diagnosed his condition as 'permanent and incurable'; for Pound, who longed to save society, this was a bitter acknowledgement that he could never now lead others to a better world. From now on, his words might be poetry, but they would be irrelevant, and this was only half of the final irony of his release. In 1946, arguing in court that Pound was mentally unfit for trial, Julien Cornell had presented Pound's insanity as the consequence of his treatment immediately after the war, and the poems he cited as proof of that madness were the cantos written in the prison camp at Pisa. In 1958, when Pound's lawyers returned to court to secure his release, they vastly expanded upon this argument. In an affidavit added to the motion, Overholser extended the diagnosis of insanity back into Pound's distant past. 'There is a strong possibility that the commission of the crime charged was the result of insanity,' Overholser explained, and in dismissing the indictment the judge emphasized exactly this claim. Pound had, they said, always been mad.

This is a specific legal point, but its consequences run wide. Now Pound's insanity was not considered temporary and the consequence of his ill-treatment; instead, his broadcasts were proof of his insanity. His words were emptied, hollowed into raving in the eyes of others, and if Pound's broadcasts were to be judged in this way, then so, too, was his poetry. 'The result of insanity,' ruled the judge: broadcasts, *Cantos*, politics, poetry. All of it was the proof of a broken mind, and Pound stood in the courtroom and watched.

After his formal discharge on 7 May, Pound remained in Washington, waiting for his passport to be issued and booking passage from New York to Genoa on a boat called the *Christopher Columbus* for 1 July. On 27 June 1958 he at last left Washington, by car, with Dorothy and Marcella Spann and Dave Horton, another young member of the Ezuversity. Now, Pound became a visitor, and they drove first to Wyncote, Philadelphia, to see the clapboard suburban house where Pound had spent his childhood. They went on to Rutherford, New Jersey, where the party spent Pound's last two nights in America staying with William Carlos Williams.

The visit was not a success. It was hot and Williams had suffered a series of strokes and then fallen into depression, and Pound did not stop talking. There is a photograph from this day, taken by the photographer Richard Avedon. Williams is seated, puzzling at the camera, and Pound stands above, his shirt undone, his hands on Williams's shoulder. Williams looks worn and Pound looks manic.

Avedon took another photograph of Pound that hot afternoon, and it is the greatest of all the portraits of this much-imagined man. I have kept a copy of it taped upon the wall above a series of desks as I wrote this book, and looked at it, waiting for it to speak to me. As always with Avedon's mineral-fine portraits, the subject is perfectly and squarely set, and Pound's giant head here fills the frame, as if all the world were his face. His eyes are shut and his mouth is just open. We cannot see his teeth. Here in the place of words there are lines: the lines wide on Pound's brow, and the crow's feet scattered from his eyes, and the furrows which hold his mouth. These are Pound's lines and they are written all over him. The photograph has a legend behind it. Avedon, they say, stepped up close and raised the camera, and said, 'You know I'm Jewish?' and before Pound could reply he clicked the shutter and froze him like this.

In the eyes of his visitors Pound took on the shine of a symbol. He was a mirror with which to compose themselves; he was raw material and an avenue to elsewhere, and they fixed him in patterns of their own. He was also a cautionary tale about the dangers of confusing life with art, and a parable of the power and peril of poetry, and even when we do not know it, we are reading him still. As Donald Davie has argued, 'Pound has made it impossible for any one any longer to exalt the poet into a seer.' After Pound it is hard to invoke the classical ideal of poets as moral leaders, for there is always his counter-example. After Pound, we are left with his warning, worry at it as we will. As he wrote to an old friend in January 1937: 'What you go on doing is thumping an unreal effigy and callin' it Ez.'

Epilogue

Trying to Write Paradise

In the Tyrolean morning, men are whaling powerful cars around the bends and cyclists click their gears up and down the curves. On the hillsides, lines of vines describe the mountains and all the view leads up. There are castles above castles, and above them cable cars, and at the edge of one fine cliff I come to a sharp turn and a signpost in two languages: EZRA-POUND-STRASSE and VIA EZRA POUND. A week ago, when I rang to confirm my visit, Pound's daughter Mary warned me about the sign, which forbids cars to drive down to the castle. Ignore that, she said, so I do. In the courtyard there are chickens and territorial geese, and American college students are carrying crates of German beer. One floor of the castle now houses a summer school, but Mary keeps an apartment at the top. I ring the bell and she says, come up all the stairs. In the turret she shows me to a room filled with books. There are Pound's poems in different languages, and the volumes of criticism, the biographies and the studies, shelf above shelf. She points. Take the Pound chair, she says, and we sit.

It was always the plan to bring Pound here after St Elizabeths, Mary tells me, so that he might have peace and write. She restored Schloss Brunnenburg with her husband, an Italian nobleman – her proper title is princess, although she laughs when I call her this – and they raised their children here. The boy was eleven and the girl was eight when Pound arrived at the castle on 12 July 1958. The next day there was a party in the village above the castle, with fireworks, and Pound danced. 'I have returned among the mountains,' he said in a short speech, for this high place reminded him of Idaho, where he was born.

Mary shows me through the rooms of the apartment. The walls are warm wood and here are portraits of him, and crucifixes, the horn of a narwhal, arrow heads and pistols. We pass up and down short flights of stairs and into the dining room. On the round table is a small sculpture of two bodies entwined, and Mary reaches out to stroke the head. He always touched it like this, she says, for he wanted to make it smooth.

A princess and her family, a castle in the mountains: this is a fairy-tale ending, but it soon came unspun. Pound had brought with him both Dorothy and his young acolyte Marcella Spann, and in the new cantos he wrote in the early months of 1959 he returns often to expressions of his love for Marcella. In September Dorothy arranged for Marcella to be sent home to Texas and Pound fell into a depression; he wrote to Marcella, 'they mistook his release for a triumph'. In 1961 he was so weak that he was admitted to a clinic for rest, and he spent a year there. Upon his release Pound was taken in by Olga Rudge, with whom he lived for the rest of his life, in Rapallo and then in Venice. He continued to work on the *Cantos*, but by now it was doubtful he would ever complete them. In 1967 a small publishing house in New York called the Fuck You Press printed a cheap, mimeographed pamphlet of the late fragments of cantos Pound had been writing, and this act of piracy prompted Pound's publishers New Directions to rush a collection into print: *Drafts & Fragments of Cantos CX–CXVII*. Because Pound had never settled on a final version, this last volume is a curiously unsteady book. The first edition differs from the later collected *Cantos*; the English and American printings do not agree.

He began with drafts, fifty years before; it is hard to end in them too. I botched it, Pound told one interviewer, and to another: My poems don't make sense.

In his last years Pound hardly spoke. He died in the municipal hospital of SS Giovanni e Paolo in Venice in the early winter of 1972. He was eighty-seven. Look at him, Mary says, and points to a portrait on the wall. In the last years we were pestering him, she tells me, and in his head, in the silence, he was composing the most beautiful . . . She breaks off, and then adds: the best poetry doesn't get on paper.

That evening I sat at a metal table outside a pizzeria on a sloping cobbled street in the town above the castle and ordered a carafe of red wine, and read the last cantos. They are things of quietness and childlike wonder: confessional, worn-down, tender, and balanced as if held between the fingertips. Sometimes there is clarity, and sometimes there are clouds. 'In mountain air the grass frozen emerald,' he writes in Canto 113,

> and with the mind set on that light
> saffron, emerald,
> seeping.

He is seeing clearly, but there is sadness too. 'Falling spiders and scorpions,' he writes in Canto 110,

> Give light against falling poison,
> A wind of darkness hurls against forest
> the candle flickers
> is faint

'No man can see his own end,' he writes, but these last poems feel like a reckoning: he is looking back over it all. 'Muss., wrecked for an error,' he writes in Canto 116, remembering Mussolini, and then

'Litterae nihil sanantes,' literature curing nothing, or poetry can bring no good.

I had asked Mary if the *Cantos* were finished, and instead of an answer she replied with a question. Is the world finished? she said, and then: Let the wind speak. That evening in my street-side pizzeria I found the line she had quoted. It is from a fragment which was excluded from the first published editions, but added later and is sometimes numbered Canto 119. The short poem runs as follows:

> I have tried to write Paradise
>
> Do not move
>   Let the wind speak
>   that is paradise.
>
> Let the Gods forgive what I
>   have made
> Let those I love try to forgive
>   what I have made.

For as long as he had been writing cantos Pound had been promising that one day they would end, and that in their finish, all would be made clear. At St Elizabeths he told his visitors that there would be 100 cantos; that he had already written the last page, which would contain only sixteen Chinese ideograms; that he was planning to give them a new title; that his Paradise would not be the Christian vision, but 'a Paradise just the same, moving towards final coherence'. The promise is still held out here. After Hell and then the purifying fires of Purgatory, Paradise is where Dante arrives at the end of his *Divine Comedy*; but Pound's concern was this world, not the next. At the close of the *Odyssey* the great wanderer Odysseus comes home to Ithaca; but home was never a certain place for Pound. Paradise: the *Cantos* that you read will not be the same as the *Cantos*

I do, and what we are left with are pieces. These are visits, too: a passing through, a moment on our way elsewhere.

There are two parts to every visit.

Mary had told me to go and see the Schloss Tirol and the following morning I had a few spare hours so I parked in the town and walked down the curving path to the square castle squatting in the valley above Brunnenburg. In this strange mountain place, which is both Italy and Austria, I found myself often under the impression that I had been turned upside down: I was constantly looking up to valleys and down on mountains. Language, place and the past were all a little unsteady. At the end of a narrow cobble lane I buy my ticket for the castle museum and pass into the first room. '01 Temple' announces a sign above the door, with the slogan 'History: What Remains?' The twelfth-century castle was constructed upon a seventh-century church and when in 1996 archeologists dug beneath the church they found an even older tomb containing a small wooden bier, large enough only for a child. In the bier was a pair of human teeth, and in front of it an altar with what the museum panel describes as 'una iscrizione enigmatica', an enigmatic inscription.

In the second room a long and well-lit case holds 'I Tesori Venuti Alla Luce,' treasures brought to light. Lined up from left to right like a sentence are objects found in the castle. There is a third-century arrowhead and an eighth-century comb; pieces of pots from between 1200 and 1500; a brooch of uncertain date; and, at the far right, closest to the present day, eight cigarette butts left by work-men in the 1980s. The museum is stuffed with moments. In the summer of 1336 a comet appeared above these skies for three months and in 1348 there was a plague of grasshoppers that stayed for two weeks and ate everything, even the women's headdresses, until they were excommunicated by the bishop and vanished. I look at lists of rules for merchants and conversion tables, which fix the rate of exchange between gold and silver and between Vienna and Bolzano.

I read about the trials of witches and the history of anti-Semitism in the region, and, walking up the stairs of the tower and through the decades, I come at last to the end of the First World War, when the Tyrol was divided into two, between Austria and Italy. Just after the display about the Second World War is a small box holding a copy of Pound's *Cantos* and a photograph of him, alongside his membership card for a local social club. There is a programme, too, for an exhibition of his works which Mary arranged in October 1958, shortly after he arrived.

On my way out I stop at the museum shop and buy a wooden sword with a lion on it for my son – he is six now – and walk down the hill to Brunnenburg, where Mary is waiting for me. Today we are a little more formal. Mary is dressed for church and we have tea, balancing the plates of biscuits on our knees. She has put out a copy of a German newspaper, which yesterday ran an article about Pound. There is so much and every day more, she says: once you get started on Pound, you do not easily get away. She longs for a complete edition of Pound's letters, and for facsimile editions of the manuscripts of the *Cantos*, but the publishers are reluctant. I don't have time to die yet, she tells me with a laugh.

After tea Mary walks me down spiral stone stairs, unlocks a small wooden door and leads me through a low arch into a tall and narrow room. There are bookshelves and museum cases upon the walls, and from the thin window a dizzying, green view. This is the Ezra Pound Room, she says, and his overcoat is here, kept behind glass, and a pair of his walking boots and the long yellow scarf embroidered with Chinese characters, which he wore on the day he was released from St Elizabeths. Beneath the cases are two low chairs Pound built, one yellow and one blue, and his box of tools. There is a cap with ear-flaps, a photograph of a marlin caught by Hemingway, an uncashed cheque from T. S. Eliot. One bookshelf is stacked with PhD theses on Pound's poetry; an American flag is draped over the other. I say to Mary, it is funny to see that here, but she stops me. Why, she says: he wanted to build the promised land.

Traitor and patriot, poet and madman, genius and fool, verse and prose, beauty and order: to all who looked upon him, Pound offered such rich contradiction, and never was he more provocative – more troublesome – than in his years at St Elizabeths. In a glass-topped case I see the inventory of his possessions from the day he entered the hospital, and on the back of an envelope a short handwritten poem. It runs:

> Hast thou 2 loaves of bread
> Sell one + with the dole
> Buy straightaway some hyacinths
> To feed thy soul.

Mary had told me, earlier in the day, that the *Cantos* are a lesson in love, and each of his visitors – Bishop and Williams, Kavka and Kasper, Olson, Seidel, Eliot, Berryman, and Lowell – loved Pound in his or her own divided way. This fragment, written on a scrap and held here high up in the mountain home that was never quite Pound's own, was a poem I could without hesitation love.

In the middle of the room an army-green canvas folding chair is set up in front of an old television set. Mary presses a button on the television, but nothing happens, so she calls to one of her grandchildren, and a slight young man in a yellow T-shirt joins us. He has the sharp, Poundian profile and a scruffy beard, and he kneels before the television and a black-and-white film starts to play. Watch this, Mary instructs me, and she shows me how to lock up, for once I am finished. She wishes me good luck with the book and she leaves me here, in the dusty gold light of the Ezra Pound Room.

The film was made by the BBC in 1959 and it shows Pound at Brunnenburg. He is wearing a plaid shirt and reading to his grandchildren; he is lying on a sofa and drawing calligraphic characters on a large sheet of card. We cannot hear it, but the director is tell-ing him what to do for the camera. His movements are stiff and his pauses abrupt. He is wearing the yellow scarf and wandering in the garden. He comes inside and takes off the scarf and his cardigan. He reaches for a book upon the shelf.

He does not know quite what he is supposed to do, so the director keeps giving him instructions. Pound rolls his eyes, and puts the car-digan back on, and knots the yellow scarf once around his shoulders, and turns to go outside again.

Essay on Sources

As I have argued throughout this book, the way to Pound is well worn. Canto 5 begins with the slightly despairing statement 'Great bulk, huge mass, thesaurus', and in reading my way after Pound I often came to think that the same might be said about both Pound's own *Cantos* and the huge reef of commentary which has grown upon them. Reading Pound is also reading about Pound, and finding him refracted in what others have said and written. Yet the most pleasing thing about him is how he is, up close, unlike anything one might expect. He is funnier and more generous than his detractors allow, for they see him only as severe and unforgiving. He is also harder and crueller than his adepts will permit. At the hospital, his visitors often felt differently about him on the way out than they had on the way in.

I wish here to acknowledge the great bulk and huge mass of previous works I have gratefully drawn upon in assembling this group portrait. This is not a complete list of relevant materials, since such a record would encompass a Poundian forty years, but instead an account of those sources which have been for me most resonant, most charged with meaning.

I have been particularly guided by several scholars, whose thinking has shaped all my own responses to Pound. The work of Donald

Davie – particularly his essay 'The Cantos: Towards a Pedestrian Reading' in *Paideuma* 1:1 (Spring and Summer 1972) and his study *Ezra Pound: Poet as Sculptor* (Oxford University Press, 1964) – is one foundation. Another is Marjorie Perloff's many writings on Pound, particularly in *The Poetics of Indeterminacy: Rimbaud to Cage* (Princeton University Press, 1981). Guy Davenport's *Cities of Hills: A Study of I–XXX of Ezra Pound's Cantos* (UMI Research Press, 1983) is full of valuable critical insights and biographical detail, observed during Davenport's own visits to St Elizabeths. Donald Carne-Ross's essay 'The Music of a Lost Dynasty: Pound in the Classroom' in the *Boston University Journal* (1972) has an admirably unfussy sense of the practicalities of reading difficult poetry.

Although I have at times disagreed with Hugh Kenner's *The Pound Era* (University of California Press, 1971), it is the most important biographical study of Pound and will always remain so. The more orthodox biographies of Pound have been an invaluable resource, both for details of the life and the ways in which that life might be told. I wish to note my gratitude to Humphrey Carpenter's occasionally bad-tempered *A Serious Character: The Life of Ezra Pound* (Delta, 1988) and A. David Moody's reverential three-volume *Ezra Pound: Poet, A Portrait of the Man & His Work* (Oxford University Press, 2007, 2014, 2015). For my purposes, Pound biographies have sometimes been more useful when less reliable: Michael Reck's *Ezra Pound: A Close-Up* (Rupert Hart-Davis, 1968), Noel Stock's *The Life of Ezra Pound* (Pantheon Books, 1970) and Eustace Mullins's *This Difficult Individual, Ezra Pound* (Fleet Pub. Corp., 1961). The greatest amassing of Poundian critical and biographical material is in the journal *Paideuma*, founded by the scholar Carroll F. Terrell. Terrell's two-volume *Companion to The Cantos of Ezra Pound* (University of California Press, 1993) is also the starting point for any serious reading of the *Cantos*.

The best of Pound is in volumes compiled by others: D. D. Paige's edition of the *Letters* (Faber and Faber, 1951); T. S. Eliot's edition of the *Literary Essays* (Faber and Faber, 1954). Richard Sieburth is the editor of the two best editions of Pound: *The Pisan Cantos* (New Directions, 2003) and *New Selected Poems and Translations* (New Directions, 2010), each of which has a hugely valuable introduction. When I went to the field at Pisa I had Sieburth's edition of *The Pisan Cantos* in my pocket. It was my Confucius, and Sieburth's *A Walking Tour in Southern France: Ezra Pound among the Troubadours* (New Directions, 1992) was an early inspiration, particularly for its simple insistence that we must walk in Pound's own footsteps. 'Of this place,' writes Pound in one of the diary scraps in this volume, 'there is nothing in the archives.'

Pound's own writings are filled with affronts which feel as if they are aimed directly at those who have the temerity to try to pin him down. 'Swinburne versus his Biographers' is the title of a 1918 essay; often he warns against any idea that the past might be known in sequence, that a man's life or story can be directly told. I mention it nowhere in the book, but Rachel Cohen's *A Chance Meeting: Intertwined Lives of American Writers and Artists, 1854–1967* (Random House, 2004) was for me a model of escape from the traditional strictures of biography, as was Richard Holmes's *Footsteps: Adventures of a Romantic Biographer* (Hodder & Stoughton, 1985).

Prologue and first approaches

For Bishop, one very rich source is her letters, as collected by Robert Giroux in *One Art* (Farrar, Straus and Giroux, 1995) and by Thomas Travisano and Saskia Hamilton in *Words in Air: The Complete Correspondence between Elizabeth Bishop and Robert Lowell* (Farrar, Straus and Giroux, 2008). It was reading the exchanges between Bishop and Lowell about Pound – and seeing him from their very different perspectives – that I first began to imagine the shape of this project, so I owe this volume a particular debt. I learned much from the reminiscences collected by Gary Fountain and Peter Brazeau in their *Remembering Elizabeth Bishop: An Oral Biography* (University of Massachusetts Press, 1994), as well as the sensitive biography by Brett C. Millier, *Elizabeth Bishop: Life and the Memory of It* (University of California Press, 1993). But Bishop's riddling poem 'Visits to St Elizabeths' was the true touchstone and prompt to all my thinking about how one might imagine and approach Pound. This is the sharpest example of a sub-genre of poetry, the poem which is also a visit to Pound, which includes John Berryman's 'The Cage', Charles Olson's 'Letter 6' in his *Maximus Poems*, the later volumes of William Carlos Williams's *Paterson*, and Frederick Seidel's 'School Days' and 'Glory'.

Pisa is the background to all of Pound's years at St Elizabeths; like a myth, it can be endlessly retold and it shifts each time, into a story of pathos or defiance, a tragedy or trick. Pound liked to tell this story. For detail on what happened at the DTC – and for the ways in which what may or may not have happened there can, in turn, be appropriated – I have taken much from the accounts by Robert Allen in *A Casebook on Ezra Pound* (Thomas Y. Crowell, 1959), edited by William Van O'Connor and Edward Stone; Michael King's 'Ezra Pound at Pisa: An Interview with John L. Steele', *Texas Quarterly* 21.4 (1978); and Stanley I. Kutler, 'This Notorious Patient' in *Helix 13/14* (1983), edited by Les Harrop and Noel Stock; as well as Julien Cornell, *The Trial of Ezra Pound: A Documented Account of the Treason Case by the Defendant's Lawyer* (Faber and Faber, 1967). A sensitive and illuminating discussion of Pound as a traitor is given in Hsiu-ling Lin's 'Reconsidering Ezra Pound's Treason Charge in the Light of American Constitutional Law' in *Paideuma* 34 (2005), a special issue on 'Ezra Pound and American Identity', edited by Hugh Witemeyer; and Pound's extensive Department of Justice file has been made publicly available online.

On the scene at St Elizabeths, I quote from Jack LaZebnik, 'The Case of Ezra Pound' in the *New Republic* (1 April 1957). On the periplum, I learned much from Ondrea Ackerman's essay 'The

Periplum of *The Pisan Cantos*' in *Paideuma* 38 (2011), as well as the discussion in Peter Makin, *Pound's Cantos* (Allen & Unwin, 1985). On the power of poetry, Pound's claim that when words fail kingdoms fall appears in his 'Affirmations . . . VI: Analysis of this Decade' in the *New Age* (1 February 1915), while the statement by E. E. Cummings is in Charles Norman's *The Case of Ezra Pound* (Funk & Wagnalls, 1968), alongside many other poets who commented upon the Pound case.

1 Olson and beginnings

All readers of Charles Olson owe a great debt to his friend and editor George F. Butterick, who is responsible for assembling the late *Maximus* poems, as well as the superbly thorough *A Guide to The Maximus Poems of Charles Olson* (University of California Press, 1980). This includes 4,000 annotations and, in revealing the full extent of Olson's allusions, raises what Butterick calls 'certain fundamental questions as to the nature of Olson's poetry and the limits of originality in art in general'. Those questions – about where one poet ends and another begins – are fundamental to my own inquiry into Olson. Other vital sources on Olson's life and works are Ralph Maud's edition of the *Selected Letters* (University of California Press, 2001), Tom Clark's biography *Charles Olson: The Allegory of a Poet's Life* (W. W. Norton, 1991), and Marjorie Perloff's essay 'Charles Olson and the "Inferior Predecessors": "Projective Verse" Revisited' in *ELH* Vol. 40, No. 2 (Summer 1973). *Charles Olson & Ezra Pound: An Encounter at St Elizabeths* (Grossman, 1975), edited by Catherine Seelye, contains both Olson's pre-meeting writings, the drama of his anticipations, and then the notes – titled 'Cantos' – he wrote upon each meeting.

The interview with Olson on 'The Art of Poetry' conducted by Gerard Malanga for the *Paris Review* (No. 49, Summer 1970) is a provocative, revealing account; Olson is characteristically slippery when the topic of his debt to the figure he calls 'Father Pound' arises. More broadly, the *Paris Review* interviews with writers on their craft remain one of the crucial sets of materials for understanding twentieth-century literature. I have gratefully consulted these throughout this project, and in this book the interviews with Pound himself (conducted by Donald Hall), Robert Lowell (conducted by Frederick Seidel), and Frederick Seidel (conducted by Jonathan Galassi and Lorin Stein) have been particularly valuable.

For my account of Howard Hall in this specific year, I have gratefully followed *The Annual Report of the Federal Security Agency, Section Six: St Elizabeths Hospital* (1945), as well as the monthly reports on St Elizabeths which are held in the National Archives: these give details of the numbers of patients and the Christmas gifts. Architectural sketches and plans for Howard Hall – including the details about doors and window guards – are from the Library of Congress and are accessible through the Prints & Photographs Online Catalog (PPOC). The Patient Case File of Ezra Pound is also now held at the National Archives; its six boxes hold what was for me an astonishingly rich and resonant set of materials, upon which I have drawn throughout this book. A useful description of the history and composition of this case file is given in the article 'Ezra Pound at St Elizabeths Hospital: The Case File of Patient 58,102' by Donald W. Jackanicz, in *Manuscripts* Vol. XLIII (No. 3, Summer 1991). The inventories – dated 26 December 1945, 28 January 1946 and 30 August 1946 – are in the National Archives case file, as are the twin mugshots taken on 26 December 1945. Dr Griffin's 'Admission Note', dated 22 December 1945, is also held here, as is Dr Kendig's Rorschach report.

In this chapter and throughout, I am indebted to Thomas Otto's *St Elizabeths Hospital: A History* (United States General Services Administration, 2013), which is the most thorough account of the hospital's planning, construction and changes over the years.

I have also gratefully drawn upon two pamphlets prepared by Dr Suryabala Kanhouwa and given to me at the hospital: 'History of Saint Elizabeths Hospital, Washington DC' and 'Blackburn Library: A Pioneer in the Field of Neuropathology', as well as a further pamphlet issued by the General Services Administration and given to me by Carter Wormeley: 'Ezra Pound at St Elizabeths'.

On Pound's own beginnings, I have learned much from Ronald Bush's monograph *The Genesis of Ezra Pound's Cantos* (Princeton University Press, 1976); *Ezra Pound to His Parents: Letters 1895–1929*, edited by Mary de Rachewiltz, A. David Moody and Joanna Moody (Oxford University Press, 2010); and Pound's own essay 'Early Translators of Homer II: Andreas Divus' in *The Egoist* (September 1918).

2   Kavka and family history

Dr Kavka's first set of case notes, dated 4 January 1946, are in the National Archives file, as is the 'Family History', dated 24 January 1946. He adds to – and reconsiders – these initial doctorly accounts in three articles: his memoir 'Olson Saved My Life' in *Paideuma* 14:1 (Spring 1985); 'Ezra Pound's Personal History: A Transcript' in *Paideuma* 20: 1 & 2 (Spring and Fall 1991); and then in 'The Dreams of Ezra Pound' in *Paideuma* 39 (2012). Further details come from 'St Elizabeth's Diary' in *Helix 13/14*; Kavka's obituary in the *Chicago Tribune* (27 May 2012) was another useful source.

Pound colourfully recounts his own early life in 'Indiscretions *or, Une Revue De Deux Mondes*', which was written in 1923 and is included in *Pavannes and Divagations* (New Directions, 1958). Here, Pound writes: 'It is one thing to feel that one could write the whole social history of the United States from one's family annals, and vastly another to embark upon any such Balzacian and voluminous endeavour,' and, as with the thwarted autobiography, this Balzacian chronicle is perhaps what Pound and Kavka were co-writing in Howard Hall.

Pound's early poems are collected in *Personae*; fittingly, given his own shifting self-presentations, he revised this edition several times, and I have here followed the texts as presented in the revised edition prepared by Lea Baechler and A. Walton Litz (New Directions, 1990).

Marjorie Perloff discusses the Malatesta Cantos and their flattening of history in *The Poetics of Indeterminacy*. The challenge of narrating the past, even a single life within it, is one of Pound's great themes throughout his writings, not only in 'Near Perigord' and the *Cantos*, but also in his extraordinary account of his friendship, *Gaudier-Brzeska: A Memoir* (New Directions, 1974). In *Guide to Kulchur* (New Directions, 1970) he insists, 'We do NOT know the past in chronological sequence. It may be convenient to lay it out anesthetized on the table with dates pasted on here and there, but what we know we know by ripples and spirals eddying out from us and from our own time.' He has borrowed the image of the patient etherized upon a table from T. S. Eliot's 'The Love Song of J. Alfred Prufrock', but in the context of a literal patient in a hospital it assumes a new – and Poundian – resonance.

Julien Cornell's correspondence with the doctors and the court testimony are from his book *The Trial of Ezra Pound*. On Frank L. Amprim, the major source was the file of materials provided by the Federal Bureau of Investigation, following my Freedom of Information Act request; and, although this may sound a little eccentric in this context, I would like to thank the FBI and the US Department of Justice for their assistance. Further details about Pound's statement at Genoa are from 'Transcript: the Interrogation at Genoa' in *Helix 13/14*.

3   Williams and America

The crucial – richest, perhaps strangest – source for William Carlos Williams is his own *Autobiography* (New Directions, 1967), particularly Chapter 51, 'Ezra Pound at St Elizabeth's', although the whole book is marked by Pound's presence. As Williams noted in his essay-memoir *I Wanted to Write a Poem* (Jonathan Cape, 1967), 'Before meeting Ezra Pound is like B.C. and A.D.,' and often when Williams is writing of other things he is thinking about – or quarrelling with – Pound. His essay 'Speech Rhythm' (1913) sets out his sense of an underlying rhythm beneath literary works; Pound praised Williams for 'eschewing the American vices' in *Poetry Review* (October 1912) in a short introduction to a selection of Williams's poems, which, as ever, reveals as much about Pound as it does about Williams. The long poem *Paterson* is Williams's most explicit engagement with Pound. I am grateful to the very useful revised edition, with extensive notes, by Christopher MacGowan (New Directions, 1992). One further illumination of Williams's turbulent, rich friendship with Pound comes from the strange poem titled 'To My Friend Ezra Pound', written by Williams in June 1956. 'I hope they do give you the Nobel Prize,' he writes: 'it would serve you right.'

I have quoted from Paul Mariani's biography *William Carlos Williams: A New World Naked* (McGraw-Hill, 1982) and Adam Kirsch's essay 'The New World of William Carlos Williams' in the *New York Review of Books* (23 February 2012). I have learned much about this most subtle, elusive of poets from these clear-sighted studies.

On Superintendent Charles Nichols, I have gratefully drawn upon the materials assembled in Thomas Otto's history. Otto's account of the practicalities of the hospital contrasts in interesting ways with Thomas Kirkbride's *On the Construction, Organization, and General Arrangements of Hospitals for the Insane* (J. B. Lippincott & Co., 1854), which describes the dream behind moral treatment. The report on St Elizabeths Hospital West Campus prepared by the Historic American Landscapes Survey (HALS DC-11) is a hugely valuable repository of plans, descriptions and details about the landscaping and gardens. The redevelopment of St Elizabeths is ongoing at the time of writing; a new plan announced in the summer of 2015 proposed to locate the main offices for the Department of Homeland Security (DHS) inside a renovated Center Building. The joke is irresistible, and it is perfectly Poundian that the old government hospital for the insane will now house the DHS. 'Ply over ply,' he wrote, following Mallarmé, as buildings shift and shimmer.

This sense that a place may be twofold, may be dream and reality, stands behind Pound's versions of the Confucian Odes. On Pound's versions of Confucius I recommend Edith Sarra's wise and thorough essay 'Whistling in the Bughouse: Notes on the Process of Pound's Confucian Odes' in *Paideuma* 16: 1 & 2 (Spring and Fall 1987). Bernhard Karlgren's glosses on *The Book of Odes* were printed in Bulletin 16 of the Museum of Far Eastern Antiquities, Stockholm, while Pound's own versions of the Confucian *Analects* – written during the Second World War, but published while he was at St Elizabeths – also shed much light on his project in the *Odes*. The *Analects* advise scholars to study the *Odes* precisely because they will, in Pound's rendering of the phrase, 'sharpen the vision, help you spot the bird', and he advises, too: 'Remember the names of many birds, animals, plants and trees.'

One hundred and twenty of Pound's broadcasts are available in Leonard Doob's *Ezra Pound Speaking: Radio Speeches of World War II* (Greenwood, 1978); Pound's letter to Ronald Duncan of 31 March 1940 is included in the Paige *Letters*. On Mahlon Loomis and early radio, I have gratefully followed Orrin E. Dunlap, Jr.'s *Radio's 100 Men of Science* (Harper & Brothers, 1944) and Alfred Thomas Story's *The Story of Wireless Telegraphy* (George Newnes, 1904), as well as *Dr Mahlon Loomis & Wireless Telegraphy* (Berea Printing Company, 1914) by his (and Pound's) cousin Elisha S. Loomis. Another useful angle on the topic of Poundian radio was provided by Richard Sieburth's essay 'The Sound of Pound: A Listener's Guide' (2007), which appears on the University of Pennsylvania's PennSound site.

This immensely valuable website includes links to all known recording of Pound speaking or reading his poetry: http://writing.upenn.edu/pennsound/x/Pound.php.

4 Eliot and modernist friendship

The extraordinary edition prepared by Christopher Ricks and Jim McCue of *The Poems of T. S. Eliot* (Faber and Faber, 2015) arrived when I was in the late stages of writing this book, but it nonetheless made me see Eliot anew. Like Patrick Heron's fascinating series of portraits of Eliot – painted in 1947 and 1948 and a great help to me in my imagining of the man – these volumes and their commentary will continue to force all future readers of Eliot to keep on reconsidering the poet and his work.

As I have suggested in this chapter, one way to understand literary modernism is through the friendship of Pound and Eliot. For the tone and feeling of that friendship, I have followed several sources. Eliot's 1928 selection of and introduction to Pound's poetry (reissued by Faber and Faber in 1948) suggested much; as did Eliot's edition of Pound's *Literary Essays* (1954). Pound's letters to Eliot, and Eliot's replies, are held among the Ezra Pound Papers, as YCAL MSS 53 in the Beinecke Rare Book and Manuscript Library at Yale. Some of the letters are fractious and some are tender; sometimes they gossip and sometimes they chide; 'yrs anonymous,' Pound signs off, from St Elizabeths, while Eliot signs 'with love' or simply 'yours'. Perhaps the most telling traces of that friendship are the editorial scrawls and corrections made by Pound upon Eliot's first draft of *The Waste Land*, which has been published in Valerie Eliot's edition of *The Waste Land: A Facsimile and Transcript of the Original Drafts Including the Annotations of Ezra Pound* (Faber and Faber, 1971). This volume is a great record of the shelving and shoring of fragments which made up the relationship between these two men and composed one of the central dynamics of literary modernism. It was also, I suggest, a kind of game, and sometimes the two great modernist pursuits of editing and tennis are joined. Guy Davenport remembered that Pound at St Elizabeths 'wore an editor's eyeshade, giving him the air of a man who had just come off a tennis court'.

On modernism more broadly, I have learned much from Lawrence S. Rainey's *Ezra Pound and the Monument of Culture: Text, History, and the Malatesta Cantos* (University of Chicago Press, 1991), Helen Carr's *The Verse Revolutionaries: Ezra Pound, H. D., and the Imagists* (Jonathan Cape, 2009), Frank Kermode's *Romantic Image* (Vintage Books, 1964) and Michael North's essay 'The Making of "Make It New"' in *Guernica* (August 2013): https://www.guernicamag.com/features/the-making-of-making-it-new. On the consequences of the Bollingen Prize, as well as the wider effects upon American poetry of the separations between life and art, I recommend the thought-provoking discussion in Jed Rasula's *The American Poetry Wax Museum: Reality Effects, 1940–1990* (National Council of Teachers of English, 1996).

Modernism was and remains an astonishingly powerful body of art and theories about art. It is also the story of specific volumes at particular moments and for me much of the wider story of modernism and Pound's place within it is encapsulated in a specific copy of a single book: the autographed *Selected Poems of Ezra Pound* (New Directions, 1949), presented by Pound to the hospital in late 1949 and held in the St Elizabeths Medical Library as item No. 13,565. There have been moments when I felt I could, like Olson, reach out and touch Pound through the page, and reading this book in the closed archive of the new hospital was one of them. Hugh Witemeyer's essay 'The Making of Pound's "Selected Poems" (1949) and Rolfe Humphries' Unpublished Introduction' in *Journal of Modern Literature*, Vol. 15, No. 1 (Summer 1988) explains the context of this edition. I am also grateful to Gregory Barnhisel's wider discussion of the strategies of repackaging Pound in his superb

James Laughlin, New Directions, and the Remaking of Ezra Pound (University of Massachusetts Press, 2005).

The whole of this study is built upon the accounts left by Pound's visitors, and in this chapter I draw explicitly upon the descriptions given in the following: A. Alvarez's autobiography *Where Did It All Go Right?* (Bloomsbury, 2002); Richard A. Cassell's 'A Visit with E. P.' in *Paideuma* 8:1 (Spring 1979); Ronald Duncan's *How to Make Enemies* (Rupert Hart-Davis, 1968); Samuel Hynes's 'Meeting E.P.' in *The New Yorker* (12 June 2006); W. S. Merwin's *The Mays of Ventadorn* (National Geographic, 2002); David Rattray's 'Weekend with Ezra Pound' in *The Nation* (16 November 1957); and Michael Reck's *Ezra Pound: A Close-Up* (Rupert Hart-Davis, 1968). Kathleen Raine gave an account in a letter to Peter Russell in 1952, and this was later published as the pamphlet 'Visiting Ezra Pound' (Enitharmon Press, 1999). Hugh Kenner gives a brief description in the chapter 'The Jersey Paideuma' in *The Pound Era*, and another in *The Elsewhere Community* (Oxford University Press, 2000), where he describes visiting Pound as 'one of the two or three turning points of my life'. His article 'Ezra Pound On Visitors' Day' in the *New York Times* (19 November 1972) mentions Pound catching squirrels with peanuts tied to string. Carroll Terrell has included a range of accounts in his short essay on St Elizabeths published in *Paideuma* 3:3 (Winter 1974), as well as interesting detail on Pound's Elizabethan pseudonyms. In 1972 a journalist called Karlyn Barker checked herself in to St Elizabeths for five days and wrote about her experiences in a series of articles in the *Washington Post*, beginning 16 July 1972; these give further, revealing context to the tenuous distinction between hospital visitor and patient.

For literary activity among the patients at St Elizabeths, I have drawn upon the annual reports, particularly for 1953 and 1954, as well as Thomas Otto's account of the patient library and production of 'Hotel St Elizabeths'. Pound was, of course, producing plays at the same time and I am grateful to Carey Perloff's edition of Pound's version of

Sophocles' *Elektra* (New Directions, 1990); Denis Goacher's introduction to the *Women of Trachis* (Neville Spearman, 1956) is also valuable as written by someone who knew and visited Pound. On Poundian and Sophoclean tragedy more broadly, I have learned much from Christine Syros's rich essay 'Beyond Language: Ezra Pound's Translation of the Sophoclean *Elektra*,' in *Paideuma* 23: 2 & 3 (Fall and Winter 1994) and Anne Carson's translation of *Elektra* (Oxford University Press, 2001). The manifesto 'Hellenists' is reprinted in *Paideuma* 6: 1 (1977). Translation – and the linked ideas that we do not all live at the same time and that we may speak with the dead – was one of Pound's obsessions. I am grateful to Eliot Weinberger's incredibly rich discussion of translation – with particular reference to Pound's *Cathay* – in his introduction to the *New Directions Anthology of Classical Chinese Poetry* (New Directions, 2003).

5   Lowell and madness

Lowell's best critic is Michael Hofmann, whose criticism has always been for me a model of the ideal relationship between poem and reader; this is the very relationship Pound spent his life considering and trying to complicate. In his essay on Robert Lowell collected in *Where Have You Been?* (Farrar, Straus and Giroux, 2014), Hofmann poses one reaction to Lowell's elegant – what he calls 'tailored' – poems, and asks, as if exasperated with the man: 'How can there be anything the matter with someone, if they express themselves so insightfully, with such wit and joy? What is defective or deficient here?' Nothing I read forced me to think more or more carefully about the relation between poetry and madness – in Lowell's poetry and in Pound's – than this essay.

I have often found a writer's letters to be his or her richest and most revealing source. I read Lowell's first in the beautiful edition by Saskia Hamilton (Farrar, Straus and Giroux, 2005) and then reread them among the Pound papers at Yale, the early ones in his manic, perfect capitals, that eerily careful handwriting. I am grateful to both Paul Mariani's biography *Lost Puritan: A Life of Robert Lowell* (W. W. Norton, 1994) and Ian Hamilton's more idiosyncratic study *Robert Lowell: A Biography* (Faber and Faber, 1983). A subtle essay by Helen Vendler – 'Lowell's Persistence: the Forms Depressions Makes', included in her collection *The Ocean, the Bird and the Scholar: Essays on Poets and Poetry* (Harvard University Press, 2015) – considers depression as poetic style. But really, Lowell was his own best biographer and analyst. Robert Giroux's edition of Lowell's *Collected Prose* (Farrar, Straus and Giroux, 1987) includes 'Near the Unbalanced Aquarium' and the interview with Frederick Seidel, as well as an illuminating interview with Ian Hamilton.

The *Diagnostic and Statistical Manual of Mental Disorders* (DSM) sets out the standard classification of mental disorders in the United States, and is regularly updated: in its shifting editions and revisions, this manual represents both the best attempt to quantify mental states and proof of the impossibility of that task. As I was writing this book, a new edition was released, in which grief was newly recognized as a kind of depression or disorder, and this is, surely, the question behind so much literature: is grief a style of madness or not? This is the question of *Antigone* and of *Hamlet*, and this small example suggests that our discussion of madness is always also a literary discussion; perhaps the reverse is equally true, that all our discussion of literature is, at some depth, a discussion of madness. On madness I have consulted and reflected upon many sources, from Lowell's poems to the 1,430 items in the Patient Case File of Ezra Pound, but one has stayed with me almost longer than all the rest. Richard Avedon's extraordinary portraits of Pound were taken, as I recount, at William Carlos Williams's home after Pound's release from St Elizabeths, but when Avedon came to publish them in his amazing collection *An Autobiography* (Random House, 1993), he placed them side by side with eerily similar images of the patients at a mental hospital in Louisiana, as well as a portrait of his own father, Jacob Israel Avedon. Avedon does not anywhere explain his intention behind this, but the point is – perhaps – clear. As we have so often seen, the context in which we place Pound works as a kind of judgement, an analysis.

Pound's madness – or not – will always remain an open question. The testimony of Dr Romolo Rossi is reprinted in *Ezra Pound: Language and Persona* (Università degli studi di Genova, 2008), edited by Massimo Bacigalupo. Dr Frederic Wertham's essay 'The Road to Rapallo: A Psychiatric Study' in the *American Journal of Psychotherapy* (October 1949) and *Readings in Law and Psychiatry* (Johns Hopkins Press, 1968), edited by Richard C. Allen and others, usefully guided my understanding of the larger controversy around the specific question of Pound's sanity. For another angle on faked or false madness, the accounts of the Rosenhan experiment, given in the article 'On being sane in insane places' in *Science* (January 1973), are relevant. In these famous and controversial tests, David Rosenhan sent eight 'pseudopatients' to admit themselves to mental hospitals and record their experiences. In the hospitals, doctors failed to distinguish between the real patients and these impostors, although, in a neat twist, the other patients could tell. In the end it came to seem to me that the attempt to tell mad from sane reveals more of the doctor than the patient, and that the history of psychiatry is therefore a history of impossible struggle. I learned of that history from *Man Above Humanity: A History of Psychotherapy* (Lippincott, 1954) by Walter Bromberg, with a preface by Overholser; and Overholser's 1952 lecture at Harvard, which was published in *The Psychiatrist and the Law* (Harcourt, Brace and Co., 1953). At the new St Elizabeths, Dr Prandoni gave me a copy of the volume of *Centennial Papers*, published by St Elizabeths in 1955, for which I thank him; Dr Prandoni and I also discussed E. Fuller Torrey's strange and revealing *The Roots of Treason: Ezra*

Pound and the Secrets of St Elizabeths (Harcourt Brace Jovanovich, 1984).

On paranoia and its relation to literary style and storytelling, I am, like so many others, indebted to Richard Hofstadter's famous essay 'The Paranoid Style in American Politics' (*Harper's Magazine*, November 1964); I have also learned from James A. Aho, *The Politics of Righteousness: Idaho Christian Patriotism* (University of Washington Press, 1990) and Mark Fenster, *Conspiracy Theories: Secrecy and Power in American Culture* (University of Minnesota Press, 1999). Eustace Mullins's books *The Secrets of the Federal Reserve* (Kasper and Horton, 1952) and *This Difficult Individual, Ezra Pound* (1961) are both oddly Poundian and crucial in understanding Pound. Mullins's website is www.eustacemullins.us, and his economic works are available there; his biography of Pound is also easily available for free on the Internet, and even this free circulation of reading material shows how deeply Mullins in his life and afterlife perpetuates the Poundian project.

For criticism on the cantos of *Section: Rock-Drill* I recommend Massimo Bacigalupo, *The Forméd Trace: The Later Poetry of Ezra Pound* (Columbia University Press, 1980); and on the ideograms I have followed Thomas Grieve's 'Annotations to the Chinese in *Section: Rock-Drill*' in *Paideuma* 4: 2 & 3 (Fall and Winter 1975). Carroll Terrell's annotations to these volumes are indispensable to those who wish to try to read them; working from a very different set of assumptions, Donald Davie's argument in *Poet as Sculptor* that the whole point of these late cantos is that they are 'unreadable' was a valuable prompt to my thinking. Samuel Hynes's article 'The Case of Ezra Pound' in *Commonweal* (December 1955) considers Pound's late cantos and their relation to his case. Allen Grossman's provocative discussion of poetic failure in his *The Long Schoolroom: Lessons in the Bitter Logic of the Poetic Principle* (University of Michigan Press, 1997) has much to say about the relationship between poetry and institutions, and underpins this chapter.

Pound's claim that poetry and prose are the expressions of opposite emotions is in a footnote to his 1918 essay on Henry James, which is included in his *Literary Essays*, while Ernest Fenellosa's essay on 'The Chinese Written Character as a Medium for Poetry', edited by Pound in 1919 and included in his *Instigations* (Boni & Liveright, 1920), contains the claim that the ideograph for 'to speak' shows a mouth with flame coming from it. This is, perhaps, an emblem for Pound's idea of the poet's role in politics: one who speaks flame. One poet who speaks flaming, provocative words is Frederick Seidel, and although I am not suggesting that Seidel and Pound share political ideals, I do here propose that Seidel's style is, at least in part, inspired by Pound. In my consideration of Seidel's style, I have been led by Wyatt Mason's profile 'Laureate of the Louche' in the *New York Times Magazine* (8 April 2009) and Benjamin Kunkel's essay 'Last things: the sinister charm of Frederick Seidel' in *Harper's Magazine* (September 2007). Michael Hofmann writes about Seidel in *Where Have You Been?* and Seidel himself kindly agreed to speak with me. William McNaughton's 'The Secret History of St Elizabeths' in *Paideuma* 30: 1 & 2 (Spring and Fall 2001) gives further details about Pound's response to Seidel.

In his study *The Characters of Shakespeare's Plays* (1817) William Hazlitt observed that 'The language of poetry naturally falls in with the language of power.' My thinking on fascism as both politics and style began with Susan Sontag's celebrated essay 'Fascinating Fascism' in the *New York Review of Books* (6 February 1975), but I have been led also by many other sources. I would like to note particularly my debt to: Tony Judt's *Thinking the Twentieth Century: Intellectuals and Politics in the Twentieth Century* (William Heinemann, 2012); Denis Mack Smith's *Modern Italy: A Political History* (Yale University Press, 1997); Christopher Duggan, *Fascist Voices: An Intimate History of Mussolini's Italy* (Bodley Head, 2012); Lucy Hughes-Hallett's superb biography *The Pike: Gabriele D'Annunzio, Poet, Seducer and Preacher of War* (Fourth Estate, 2013), particularly for the vexed entanglement between high art and low politics; R. J. B. Bosworth's *Mussolini's Italy: Life Under the Dictatorship 1915–1945* (Allen Lane, 2005); and Sergio Luzzatto's strange and compelling *The Body of Il Duce: Mussolini's Corpse and the Fortunes of Italy* (Picador, 2006). The political scientist James C. Scott discusses modernist architecture and the perfect fascist city in his *Seeing Like a State: How Certain Schemes to Improve the Human Condition Have Failed* (Yale University Press, 1998), which is a book I have been thinking about – and with – for many years.

Pound's politics and political writings have at times been obscured in the consideration of his poetry. I am very grateful to recent work by several scholars, particularly Tim Redman's *Ezra Pound and Italian Fascism* (Cambridge University Press, 2009) and Matthew Feldman's *Ezra Pound's Fascist Propaganda, 1939–45* (Palgrave Macmillan, 2013), for their clear treatment of the vexed and occasionally tricky discussion of Pound's political engagement. Robert Casillo's *The Genealogy of Demons: Anti-Semitism, Fascism and the Myths of Ezra Pound* (Northwestern University Press, 1988) contains very useful analysis and translation of Cantos 72 and 73.

Pound's journalistic prose has been collected in the multi-volume edition *Ezra Pound's Poetry & Prose: Contributions to Periodicals* (Garland Publishing Inc., 1991), edited by Lea Baechler, A. Walton Litz and James Longenbach. Noel Stock's *Reading the Cantos: A Study of Meaning in Ezra Pound* (Routledge and Kegan Paul, 1967) is written from the perspective of one who knew – and worked with – Pound during these years, and emphasizes the links between the style and content of the journalism and the *Cantos*. The CasaPound website also features much material which attempts to connect Pound's poetry and thought with our own contemporary concerns. The report prepared by Jamie Bartlett and Jonathan Birdwell, 'Populism in Europe: CasaPound' (Demos, October 2012) contains much useful context to this fascinating movement, while Kasper's FBI file is also openly available online.

7   Berryman and academia

Of all the poets in this book, John Berryman is the one I am closest to. I have been reading and rereading him for many years, and I had not thought of him at all in the context of this project when I began, but was pleasantly unsurprised to find in his *Dream Songs* another encounter with Pound. This least Poundian of poets was in his own way deeply touched by Pound.

Berryman's complicated identification with Pound is implicit in his poems 'The Cage' and 'A Winter-Piece to a Friend Away'. It is made explicit in Robert Lowell's obituary for his friend, published in the *New York Review of Books* (6 April 1972), where he observes that Berryman, shortly before his death, was almost turning into 'Pound at St Elizabeth's, emphatic without pertinence, then brownly inaudible'. Berryman's account of his visit to Pound was published in the *Michigan Quarterly Review*, Vol. XLV, No. 4 (Fall 2006); and Amanda Golden usefully discusses Berryman's annotations to Pound's letters in her essay 'John Berryman at Midcentury: Annotating Ezra Pound and Teaching Modernism' in *Modernism/ modernity*, Vol. 21, No. 2 (April 2014). Berryman's copy of Pound's *Letters*, as well as the drafts of his account of his visit and the letters from Olson, are in the John Berryman Papers (Mss 43), Literary Manuscripts Collection, University of Minnesota Libraries, Minneapolis. Here, too, is the manila folder marked 'Pound biog': like much else in Berryman's life, the project here hinted at remained unfinished. Berryman's life has been subtly and thoroughly recounted by John Haffenden in *The Life of John Berryman* (Routledge, 1982) and Paul Mariani in *Dream Songs: The Life of John Berryman* (William Morrow & Co., 1990). For Berryman as a skilled yet thwarted academic, Haffenden's edition of his writings on Shakespeare is invaluable: *Berryman's Shakespeare: Essays, Letters and Other Writings* (Farrar, Straus and Giroux, 1999).

Pound's passion for teaching – and his self-presentation as a kind of rogue, dissident academic – is evident across his writings and broadcasts, but perhaps nowhere made clearer than in his letters to Iris Barry, included in the Paige edition of his *Letters*. He told Kavka that his nickname at school had been 'professor', while Marcella Booth's essay 'Ezrology: The Class of '57' in *Paideuma* 13:3 (Winter 1984) describes him lecturing on the lawns at St Elizabeths. Michael Davidson's essay 'From the Latin "Speculum": The Modern Poet as Philologist' in *Contemporary Literature*, Vol. 28, No. 2 (Summer 1987) argues that philology – the archetypal academic practice – is central to modernist poetry, and particularly Pound's. Sheri Martinelli's memoir published in *Paideuma* 15: 2 & 3 (Fall and Winter 1986) was a valuable and moving source, on both the late cantos and the feeling of loving and being loved by Pound; even more so are the eighteen uncatalogued, pale green folders of Martinelli papers now held in Yale, alongside Omar Pound's papers and the broken teeth.

The statistics for patient admissions and discharges, revealing the impact of the new tranquillizing drugs, are from the annual reports. Pound's last days at the hospital, and his departure, are described in Harry M. Meacham's *The Caged Panther: Ezra Pound at Saint Elizabeths* (Twayne Publishers, 1967), as well as in Eustace Mullins's *This Difficult Individual*, which quotes Pound's concern at lamp posts and street signs in Washington, DC. Michael Reck's *Ezra Pound: A Close-Up* recounts the scene on his ship back to Italy.

Epilogue and endings

Pound in his last years was a powerfully symbolic, moving, silent figure. Donald Hall's account of Pound's late life and the printing of the final cantos is given in *Their Ancient Glittering Eyes: Remembering Poets and More Poets* (Ticknor & Fields, 1992), as well as in his 1962 interview with Pound for the *Paris Review*. Guy Davenport's short story 'Ithaka' in his collection *Da Vinci's Bicycle* (New Directions, 1979) describes a visit to an elderly Pound at Rapallo. Pound's late work has attracted very sympathetic and subtle commentary, most notably Peter Stoicheff's *The Hall of Mirrors: Drafts & Fragments and the End of Ezra Pound's Cantos* (University of Michigan Press, 1995), while Christine Froula also usefully discusses the idea of error as central to the whole project of the *Cantos* in her *To Write Paradise: Style and Error in Pound's Cantos* (Yale University Press, 1984). D. G. Bridson of the BBC visited Pound at Brunnenburg in April 1959 and filmed him there.

Although I do not discuss it here, Allen Ginsberg's meeting with Pound in Venice in October 1967 stands behind my consideration of Pound's own endings. As Ginsberg recounted in an article published in the *Evergreen Review* 57 (June 1968), the young Jewish poet praised Pound's technique and tried to explain his debt to Pound's poetry. In reply, Pound apologized for what he described as 'that stupid, suburban prejudice of anti-Semitism'. 'You must go on working,' Ginsberg told Pound, and the scene remains for me a moving one. It suggests, simply, what we all must do: which is to make our peace, as best we can, with this most difficult man.

Acknowledgements

My first debt is to those who knew Pound and agreed to speak with me about him. I would like to thank A. Alvarez, Donald Hall, Samuel Hynes, Annie and Winfred Overholser, Jr., and Frederick Seidel, each of whom patiently answered my many questions. I am particularly grateful to Mary de Rachewiltz, who invited me to visit her at Brunnenburg. At St Elizabeths, Dr Jogues Prandoni and Dr Suryabala Kanhouwa were expert guides to the hospital's present and past, while Carter Wormeley kindly showed me around the General Service Administration development, and I am grateful for both his time and enthusiasm.

I have incurred many debts during the writing of this book. I wish to note my gratitude to: Laura Barber, April Bernard, Catherine Brown, Hannah Dawson, Jonathan Galassi, David Godwin, Philip Gwyn Jones, Kathryn Hujda, John Kaminski, Jane Kramer, Julian Mitchell, Caroline Moorehead, Turi Munthe, Adrian Overholser, Ian Pindar, Miranda Popkey, Josh van Praag, Adriano Scianca, Richard Sieburth, James Shapiro, Michal Shavit, Ellie Steel, Leon Surette, Jeremy Swift, Hayley Wagreich and Eliot Weinberger.

Index

Adams, Henry Brooks 108
Adams, John, US President 89
Aeschylus 146
Agassiz, Jean Louis 201, 203
Allen, Robert 7
Alvarez, A. 11
American Journal of Psychotherapy 173
American Psychiatric Association:
    Diagnostic and Statistical Manual
    of Mental Disorders (DSM)
    160–61, 191
Amprim, Major Frank
    Lawrence 73–6
Anderson, Donald 71
Apocalypse Now (film) 209
Arnold, Thurman 28, 247
Avedon, Richard: photographs of
    Pound 251–2, *253*

Baldpate hospital, Massachusetts 183
Barnard, Mary 51
Barnhisel, Gregory: *James Laughlin,*
    New Directions, and the
    Remaking of Ezra Pound 128
Beats, the 25, 198, 227
Bentley, Richard 237, 238
Berryman, John 164, 221, 222–5,
    228, 235, 261; Pound's letters
    to 223, 224; visits Pound at St
    Elizabeths 11, 24, 155, 221–2
'The Cage' 222, 245, 249, 266

Dream Songs 224–5
Bertran de Born 76, 77
Bird, Robert S.: articles about
    Kasper 201–2
Bishop, Elizabeth 14, 261; letters to
    Lowell 14, 16; visits Pound at
    St Elizabeths 12, 14–16,
    24, 155
    'Keaton' 14
    'Visits to St Elizabeths' 12–13,
    14, 15–16, 266
Blackburn, Paul 11
Bollingen Prize (1949) 24, 132–3
Bookman (magazine) 51
Bottai, Giuseppe 218
Bradbury, Ray: *Fahrenheit 451* 210
Braque, Georges 148
Briarcliff Quarterly 90
Bromberg, Walter and Overholser,
    Winfred: *Man Above*
    Humanity: A History of
    Psychotherapy 175
Brooke, Rupert 122
Brown v. Board of Education of
    Topeka (1954) 26, 198–9
Browning, Elizabeth Barrett 4
Browning, Robert 4, 63,
    64, 153
Brunnenburg, Schloss, South
    Tyrol 17, 255–6, 260–62
Butterick, George 56

Carpenter, Humphrey: *A Serious Character: The Life of Ezra Pound* 174, 216, 264
Carrington, Dora: *Lytton Strachey* 4
Carson, Anne 145, 146
CasaPound, Rome 205–14, 219
Casillo, Robert 216
Catholic War Veterans Authority 250
Cavalcanti, Guido 143
Chatel, John 227
Christopher Columbus (boat) 251
Churchill, Winston 23, 192
Cocteau, Jean 246
'Cold War' 23
collage 148
Commonweal (journal) 182
Confessional poets, the 164–5
Confucius 4, 6, 9, 33, 36, 43, 77, 113–14, 138, 143, 221–2, 233
    Analects 116
    see also The Classic Anthology Defined by Confucius; *Confucian Odes under* Pound, Ezra
Cornell, Julien: as Pound's defence lawyer 8, 9, 24, 42, 71, 72, 79, 120, 121, 250; and Lowell 155
Crommelin, Rear Admiral John G. 199
Cruvant, Dr Bernard 160, 161
Cummings, E. E. 4–5, 21

Daniel, Arnaut 143
Dante Alighieri: *Divine Comedy* 258
Davenport, Guy 11, 25, 150, 229, 264
Davidson, Michael: 'From the Latin Speculum . . .' 235
Davie, Donald 17, 252, 263–4
    Poet as Sculptor 189–90, 264
Dial magazine 103, 104
Dickey, James 11
Dix, Dorothea 100, 123, 175–6, 194

Dragnet (radio drama) 24
DSM *see* American Psychiatric Association
Dublin: Ezra Pound International Conference (2013) 230, 234, 235, 236
Duncan, Robert 11
    How to Make Enemies 137, 140
Duval, Dr Addison 10

Edge (magazine) 27, 200
Eisenhower, Dwight D., US President 25
electroconvulsive therapy (ECT) 125, 126, 155, 171, 183
Eliot, T. S. 148, 154; friendship with Pound 69, 122, 129, 130, 138, 140, 148, 207, 260, 261; advises him 132; Overholser's letter to 174; visits Pound at St Elizabeths 11, 23, 25, 122, 137–8, 141, 148; wins Légion d'honneur and Nobel Prize in Literature (1948) 138; as Bollingen Prize judge (1949) 132–3; and Seidel 196, 197; memorial service 225
    'Burnt Norton' 138
    The Cocktail Party 147–8
    The Confidential Clerk 148
    The Elder Statesman 148
    Ezra Pound (1946) 138
    Ezra Pound and His Metric and Poetry 129
    (ed.) *Literary Essays of Ezra Pound* 26, 264–5
    'The Love Song of J. Alfred Prufrock' vii, 129, 139, 142
    'Tradition and the Individual Talent' (essay) 131–2
    The Waste Land 4, 129–30, 136, 139, 148

Eliot, Vivienne 148
Emery, Clark 229
  Ideas Into Action 229
EPIC *see* Ezra Pound International
  Conference
Esquire (magazine) 246
Euripides: *Alcestis* 147; *Ion* 148
Ezra Pound International Conference
  (EPIC) 229–30; Rapallo (2005)
  171; Dublin (2013) 230, 234,
  235, 236

Faber and Faber 9, 132
  Selected Poems of Ezra Pound 132
  The Translations of Ezra Pound
  25, 143
fascism 211–12, 213, 215, 217–18;
  see also Pound, Ezra: *views*
Faubus, Governor Orval 27
FBI 6, 74, 88, 90, 198; *see also*
  Amprim, Major Frank Lawrence
Fitzgerald, F. Scott: *Tender Is the*
  Night 162
Fitzgerald, Robert 157–8
Fleming, Rudd 146
Ford, Ford Madox 51, 140, 235;
  Williams to 89
Freeman, Dr Walter J. 85
Freud, Sigmund 4, 44, 162
  Moses and Monotheism 44
Frost, Robert 246
Fuck You Press 256

Galileo Galilei 192
Gallup, Donald 199
Garfield, James A., US President
  123, 180
Gillespie, Dizzy 25
Ginsberg, Allen: *Howl and Other*
  Poems 27
Golding, Arthur 108
Gordon, David 227

Grenfell, Russell: *Unconditional*
  Hatred 192
Grieve, Thomas 190–91
Griffin, Dr Edgar 22, 33
Guiteau, Charles J. 123, 180

Hamilton, Ian 239
  Robert Lowell: A Biography
  184, 187
Hammarskjöld, Dag 246
Hanno the Navigator 18, 86
  Periplus of Hanno 18
Hardwick (Lowell), Elizabeth
  156, 187
Hardy, Thomas 4, 16, 153
Harvard University Press 26
H.D. (Hilda Doolittle) 50
Health Insurance Portability and
  Accountability Act (HIPAA) 124
Hemingway, Ernest 4, 26, 45,
  246, 260
Hillyer, Robert: 'Treason's Strange
  Fruit' 133
Hinckley, John, Jr 180
Hitler, Adolf 8, 94, 153, 179, 218
Holder, Lt Colonel P. V. 9
Homer: *Odyssey* 39, 40, 41–2, 59, 60,
  157, 258
Horton, David 227, 251
Hudson Review 26, 139, 143, 157
Hynes, Samuel 135, 181
  'The Case of Ezra Pound' 181–2

Ibbotson, Joseph Darling 236–8

Jackson, Andrew, US President 180
James, Henry 227
Jarrell, Randall 11, 24, 155
Jefferson, Thomas, US President 89
John, Augustus: *Dylan Thomas* 4
Joyce, James 84, 129, 193–4, 207
  Ulysses 5, 84, 116

Joyce, William ('Lord Haw-Haw') 22
Judt, Tony 211

Kaminski, John 179–80
Karlgren, Bernhard: *The Book of Odes* 117, 118, 119
Kasper, John 27, 198, 199, 201–4, 227, 261; letters to Pound 24, 199; visits Pound at St Elizabeths 24, 195, 198
'Segration or Death' 201
Kavka, Dr Jerome: early interviews with Pound 22, 47, 61–4, 67, 68–70, 79, 80, 95, 113, 189, 261; and Olson 54–5; leaves Howard Hall 72
Keats, John 3
Kees, Weldon 14
Kendig, Dr 40, 41, 160
Kenner, Hugh 168, 229
The Poetry of Ezra Pound 228
The Pound Era 168, 234–5, 264
Kermode, Frank 139
Kerouac, Jack 206–7
King, Dr Marion 9–10, 71–2
Kirkbride, Thomas 101, 103
On the Construction . . . of Hospitals for the Insane 101–2
Kirsch, Adam 111
Korean War (1950–53) 25
Kutler, Stanley 173

Laughlin, James 42, 132, 232; sends Pound's books to Dr Kavka 54, 70; publishes Pound's *Selected Poems* 127–8; and Berryman 223; and Lowell 154; and Olson 42, 53, 55; and Williams 107
Lawrence, Richard 180
Laws, Judge Bolitha J. 22
LaZebnik, Jack 10

Legge, James: translation of Confucian Odes 113, 115, 117, 118, 119
Lewis, Percy Wyndham 5
Library of Congress, Washington, DC 14, 90, 132, 155, 165, 177, 221
Life magazine 246
Longfellow, Henry Wadsworth 62, 63
Loomis, Elias 95, 96
Loomis, Elisha S. 95, 96
Loomis, Joseph 95
Loomis, Mahlon 95, 96
Loomis family 61, 96
Lowell, Elizabeth *see* Hardwick, Elizabeth
Lowell, Robert: wants to study under Pound 154; arrested for denouncing the war 154–5; becomes a poet and Consultant in Poetry at Library of Congress 155, 164; madness and hospital treatment 155, 165, 182–4, 186–7; divorces and marries again 153, 155, 156; letters to Pound 153–4, 155, 157, 166, 186; and Elizabeth Bishop 14; visits Pound at St Elizabeths 11, 14, 24, 155, 156–7, 168, 221, 261; as Bollingen Prize judge (1949) 132–3; meeting with Pound after his release 188–9
'Adolf Hitler von Linz' 154
Collected Poems 156
The Dolphin 187
'Ezra Pound' 187–8
'Florence' 151, 156
For Lizzie and Harriet 187
'For the Union Dead' 165
History 187, 188
'Home After Three Months Away' 184–5, 186
Life Studies 184, 185–6, 187

Lord Weary's Castle 155, 184
'Near the Unbalanced Aquarium'
   165
Notebook 1967–68 187
'Sailing Home from Rapallo' 185
'To Delmore Schwartz' 164
'Waking in the Blue' 185

McLean Hospital, nr Boston 185
MacLeish, Archibald 246; visits
   Pound at St Elizabeths 11
McNaughton, William 217
Malatesta, Sigismondo, of Rimini 78
Man Ray (Emmanuel Radnitzky) 51
Marconi, Guglielmo 96
Mariani, Paul: *William Carlos
   Williams* 93
Marinetti, Filippo 210, 215
Martinelli, Sheri/Cheri 187,
   227, 239, 240, 241–2, 243;
   correspondence with
   Pound 25, 241, 245;
   visits Pound at St Elizabeths
   25, 168, 242–3
Massachusetts Review 104
Maximus of Tyre 56
Mayo, Robert 228
Meacham, Harry 247–8
Merwin, W. S. 11
   The Mays of Ventadorn 134,
   135, 136
Metato, Italy 1–2
Michaux, Elder Lightfoot
   Solomon 193
Miller, Arthur 147, 148
   Death of a Salesman 147
Millier, Brett: *Elizabeth Bishop* 14
Milton, John: *Paradise Lost* 237
Mingus, Charles 25
modernism/modernists 2, 3, 11, 14,
   38, 41, 43, 45, 65, 93, 113,
   128–9, 132, 139, 140, 148,
   150, 193, 235

Moody, A. David: *Ezra Pound . . .*
   174, 264
Moore, Marianne 11, 163, 167
Mullins, Eustace 26, 176–80, 248
   A Study of the Federal Reserve
   177, 203
   *This Difficult Individual, Ezra
   Pound* 178, 264
Muncie, Dr Wendell 71
Mussolini, Benito 2, 8, 55, 70, 75,
   94, 209, 210, 211, 215, 218,
   220, 257; Pound's meeting with
   216–17

Nabokov, Vladimir: *Lolita* 27
National Archives, Washington, DC:
   St Elizabeths' files 19, 166–71,
   174, 175, 226
National Portrait Gallery, London 4;
   Statesmen's Gallery 4
New Directions (publishers) 9, 24,
   73, 126, 127, 128, 224, 256; *see
   also* Laughlin, James
New Republic (magazine) 10
New Times (Melbourne) 27, 200,
   218, 232–3
New York: Make It New, Bleecker
   Street 198, 203; San Remo Café
   198
New York Herald Tribune 201–2
New York Times 9, 27, 133, 147,
   167, 246
New Yorker (magazine) 52, 135
Newsweek 167
Nichols, Charles 100–1, 181
Nine (magazine) 219
Nixon, Richard M., US President 124
Nuremberg Trials (1946) 23, 46

Olson, Charles *30*, 31, 38, 44–5,
   223, 261; interviews Pound for
   PM magazine 31; and Pound's
   trials 32, 45, 46; visits Pound at

Olson, Charles (*cont.*)
  St Elizabeths 11, 22, 38, 43, 44,
    46–8, 49, 52–3, 54, 55, 56, 59;
    letter to Dr Overholser 42–3;
    and Dr Kavka 54–5, 69;
    copies from Pound's
    Cantos 55–6
  Call Me Ishmael 52–3
  'Human Universe' (essay) 59
  The Maximus Poems 29, 46–7, 48,
    49, 56–8, 59, 266
  'La Préface' 59–60
  'Projective Verse' (essay) 58
  A Translation' 43–4
  X&Y 60
Olson, Connie 38, 43, 44, 48, 49, 53
Orwell, George 211
Otto, Thomas 102, 103, 181
Overholser, Annie 140–42
Overholser, Dr Winfred 8, 42, 112,
    124, 140, 174–6, *175*; court
    reports on Pound 8, 53, 79–80,
    105; Williams's letter to 106,
    110; attempts to limit Pound's
    visitors 24, 133–4; diagnoses
    Pound 26; and Mussolini's brain
    220; and Torrey's conspiracy
    theory 172, 173–4, 176
Overholser, Dr Winfred, Jr 140,
    141, 157, 161, 171,
    183, 250
  Handbook of Psychiatry 159
Ovid: *Metamorphoses* 108,
    227–8, 229

Paideuma (journal) 69, 264, 266
Paris Review 187
Parker, Charlie 25, 198
Parks, Rosa 27
Payne Whitney Psychiatric Clinic,
    New York 183, 186
Perloff, Marjorie 58, 78, 264
Picasso, Pablo 148

Pinel, Philippe 159, 175
Pisa, Italy: US Disciplinary Training
    Center (DTC) 6–8, 17, 33, 38,
    52, 53, 71, 222, 250
PM magazine 31, 35
Poetry magazine 3, 38
Poetry Review 89
Poetry Society of Virginia 248
postmodernism/postmodernists 11,
    31, 58–9
Pound, Dorothy (*née* Shakespear):
    in Italy with Pound 33; visits
    Pound at Pisa DTC camp 7;
    remains close to him 243; her
    son, Omar 244; takes control of
    Pound's legal affairs 23, 42, 79,
    127; visits Pound 19, 23, 24,
    134, 137, 168; and Williams
    106, 108, 109; withdraws
    petition for Pound's release
    120–21; and frequency of
    Pound's visitors 133; pleads with
    Berryman to visit Pound 223;
    alternates visits with Martinelli
    242–3; and Pound's release 247,
    248, 251; sends Marcella Spann
    home 256
Pound, Ezra: background 61–2,
    63–4, 95–6; birth 127;
    childhood 63; at school 49–50,
    63; at Military Academy 50;
    at University of Pennsylvania
    50, 63, 88, 230–31; begins
    friendship with William Carlos
    Williams (*see entry*) 88–90;
    at Hamilton College, New
    York 50, 63, 231, 237, 238;
    in London 50–51, 53, 88–9;
    lectures at London Polytechnic
    232; early poetry 64–7, 76–7;
    in Paris 51; receives honorary
    degree from Hamilton College
    (1939) 51, 233; in New York

51; moves to Italy 33; children 63; meets Mussolini 216–17, 218; starts journal 89; wartime anti-American broadcasts from Rome 2, 5, 7, 33, 52, 75, 87–8, 90–92, 93–5, 96, 127, 178, 180–81, 191, 215, 216, 251; captured by Communists 5; questioned by FBI in Genoa 6, 8, 73–4, 76; imprisoned by Americans in Pisa 6–7, 33, 38, 52, 132, 222; has nervous breakdown 6; indicted for treason 5, 7, 75, 127; taken to US 8, 48, 90; gives *PM* magazine interview 31; and Mussolini's death 220; and treason trial 7–8, 32, 45, 46, 76, 90; found to be insane 8, 9–10, 11, 32; admitted to St Elizabeths 8, 11–12, 19, 32–3, 35–7, 52, 261; timeline at St Elizabeths (1945–58) 22–8; first interview with Dr Griffin 33; 'delusions of persecution and grandeur' 33; interviews with Dr Kavka 47, 61–4, 67–70, 79; visitors 10–11, 17, 18–19, 133–7, 168, *see also* Berryman, John, Bishop, Elizabeth, Eliot, T. S., Kasper, John, Lowell, Robert, Martinelli, Sheri, Mullins, Eustace, Olson, Charles, Pound, Dorothy, Seidel, Frederick, Williams, William Carlos; takes Rorschach test 40–41, 54, 160, 162; daily life at Howard Hall 79; sanity hearing 22, 23, 43, 46, 53–4, 71–2, 250; defence lawyer appeals for his discharge 42; allowed to walk in 'the Moat' 23, 47; asks publishers to send Dr Kavka all his books

54; corrects page proofs of cantos 52, 53; power of attorney given to Dorothy Pound 23, 42, 79, 127; writes to Professor Ibbotson 236–7; denied bail 79; a further hearing (1947) 79, 105; moved to Cedar Ward, Center Building 23, 79–80, 105; given own room with typewriter 112–13; petition for habeus corpus withdrawn 120; and Berryman 221–5; moved to Chestnut Ward 120, 133, 142, 173–4; mother dies 24; wins Bollingen Prize (1949) 24, 132–3; translates Sophocles' *Elektra* 24, 143 (*see below*); and Sheri Martinelli 241–2 (*see entry*); a 'narcissistic personality type' (1953) 25; his insanity questioned 157–64, 170–71; and relaxation of rules 226–7; 'psychotic disorder, undifferentiated' (1955) 26; visited by Olga Rudge 243 (*see entry*); journalistic pieces 199–201, 218–19; ageing 200–1; association with Kasper (*see entry*) becomes public 201–4; treason indictment dismissed (1958) 28, 245, 246–7, 250–51; discharged from St Elizabeths 28, 245–6, 247--8, 249–51, 260; his medical records 124–5; in Washington 251; visits childhood home 251, and Williams 251; photographed by Avedon 251–2, *253*; joins his daughter, Mary (*see* Rachewiltz, Princess Mary), at Schloss Brunnenburg 255–6, 260, 261–2; brings Dorothy and Marcella Spann (*see entry*) with

Pound, Ezra (*cont.*)
him 256; exhibition of works arranged by Mary 260; falls into depression 256; in clinic 256; at Eliot's memorial service 225; and conspiracy theories 172–3, 174, 176, 182; spends last years with Olga Rudge 256, 257; death and funeral 245, 257; his will 245; archive at Yale University 245, *see also* National Archives, Washington, DC
appearance and characteristics: appearance and clothes 10, 33, 37, *37*, 38, 49–52, 164, 200, 247, *253*; contradictions and failings 2–3, 10, 21; eyes 164; facial expressions 68; gesticulations 68; knowledge of Latin 18, 40; legacy 2–3; his letters 42; loves movies 193; love of nicknames 15, 68, 42, 70, 138; loves tennis 112, 138, 140, 141; as philologist 235, 241; pseudonyms 199–200, 218; reading lists 108; self-analysis 189; singing/humming 69, 113, 114, 159, 167, 221, 225; speech habits/soliloquies 64, 70, 72–3; teeth 170, 245, 248–9
views on: America/American culture 2, 44; anti-Semitism 2, 178, 180, 200, 252; Chinese philosophy 3, 5, 33, 36, 43, *see also Confucian Odes*; critics 16; fascism 2, 3, 11, 43, 44, 53, 128, 132, 192, 205, 213, 215–16, 219; modernism 2, 3, 14, 41; poetry/poets 16–17, 20, 73; racism 2–3, 200, 204; universities 230–33; US presidents 180–81

ABC of Reading 16, 162, 201, 231
autobiography 127–8
'The Beautiful Toilet' 162–3
Cantos 2, 18, 31, 36, 44, 52, 70, 77, 89, 91, 93, 94, 109, 114, 150, 225, 228–9, 238–41, 243, 251, 256, 258–9, 260, 261; No. 1 41–2, 60; No. 2 164; No. 4 164; No. 5 164, 263; No. 8 77–8, 130–31; No. 9 228; No. 13 77; No. 24 78; No. 25 78–9; No. 40 86; No. 45 107, 208; No. 46 91–2; No. 53 43; No. 59 18; No. 72 9, 214–16; No. 73 9, 215–16; No. 110 257; No. 113 257; No. 116 257–8; No. 119 258; *see also A Draft of Cantos XXXI–XLI; A Draft of XVI Cantos; A Draft of XXX Cantos* 77; *Drafts & Fragments of Cantos CX–CXVII; The Pisan Cantos; Thrones de los cantares* (*below*)
Carta da Visita (*A Visiting Card*) 212–13
Cathay 113, 139, 143, 162–3
The Classic Anthology Defined by Confucius 26, 153, 157
Confucian Odes 23, 36, 43, 77, 113–14, 117–21, 138, 157, 196, 197
'De-Segregation' (article) 200
'The Development of Literature in Southern Europe' (lecture) 232
'Dr Williams' Position' (essay) 103–4
A Draft of Cantos XXXI–XLI 77, 89
A Draft of XVI Cantos 38–40
A Draft of XXX Cantos 77
Drafts & Fragments of Cantos CX–CXVII 256–7
'Francesca' 65

The Great Digest 196
Guide to Kulchur 16–17, 163, 231
'How to Read' (pamphlet) 231, 232
'In Durance' 65–6
Jefferson and/or Mussolini 31
Literary Essays of Ezra Pound 26
Make It New (essays) 70
'Near Perigord' 76–7
'Patria Mia' (essays) 88–9, 232
Personae 64–5, 70, 131
The Pisan Cantos (Cantos 74–84)
    6–7, 24, 52, 53, 57, 71, 132,
    133, 134, 139, 148, 150, 156,
    237–8; No. 74 8, 55–6, 220;
    No. 75 55–6; No. 79 164; No.
    81 224, 245
'The Return' 94
'The Seafarer' 66–7, 237
Section: Rock-Drill de los cantares
    (Cantos 85–95) 27, 158,
    189–93, 194; No. 85 27; No. 86
    27; No. 87 27; No. 88 27; No.
    89 27; No. 90 26, 27, 162; No.
    91 26, 27, 158; No. 92 26, 27,
    158; No. 93 26, 27, 158, 239,
    240, 241; No. 94 26, 27, 158;
    No. 95 26, 27, 158
The Selected Poems of Ezra Pound
    24, 126, 127–8, 134
Sophocles' *Elektra* (translation) 24,
    143, 144–7, 148–9
Sophocles' *Women of Trachis*
    (translation) 25, 26, 143,
    148–9, 157
Thrones de los cantares (Cantos
    96–109) 27, 28, 233–5; No. 96
    233; No. 97 242; No. 98 233,
    235; No. 99 17, 27, 233–4,
    248; No. 100 28; No. 107 28;
    No. 108 28; No. 109 28
The Translations of Ezra Pound 25,
    143

'The Tree' 64–5
'Yiddisher Charleston Band' (song) 69
Pound, Homer (father) 50, 61–2;
    Pound to 84
Pound, Isobel (mother) 24, 50, 62
Pound, Omar 7, 63, 244–5, 247
    'Epigram' (translation) 244
Powell, Bud 25
Prandoni, Dr Jogues 123, 124–5,
    126
Presley, Elvis 27
Protocols of the Elders of Zion, The
    179, 203
Pusey, Dr Nathan M. 196

Rachewiltz, Prince Boris de 255
Rachewiltz, Princess Mary de: birth
    63, 243; gives birth 23; in
    Washington 25; and Pound 63,
    245, 255–6, 257, 258, 260, 261;
    at his funeral 245; at Schloss
    Brunnenburg 17, 255–61;
    Pound's letters to 26, 250
Rachewiltz, Walter de 23, 234
Raine, Kathleen 11, 135, 136
Rapallo, Italy 52, 73, 94, 140, 153,
    154, 186, 245, 256; 21st Ezra
    Pound International Conference
    (2005) 171
Reagan, Ronald, US President 180
Reck, Michael 135; visits Pound 168,
    177, 193
    Ezra Pound: A Close-Up 135, 264
Redman, Tim: *Ezra Pound and Italian
    Fascism* 211
Reed (Walter) Army Hospital 105
Roach, Max 25
Rome 215, 218; CasaPound
    205–14, 219
Roosevelt, Franklin D.,
    US President 180–81
Rossi, Dr Romolo 171

Rousselot, Abbé Pierre-Jean 94
Rudge, Olga 243, 244, 245, 256

St Elizabeths Hospital, Washington,
    DC 8, 10, 17, 32, 36, 61, 83,
    84–7, 100–1, 102–3, 105,
    123–4, 159, 180, 181, 219,
    240, 249–50; *Annual Reports . . .*
    125–6; Blackburn Laboratory
    85–6; Cedar Ward 19, 24,
    80, 109, 110, 112–13, 115,
    120; *Centennial Papers* 183;
    Center Building 80, 83, 85, *97*,
    97–100, 101–2, 105, 111, 115,
    121, 124, 142, 202, 226, 249,
    250; Chestnut Ward 19, 24,
    98–9, 115, 120, 133–4, 142,
    168, 174, 202, 226, 229, 247,
    249; *Cry of Humanity* (play)
    194; files *see* National Archives,
    Washington, DC; Howard Hall
    19, 22, 23, 32–3, 34–5, 38, 42,
    46–7, 52, 54, 70, 79–80, 87,
    103, 105, 112, 113, 119–20,
    236, 238; Medical Library 126;
    Oak Ward 115; occupational
    therapy 123, 126, 158–9, 250;
    patients' library 126, 142;
    timeline of Pound's years at
    22–8
Salinger, J. D.: *The Catcher in the
    Rye* 25
Sandburg, Carl 3
Sant'Ambrogio, Italy 5
Saturday Review of Literature 133
Scheiwiller, Vanni 158
Schwartz, Delmore 164
Scianca, Adriano 205, 206–9,
    212, 219
    Ezra Fa Surf 209
'Seafarer, The' (Anglo-Saxon poem)
    66–7, 237

Seidel, Frederick 187, 195,
    196–7, 261; visits Pound at St
    Elizabeths 11, 26, 195–6, 197–8
'Glory' 197–8, 266
My Tokyo 197
Nice Weather 197
'Poem by the Bridge at
    Ten-Shin' 197
'School Days' 197, 266
Senate House, London: reading
    group 238–40
Sexton, Anne 164, 165
'You, Doctor Martin' 165
Shakespeare, William 63, 130
    As You Like It 102
    A Midsummer Night's Dream 102
    Sonnets 58
Shelley, Percy Bysshe 20
Sidney, Sir Philip 20
Sieburth, Richard 94, 265
Silver Hill, Maryland: Federal
    Communications Commission 92
Slatin, Myles 229
Smith, Denis Mack 211
Sophocles 149–50
    Elektra 24, 143, 144–7, 148–9
    Oedipus at Colonus 148
    Women of Trachis 25, 26, 143,
        148–9, 157
Spann, Marcella 227–8, 243, 251, 256
    Confucius to Cummings 227
Stalin, Joseph 8, 25
Steele, Lt Colonel John L. 7
Stevens, Dr Harold 72
Stevens, Wallace: 'The Man with the
    Blue Guitar' 163
Stock, Noel 200
    The Life of Ezra Pound 199–200,
        201
Strachey, Lytton 4, 239
Stravinsky, Igor 246
Strike (journal) 27, 200, 217

Sun, Veronica 122, 138
Szasz, Thomas 173; *Law, Liberty, and Psychiatry* 173

Tate, Allen 11
Tirol, Schloss 259–60
Torrey, E. Fuller 172
   The Roots of Treason: Ezra Pound and the Secrets of St Elizabeths 172, 173
Truman, Harry S., US President 38; Williams to 100, 104–5
Tzara, Tristan 51

Vietnam War 27
Village Voice (magazine) 203
Voice (magazine) 27, 200

Washington *Evening Star* 220
Watling, F. E. 146
Wertham, Dr Frederic 173
Williams, Flossie 87, 88
Williams, William Carlos 87–8, 89, 100, 103, 104–5, 114, 121, 184, 251, 261; friendship with Pound 88–90, 92, 93, 103–4,

106–7; visits Pound at St Elizabeths 11, 23, 83, 105–11, 136
   Autobiography 109–11, 136
   'Between Walls' 111
   'The Crimson Cyclamen' 111
   Kora in Hell: Improvisations 89–90
   Paterson 92–3, 107–8, 109, 266
   'The Red Wheelbarrow' 111
   'A Study of Ezra Pound's Present Position' 81, 104
Windsor, Edward, Duke of 192
Witemeyer, Hugh 127
Woolf, Virginia 193–4
Wormeley, Carter 84–5, 86, 87, 97, 98, 99, 112, 123
Wright, Frank Lloyd 246
Wyncote, Philadelphia 251; Public School 49–50

Yaddo, Saratoga Springs (writers' colony) 166, 182
Yale University: Pound archive 245
Yeats, W. B. 139, 236

Zukofsky, Louis 11

Permissions Acknowledgments

Illustration Credits

pp. x–xi: Second-floor plan of Center Building, St. Elizabeths Hospital, from the Historic American Buildings Survey. Library of Congress, Prints & Photographs Division.

p. 30: Photograph of Charles Olson reading the *Cantos*, courtesy of the Charles Olson Research Collection, Archives and Special Collections at the Thomas J. Dodd Research Center, University of Connecticut Libraries. Used with permission.

p. 34: Architectural floor plan of Howard Hall. Held in the Prints and Photographs Online Catalog of the Library of Congress.

p. 37: Photograph of Ezra Pound on 26 December 1945. Picture by: /AP/Press Association Images (PA.3346885).

p. 53: Drawing of containers, courtesy of the Charles Olson Research Collection, Archives and Special Collections at the Thomas J. Dodd Research Center, University of Connecticut Libraries. Used with permission.

p. 97: Front elevation of St. Elizabeths, Washington, DC. Library of Congress, Prints & Photographs Division, 12359-10A.

p. 175: Photograph of Dr Winfred Overholser. Held in the Prints and Photographs Online Catalog of the Library of Congress.

p. 190: Detail of page of Canto 85 from *The Cantos of Ezra Pound*, copyright © 1948 by Ezra Pound. Reprinted by permission of New Directions Publishing Corp.

9 780374 538040